纪念孙中山诞辰一百四十五周年
（1866—2011）

暨

辛亥革命一百周年
（1911—2011）

伦敦蒙难记

我被伦敦中国公使馆拘押和释放的经历

孙中山 著

庾燕卿　戴桢　译注

中国社会科学出版社

图书在版编目（CIP）数据

伦敦蒙难记 / 孙中山著. —北京：中国社
会科学出版社，2011.6
ISBN 978-7-5004-9758-5

Ⅰ.①伦… Ⅱ.①孙… Ⅲ.①孙中山（1866~1925）
—生平事迹 Ⅳ.①K827=6

中国版本图书馆CIP数据核字（2011）第075072号

责任编辑　武　云
特约编辑　赵　薇　段　珩
责任校对　刘晓红
封面设计　3A设计艺术工作室
技术编辑　王炳图　王　超

出版发行　中国社会科学出版社
社　　址　北京鼓楼西大街甲158号　　　　邮　编　100720
电　　话　010-64036155　84029450（邮购）
网　　址　http://www.csspw.cn
经　　销　新华书店
印　　装　三河市君旺印装厂
版　　次　2011年6月第1版　　　　　印　次　2011年6月第1次印刷
开　　本　710×1000　1/16
印　　张　17.75
字　　数　248千字
定　　价　39.00元

孙中山1912年1月任中华民国临时大总统

孙中山流亡欧洲时摄影

孙中山1883年17岁照

孙中山的恩师康德黎先生

孙中山1896年流亡美国旧金山时照相

1909年8月在伦敦

《伦敦蒙难记》1912年中译本

上海三民书店版中译本

孙中山《伦敦蒙难记》最早的版本
——1897年英文原版书

上海新民社1927年版

孙中山书赠黄兴对联

自序

自建國方畧之心理建設物質建
設社會建設三書出版之後予乃
從事於草作國家建設以完成此
悅國家建設一書較前三書為獨

大內涵有民族主義民權主義民生
主義五權憲法地方政府中央政
府外交政策國防計畫八冊而民
族主義一冊已經脫稿民權主義
民生主義二冊亦草就大部其他

正條理使成為一完善之書以作宣
傳之課本則其造福於吾民族吾國
家誠未可限量也民國十三年三月
三十日孫文序於廣州大本營

孙中山手书《三民主义》自序

1911年孙中山（后排中）、冯自由（后排右三）在温哥华与洪门会成员

目 录
Contents

附 录

译者前言

　　孙中山《伦敦蒙难记》英文原著于1897年1月在英国伦敦和布里斯托尔出版发行。15年之后，即辛亥革命胜利之后，于民国元年（1912）由上海商务印书馆出版了这本书的中文译本，译作《伦敦被难记》。不过中文本并非孙中山本人所译，尽管当年它在海外的轰动性效应对朝廷的震动实不亚于书中所述的那次暴动，但是时过境迁，他早已无暇顾及他早年的这本成名之作了。直至今天此书最流行的版本仍是一个世纪以前的这个译本，目前中华书局出版的《孙中山全集》编入的正是这个中文版本，并且没有收录孙中山的英文原著。

　　我们的这篇译文是根据台湾1973年版《国父全集》第五册英文著述卷译出的。台湾本全集是否另外编入了中文翻译，因为手边无全书，未能查检；不过目前坊间见到的翻印本，与中华书局版全集刊本均同，即所采用的都是1912年上海商务印书馆印行的译本。这个译本距今已经100年了，又系文言意译，且做了大量删节，因此我们认为，为读者提供一个全新的译本对于阅读和研究应该是有所帮助的；至少对于以往旧的翻译可以起到英文校订的作用。下面可以举几个具体的译例来说明这一点。

　　旧译"序"结尾一句："使非然者，予万不敢贸然以著作自鸣也。"[①]英文原著是："…，I could never have ventured to appear as the

① 《孙中山全集》第1卷，中华书局1981年版，1986年重印本，第49页。

Author of an English book." 此句中 "as the Author of an English book" 一语是不可不译的，如果不是以"英文著述者"的身份发表，对于一个早就已经在《万国公报》上发表过《上李傅相书》（即《上李鸿章书》）这样文章的极为自信、非常具有胆识的政治家来说还不至于谦虚到"万不敢贸然以著作自鸣"的地步。

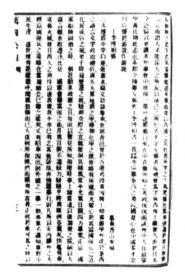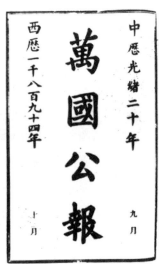

孙中山1894年在《万国公报》上发表了《上李傅相书》

旧译第一章："初不料四年后竟被幽于伦敦中国使馆……虽然，予之知有政治生涯，实始于是年；予之以奔走国事，而使姓名喧腾于英人之口，实始于是地。"[①]此一段话很有些歧义。据前文，所谓四年之后是指1896年，这一年孙中山自伦敦绑架事件披露后即享誉英伦，这是不错的；但是说"予之知有政治生涯，实始于是年"就不对了，即使是理解为四年之前的1892年，前后的话仍不能照应。查对原文就清楚了，原来英文原著在"知有政治生涯"、"奔走国事"这样意思的话之前，明确地交代了"at Macao"，即在澳门，并非说是在

① 《孙中山全集》第1卷，第49—50页。

伦敦，这样开始政治生涯的时间和地点就说得很清楚了，没有任何歧义。

原著在写到自己的学历时是这样说的："After five year's study（1887—1892）I obtained the diploma entitling me to style myself 'Licentiate in Medicine and Surgery, Hong Kong.'"旧译则为："阅五年而毕业，得医学博士文凭"[①]。这句翻译得很不准确，原文并没有说自己获得医学博士文凭，只是说取得了大学文凭；这还关系不大，关键是译文漏译了一个比学位重要得多的证书："Licentiate in Medicine and Surgery, Hong Kong"，即"香港内外科行医执照"。这个证书，当时不仅关系孙中山的生计，而且还是掩护孙中山从事革命工作的一个重要身份证，实际上它比博士学位重要得多，在孙中山的生平大事记里或年谱中，这一学历资格是必定要记载的。如果需要强调学位，"Licentiate"相当于硕士，是一个具有开业资格的医学硕士。虽然习惯上有称呼孙逸仙博士的，这是因为医生和博士均为Dr.（Doctor），他的名片上就是写着"Dr. Y. S. Sun"，但并不等于他获得了医学博士文凭。

《伦敦蒙难记》这篇自述由于当时面对的是英国读者，同时鉴于当时国内的政治环境，文中孙中山特意隐蔽了自己的激进的政治主张，以及地下党革命组织，只字不提兴中会；但是旧译没有依照原著，而将"'Young China' Party"、"Committee of Reformers"均译作了"兴中会"，比如像这样的句子："此兴中会之所由设也。此兴中会之所以偏重于请愿上书等方法……"[②]这就明显地不符史实了。兴中会自成立起，就是彻底地以推翻清朝政权为己任的革命组织，它何时改变过其革命宗旨，"偏重于请愿上书等方法"呢？这样改译显然不合原著文意，同时在一定程度上也抹去了孙中山早年所存在的某种较温和的改革政治的理念。

---

① 《孙中山全集》第1卷，第50页。

② 《孙中山全集》第1卷，第52页。

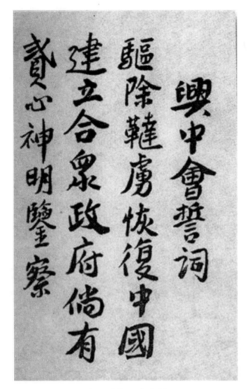

孙中山手书兴中会誓词

关于清廷的腐败，第一章里提到两广总督李瀚章："The Viceroy，Li Han chang（brother of the famous Viceroy Li），…"旧译为："时为两广总督者曰李瀚章，即李鸿章之弟〔兄〕也"①。旧译将李瀚章误为李鸿章之弟，《孙中山全集》编校者订正为"兄"，这是不错的；但此语并非就此一点译得不准确，其他不确之处应当一并订正。首先，当时的两广总督为谭钟麟（1822—1905），早在乙未（1895）起义半年以前李瀚章即被参劾以病免职，已不在总督任上了，译为"时任"不妥，原文的意思也只是说李氏任总督时所制定的一项劣政更激化了人们反政府的情绪；另外英文原著没有出现李鸿章的名字，只说是"brother of the famous Viceroy Li"，即"著名的李总督的兄弟"。

① 《孙中山全集》第1卷，第53页。

孙中山此时在伦敦写的另一篇英文论文《中国的现在和未来——革新党呼吁英国保持善意的中立》（China's present and Future; The Reform Party's Plea for British Benevolent Neutrality，1897.3）提到此事时倒是指名道姓了："在最近以前还没有为出卖官职而制定一个固定的价目表的事情，现在当局的大官变得这样无耻，就是前任总督李瀚章——李鸿章的兄弟——对于两广（广西、广东）的每个官职曾定下一个正规的价格表。"①

　　大概是讲究语言的简洁吧，旧译文许多语句都大大浓缩，如第一章结尾的一段原文："Having informed him that I was in trouble through having offended the Cantonese authorities， and fearing that I should be arrested and sent to Canton for execution."意思是："告诉他我正在麻烦中，因为获罪于广东当局，恐怕我会被逮捕并押回广州施行处决。"可是旧译改成了这么简单的一句："康德黎君闻予出奔之故。"像这样不到位的译法确实是不胜枚举，俯拾皆是；而大段文字随意的删节也不乏其例，如第五章开头一段话："公使馆外面正在发生的事情，当然我一点也不知道。我所有的求援字条，所有的碎纸片都丢到窗外去了，所有的信件我都已正式递交给了哈里代·马卡尼（旧译为马凯尼）先生和邓，我知道这都没有用，然而更糟的是他们对我施行了更为严密的看守，这样我和朋友的联系就越来越不可能了。"整个这一段都给删掉了。康德黎先生和孟生博士向伦敦警察厅报案没有结果，文中写到他们焦虑的心情："现在最紧迫的是要知道到何处去诉说这个事实：一个人的生命已在危险中；国家的法律已被践踏；而这个人实际上是在英帝国的京城被人谋杀的。"像这种表达他们维护人权、维护大英帝国主权的法律观念的重要文字，这也是他们营救政治囚犯的法律根据，也都被毫无理由地删掉了。

　　整段整句删节最长的是第七章中一篇题作"营救方案之一"的报纸新闻，删去原文（英文）181个单词。而此章结尾所引科尔的一封密

---

　　① 《孙中山全集》第1卷，第105页。

信，旧译未按照书中所引的原信翻译，而是以作者转述的形式译出，这就失去了这封"密信"作为档案材料（原始资料）的价值，虽然这封信的真实性还有待考证。

关于孙中山获释的情形，旧译本译得过于简练，比如其中一段："兹事虽微，然以英政府之代表而竟令从后门出，在中国外交家方且自诩其交涉之间又得一胜利，其为有意简亵，固无可讳言。"①此一段省略了很多意思，原文这里不必列出，只说一说其大意："英国政府的代表像下等人一样被人从后门送出，这一事实会影响首相及其内阁成员的声誉。实际上那是有意的怠慢和侮辱……"在这一段文字中，孙中山对于一个立宪制国家没有坚决地维护人权和自己国家的尊严所流露出来的遗憾的心情是很明显的，但是这在旧译里就不容易看出。

孙中山获释之际，清使馆英籍参赞、绑架阴谋之策划者哈里代·马卡尼虚伪地和他、康德黎先生以及英国政府派来接他的人一一握手，在孙中山眼里，马卡尼是一个犹大式的伪君子，而这种深刻的憎恶心理，在旧译本里却被抹掉了。

对于将近100年前的翻译本来无须吹毛求疵，那时翻译的理念与现在大不相同，即使如主张"信、达、雅"原则的严复，他的译文也多属于改译；况且今天的翻译也并非无可挑剔，拙译显然也只能是抛砖引玉而已，事实上初译稿在杂志上发表后我们自己就已经发现一些不妥之处了，这里也且举几个例子为证。

先说翻译得不准确的，如第一章中谈到封建王朝对于思想的禁锢，原文中有一句是这样的："The so-called 'Literati' of China are allowed to study only the Chinese classics and the commentaries thereon." 我们的初译稿是："所谓中国的文人学士是允许读中国的文学艺术名著及其注释的一些作品的。"这样翻译似乎并不算错，但显然不合原意，看下面一句就发现自己是译得多么的外行了。接下来的一句是：

① 《孙中山全集》第1卷，第75页。

"即由古代哲学思想家编纂的作品，如孔夫子和其他作家的著作。"这显然指的是四书五经，译作"文学艺术名著"未免太宽泛了；并且除了经书注疏，在科举时代，还有别的闲书杂著能够为之作注，并可供文人学士们去研究阅读吗？这一句现在已修订为："所谓中国的'文人'仅允许研读中国经典及其注释。"

第三章中有解释"大人"和姓氏的一句："…Kung-Ta-Yen. Kung is his family name or surname."拙译最初是这样的："……比如龚大人。龚是他的家族姓氏或别姓"。这样的翻译实在蹩脚、笨拙，这是由于对"family name"和"surname"这两个同义词汇以及对于"or"这个单词理解不正确所导致的。由于"surname"还有别名和绰号的意义，当初似乎就解决了"family name"和"surname"词语重复的问题了，但是原文哪里会这样的别扭呢？这样翻译显然曲解了原意。细致考虑，"family name"在这里绝不应该简化为"姓氏"，必须翻译成"家庭"或"家族"的"名"，哪怕意译为"父名"都行；而"surname"倒是不该刻意采用其他义项，如绰号、别名别姓之类，译

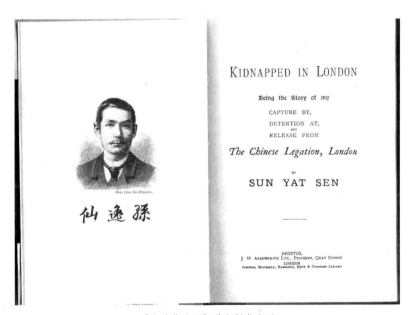

KIDNAPPED IN LONDON

Being the Story of my
CAPTURE BY,
DETENTION AT, AND
RELEASE FROM

The Chinese Legation, London

BY

SUN YAT SEN

BRISTOL
J. W. ARROWSMITH LTD., PRINTERS, QUAY STREET
LONDON
SIMPKIN, MARSHALL, HAMILTON, KENT & COMPANY LIMITED

《伦敦蒙难记》英文版书名页

为"姓氏"就可以了。此一句现在已改译为："……比如龚大人。龚是他的家族名，即姓氏"。这样"or"在这里自然也就不会误解为连接词了，而是判断性词语。

第六章中描写康德黎去见《泰晤士报》编辑时有这样一句话："There he was received in 'audience'."这一句初译稿是这样的："在那里他被'接见'了"。当初认为"be received in audience by"，这是一个习惯用语，即"被……召见"的意思；但是《泰晤士报》编辑对一个来访者而且是一位绅士会这般无缘无故地傲慢无礼吗？这是上级对下级的态度，这样表达就带有一种莫名其妙的盛气凌人的情绪了。后来意识到"in 'audience'"这个介词短语中的"audience"是带有引号的，才想到报社编辑对于这个肩负着特殊使命的访问者的来意是并不了解的，所以并没有引起他们的足够重视，当时不过以为只是平时一般"读者"的寻常来访罢了。毫无疑问，原来的理解是不对的，"audience"译为"接见"是错误的，应译为"读者"，"in 'audience'"的意思是："作为'读者'"。这是一个名词结构。此句的意思是《泰晤士报》的编辑把来访者康德黎先生当做他们报纸的一般读者接待了。

第七章中有一段说到试图运用"人身保护令"法律使被囚禁者获释的措施，原文是这样写的："a writ of **_Habeas Corpus_** was made out against either the Legation or Sir Halliday Macartney, I know not which, but the Judge at the Old Bailey would not agree to the action, and it fell through." 初译稿是："英国政府发出一份针对公使馆或哈里代·马卡尼先生的人身保护令公文，我不知道这件事，但伦敦中央刑事法院的法官没有同意这一行动，因此此事成为泡影。"原文中并没有"英国政府"这个词语，译成由政府发出一个法律命令，这说明译者对"'人身保护法'令状"以及司法独立的概念是模糊不清的；而且这么翻译行文上还有歧义，似乎这个"人身保护令公文"是支持中国公使馆和马卡尼先生拘押人犯的。以后我们看到康德黎与《环球报》

（旧译为《地球报》）记者的谈话资料才知道，是康德黎先生与孟生博士向伦敦高等法院申请保护人权令的。报纸上这样报道："据说他们（指康德黎与孟生）已向法官申请人权保护令；但在授予这种法令权利方面似乎有困难，因为还不清楚英国司法当局究竟能对一个外国公使馆行使权力到何种程度。"因此，这一句译文即订正为："一份申请针对公使馆或哈里代·马卡尼先生的'人身保护法'令状已经提交，我不知道这件事，但伦敦中央刑事法院的法官没有同意这一行动，因此此事未能实现。"修订这一句真使人惭愧，翻译岂止语言问题，若缺乏常识，对于语言的理解必定模糊，一经翻译即贻误读者（我们深恐读者再读到《鲁迅研究月刊》上的这一句误译，同时也很庆幸现在能够纠正）。顺便提一下，文言旧译本此处也误译为："英政府缮就保护人权令，拟饬中国使馆或马凯尼将人犯交出审讯……"[①]

在修订过程中我们还得感谢友人们的帮助，他们给我们提出了极有价值的意见。书中关于澳门行医一节，有一句原来是这么翻译的："这件事值得特别注意的是西医在中国为一项前所未有而又意义重大的创举"。黎维新先生来信指出："此句似可斟酌：西医在中国的流传是否称其为'创举'？"查对原文后发现我们对原文的理解的确错了，原文并不是说明"西医"在中国流传的意义，而是强调著者在澳门的行医活动能够得到当地华人士绅的鼎力支持，这在当时的中国可谓破天荒的新鲜事物。现在这一句已订正为："这件事在中国作为一个新的和重大的尝试值得特别注意。"

傅白芦先生的意见对我们也很有启发。他在信里说："问题在，'少年中国党'又不见于史事，它是个什么组织？不知道英文中的'政党'一词与'社团'一类是否都可以是party？如果可以，那么，这个组织名称不妨叫作'少年中国社团'。"他的话谦虚委婉，意思却是很明确的，即：party还有社团、会党的意义，应该考虑译得更准确一些；此外就是"少年中国党"究竟是一个什么组织，广州起义前

————————
① 《孙中山全集》第1卷，第71页。

夕，说到这个组织无疑是暗指兴中会，但是这个组织在兴中会成立前就已经存在了，对这个问题应该如何解释呢？鉴于他的意见，我们努力重新理解原文，去更多地翻阅文献资料。现在已将"Young China Party"（原译"少年中国党"）改译为"'中国少年会'"了，并写了一个较长的译注。我们认为这个组织指的就是"教友少年会"，孙中山是该组织的发起人之一，有他撰写的一篇发起缘起性质的文章为证。此文题作《教友少年会纪事》，发表于1891年6月上海广学会出版的《中西教会报》。这就是说，此会实际上是孙中山在香港西医书院做学生时就已经创建了。《教友少年会纪事》这一篇逸文已收入上海人民出版社出版的《孙中山集外集》。当然这个问题还可以讨论，目前就我们的力所能及，或许可以说已推进了一步吧。有兴趣的读者还可以参阅冯自由《革命逸史》中的《兴中会始创于檀香山之铁证》、《孙总理修正〈伦敦被难记〉第一章恭注》这两篇文章，此二文专门讨论了这一问题。

诸如此类的修订有不少，这里就不一一列举了。拙译初稿在《鲁迅研究月刊》上发表时，责任编辑陆成先生也订正了多处误译；此次出版单行本，又承蒙中国社会科学出版社编辑对译稿再次作了修订，因我们素不相识，只能借此向他们深表谢忱。

19世纪的伦敦英语与当代英语尤其是美语的差异已经很大，近似汉语文言与白话的区别；我们不敢说对于原著的理解已经十分明白无误，我们相信译文需要修订、值得商榷的地方远不止现在已经做的，我们期待着更多的朋友的指正。

关于*Kidnapped in London*的"附录"，译文中已有说明，这里再作一点补充。这个"附录"是孙中山摘编的当时报载对于绑架事件之评论，因并非孙中山本人著述，我们决定采用商务印书馆的旧译文，不再另行翻译。但"附录"之末附有一封孙中山向英国政府及新闻界朋友表示感谢的英文信函，这是孙中山的一篇完整的文字，是可以单独收入他的全集和书信集里的，而此信的旧译文与原文出入较大，这里有必要重新翻译。下面是原文：

The following is a copy of the letter I sent to the newspapers thanking the Government and the Press for what they had done for me：

To the Editor of the——

Sir，－Will you kindly express through your columns my keen appreciation of the action of the British Government in effecting my release from the Chinese Legation？ I have also to thank the Press generally for their timely help and sympathy. If anything were needed to convince me of the generous public spirit which pervades Great Britain， and the love of justice which distinguishes its people， the recent acts of the last few days have conclusively done so.

Knowing and feeling more keenly than ever what a constitutional Government and an enlightened people mean， I am prompted still more actively to pursue the cause of advancement， education， and civilisation in my own well－beloved but oppressed country.

Yours faithfully，

Sun Yat Sen.

46 Devonshire Street，

Portland Place， W.，

Oct. 24

中译文：

以下是这封信的副本，我寄给各报纸以感谢政府和新闻界为我所做的一切。

致各报编辑

先生：

　　我不知道能否通过你们的专栏，对于英国政府的援救促使我从中国公使馆获得释放，深切地表达我的诚挚的感激之情？我也很感激新闻界普遍地给予我的及时声援和同情。如果有什么事能让我信服遍布英国的宽厚的公德精神以及热爱正义的人民，那么最近几天的行动已使我深信不疑。

　　我比过去更加深切地体会到立宪政体以及国人开明的意义，这将促使我更积极地追求进步事业，为我深爱而又受压迫的国家继续努力促进教育和文明事业的发展。

你的忠实的，

孙逸仙

10月24日

于波特兰区德文榭街46号

　　除了上面这一封感谢信外，孙中山在离开英国时还特向《环球报》（一译为《地球报》）写了一封感谢信，当时即发表在该报上。因找不到英文原文，这里只能转引《孙中山年谱长编》中的译文：

致伦敦《地球报》函

先生：

　　您一直对我的事给予善意关怀，出于礼貌，现告知《地球报》及公众，我将于7月1日星期四乘船离开利物浦去远东，取道加拿大经太平洋越过美洲。对于您在我被囚禁于中国公使馆时的迅速行动深表感谢，永志不忘。

您忠实的孙逸仙，

波特兰均[区]覃文省街四十六号，

（1897年）6月29日。①

此函另可参阅《孙中山集外集补编》编入的译文：《致伦敦〈地球报〉函（一八九七年六月二十九日）》。

关于原著的初版，几乎所有的资料介绍都是说1897年初在英国的布里斯托尔出版，原来我们也是这么认为的，这次因编单行本特别留意了英文原著的版本记载，才发现这是不准确的。实际上这本书只是在布里斯托尔的一家印刷厂印制，当然在某地印刷，也可以说就是在某地出版吧，但是编辑发行应该还是在伦敦。有一个版本记录写得很具体：Bristol：J. W. Arrowsmith Ltd.，Printers，Quay street ／ London：Simpkin，Marshall，Hamilton，Kent and Company Limited. 应该说这本书的初版是在 London 和 Bristol 两地出版的。

这里有必要说明一下中文译本的书名。上海商务印书馆1912年译本书名是：《孙大总统自述·伦敦被难记》（书内又题作：《伦敦被难记——广东孙文自述》）。以后的版本基本都依据这个书名，如题为《孙逸仙伦敦被难记》、《孙中山伦敦被难记》等。书名上冠以"孙大总统自述"等字样显然是译者或编辑所加，《孙中山全集》刊本即作《伦敦被难记》，这是符合著作文集体例的；但是书名仍然翻译不完全，原著全名是：

Kidnapped in London

Being the Story of My Capture by, Detention at, And Release from the

---

① 转引自陈锡祺主编《孙中山年谱长编》上册，中华书局1991年版，第138页。

1925年3月12日孙中山在北京逝世，宋庆龄（右）与孙科（左）在北京行辕灵堂守灵

Chinese Legation, London

在*Kidnapped in London*书名之后还有长长的一个副标题："我被伦敦中国公使馆拘押和释放的经历"。这个副标题是对"伦敦绑架记"或"伦敦绑架案"这一主题的补充说明，并非可有可无的文字，不应该省略掉。本书初译稿发表在期刊上时也没有翻译这一全名，这次补译上算是弥补了一个缺陷。至于*Kidnapped in London*则保留了传统的译法，因为《伦敦蒙难记》这个书名今天已为广大读者所熟知，而且益于读者理解书的内涵，就不刻意直译了。

当下有一种言论，说孙中山被清使馆绑架后如何如何贪生怕死，屈膝求饶，而且此种言论在网上广为传布。这种流言在学界，在研究者当然是视为垃圾，但是对于一般读者可能还是有着一定蛊惑作用的，因为既然有这种言论流布，当然就有这样的社会氛围。孙中山去世时鲁迅写过一篇杂感《战士和苍蝇》，说战士死了的时候，苍蝇们就以为发现了战士身上的污点，颇为得意，围着营营地叫，嗤着，以为比死了的战士更英雄。鲁迅解释这篇杂感的寓意时说："所谓战士者，是指中山先生和民国元年前后殉国而反受奴才们讥笑糟蹋的先烈；苍蝇则当然是指奴才们。"（《这是这么一个意思》）孙中山逝世时中国还处于革命尚未成功、军阀割据的乱世；然而在今天，令人不愿看到的事实是，在海峡两岸都已进入高度发展的文明时代后，仍然存在着这种传播流言的苍蝇和奴才。这更使我们深切地感到《伦敦蒙难记》这篇历史文献的珍贵，同时也感到应该有一个全新的译本。

2009年10月初稿
2011年元月改定

伦敦蒙难记

Kidnapped in London

序 言

    我最近被拘留在伦敦波特兰区49号的中国公使馆，这引起了广泛的注意，也给我带来了许多朋友，同时提出了许多法律上的、学术的以及国际性的法律观点，如果我不把与事件相关的所有情况公布于众，那我真是太不尽责了。

    由于我英文著述的浅陋，须请广大读者谅解，坦白地说，在表达意思上，如无一位好友给予的帮助，我决不敢作为英文著述者出版此书。

孙逸仙

1897年于伦敦

伦敦蒙难记[*]
Kidnapped in London

第一章　革命事由

这是一个封建制度，一个专制极权统治，一个非正义的独裁政体，它是靠自身的腐败而生存发展的。在这个以使腐败合法化为最终目的的政权下，谁还能怀疑一股强大的不满情绪的潜流存在于民众之中呢？

---

　　* 英文原著书名为*Kidnapped in London*，直译为《伦敦绑架记》。本书译为《伦敦蒙难记》。关于中文译名，参阅"译者前言"。第一章标题原文为The Imbroglio，意为纷乱、纷扰、纠纷，指一种错综复杂的政治局势，这里即译为"革命事由"。

1912年5月25日，孙中山在澳门卢园春草堂与镜湖医院值理等合影

　　1892年我定居在离珠江口很近的一个小岛澳门从事医业。我做梦也没想到四年后我竟然成了中国驻伦敦公使馆的一名囚犯，更没想到因此竟引起了政界的轰动，在英国政府的积极干预下，我才获得了释放。然而就在这一年，在澳门，我开始认识了自己的政治人生；同时在那里开始了我的另一职业生涯①，一个已经给我在英国民众中带来如此显著名声的政治生涯。

　　1886年我学医于广州英美传教会②，该会由德高望重的戈尔博士主持；1887年我听说在香港创办了一所医科大学③，便立刻决定去该

----

　　① 这里原文为"part of my career"，直译为："我的职业（生涯）的一部分"，或"我的事业的一部分"。孙中山当时是一位开业医生，从事政治可以说是他的职业的一个部分，属于他的另一职业。

　　② 孙中山在《复翟理斯函（1896.11）》中说："二十一岁改习西医，先入广东省城美教士所设之博济医院（Canton Hospital）肄业。"（见本书所收此封信函）

　　③ 即香港西医书院（因医学院附设于雅丽氏医院，又称雅丽氏医学院），创建于1887年10月1日。孙中山在《复翟理斯函》中说："二十一岁改习西医……次年转入香港新创之西医书院（College of Medicine for Chinese, Hong Kong）。"（英文名直译为：香港·中国医学院）又，在《孙文学说》第八章"有志竟成"中说到转学的原因："予在广州学医甫一年，闻香港有英文医校开设，予以其学课较优，而地较自由，可以鼓吹革命，故投香港学校肄业。"（见《孙中山全集》第6卷，第229页）香港西医书院即今香港大学医学院之前身。

孙中山在香港西医书院所获医学文凭　　　　1892年7月孙中山在香港西医书院学习
（中英文双语本）　　　　　　　　　　　　时的学生装照

校学习，以便利用该校所拥有的诸多优越条件。

学习五年后（1887—1892）我取得了大学文凭，获得了"香港内
外科行医执照"①。

澳门属葡萄牙已360年；②尽管其政权已由欧洲人掌握，而居民大
多为华人，人口中有一部分自称是葡萄牙人，其实他们已是经历几代
人繁衍的欧亚混血人了。

在我新近选择的家，我感到当地医院的华人董事极愿意帮助我并

---

① 孙中山所获医学文凭（执照）为中英文双语本，中文为："香港西医书院
掌院并讲考各员等，为给执照事：照得孙逸仙在本院肄业五年，医学各门历经考
验，于内外妇婴诸科，俱皆通晓，确堪行世，奉医学局赏给香港西医书院考准权宜
行医字样，为此特发执照，以昭信守。须至执照者。右仰该学生收执。一八九二年
　　月　　日。"（执照副本今存。参阅罗刚《中华民国国父实录》第1册，台湾正中
书局1988年版，第246页；陈锡祺主编《孙中山年谱长编》上册，中华书局1991年
版，第58—59页）英文本学历资格为"Licentiate"，此为欧洲大学所颁学士与博
士之间的学位，并具有开业资格。

② 明嘉靖三十二年（1553）澳门即为葡萄牙强行租借，至19世纪末澳门已被
葡萄牙殖民者占领了300多年。

孙中山施行义诊的澳门镜湖医院旧址

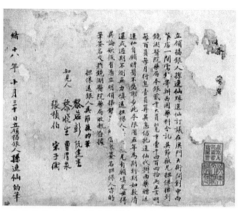

孙中山在澳门行医时与镜湖医院订立的贷款合同

且在从事欧洲内外科医疗业方面提供很多机会。①他们安排一间病房给我任意使用，并从伦敦为我购置药物和医疗器械，同时给予我一切特权，借此，使我所采取的新的医疗措施在当地能够得到充分实施。

这件事在中国作为一个新的和重大的尝试值得特别注意。遍及整个清帝国从来没有任何一个中国医院的董事会给予西医任何直接的正式的支持鼓励。然而很多病人，特别是需要外科手术的许多患者前来求医。在主管面前我做了几例大外科手术。另一方面，从一开始和葡萄牙当局就难以相处。现在阻碍西医发展的不是东方的愚昧，而是西方的嫉妒，他们干预、阻止我的发展。葡萄牙的法律禁止任何无葡萄牙执照的人在葡萄牙辖区行医，而这种执照只能在欧洲获得。葡萄牙医生在这项规定的庇护下和我在行医权利上发生了冲突。他们禁止我在他们之中行医，同时也不许我给葡萄牙人开药方，凡外籍医生签字的处方药剂师不给配药；因此我的医业的发展从一开始就受到阻碍。在澳门创业的尝试遭受挫折后，同时在经济上也受到相当大的损失，

---

① 孙中山从香港西医书院毕业后即到澳门行医，得澳门士绅襄助为镜湖医院施行义诊，并借银开设中西药店，租赁房屋做医疗室。

陷此困境是我始料不及的，于是我不得已去了广州。①

在澳门我才知道有一种政治运动，我认为那是一个最理想的组织，这个组织名称叫"中国少年会"②。它的宗旨是如此贤明，如此温良，如此充满希望，因此我赞同他们的宗旨，并立刻加入成为该会成员，而且我自信入会后定能尽全力为国为民牟取福利。我们计划采用和平的改革手段，希望呈递一份有理有节的改革方案给朝廷，③促使其创行一种与现代时势相符合的新政体。这个运动最主要的目标是制定立宪政体以代替守旧、腐败和衰弱不堪的旧政体。中国就正在这个破旧体制下呻吟着。

---

① 英文原文为Canton，广东的音译，以后也指广州。孙中山被迫离开澳门后即前往广州行医，1893年春在广州西关冼基开设东西药局。

② "中国少年会"（"Young China Party"） 当指"教友少年会"。孙中山在《教友少年会纪事》一文中写道："辛卯之春，二月十八（按：即1891年3月27日），同人创少年会于香港，颜其处曰'培道书室'。""是晚为开创之夕，同贺盛举，一时集者四十馀人，皆教中俊秀。曰（按：此文署'后学孙日新稿'）叨从其列，喜逢千古未有之盛事。又知此会为教中少年之不可少者，望各省少年教友亦有仿而行之……"（见《孙中山集外集》，上海人民出版社1992年印本，第597—598页；《孙中山年谱长编》1891年3月所录《教友少年会纪事》一文）"Young China Party"，《孙中山全集》刊本（即1912年商务印书馆译本）译为"少年中国党"，译者注为"兴中会"（见《孙中山全集》第1卷，第50页），实际此时"兴中会"尚未成立。辛亥革命爆发后，孙中山在伦敦与记者谈话时提到早年曾参加"中国少年会"之事："一八九二年，我得到了一张准许以内外科医生行医的文凭。……正当我在澳门为开业而奋斗，而我的奋斗又由于葡萄牙医生的歧视而四处碰壁的时候，一天晚上，有一个岁数和我差不多的年轻商人来访，问我是否听到北京传来的消息，说日本人就要打进来了。……'天命无常。'我的朋友说。'对，'我表示同意，并且引述一句帝舜的话，'天听自我民听。'那一晚我加入了少年中国党（Young China Party）。"（《我的回忆——与伦敦〈滨海杂志〉记者的谈话（一九一一年十一月中旬）》，《孙中山全集》第1卷，第547—548页）这里所说"少年中国党"即指"教友少年会"。孙中山在《中国之司法改革（一八九七年七月）》一文中又称为"Reform Party of Young China"，中译名为"少年中国改革党"（见《孙中山集外集》，上海人民出版社1992年印本，第17页）。

③ 关于请愿改革事参阅第二章第29页注②。这之前，1894年春孙中山起草了《上李鸿章书》，发表于当年9月和10月号《万国公报》。

1886年，孙中山学医之博济医院附设的南华医学堂

香港西医书院（今香港大学医学院前身），孙中山于1887年至1892年在此学医

雅丽氏医院创立人何启（1859—1914），香港西医书院法医学教授。兴中会会员，参加策划了乙未广州起义

    关于中国现行的是什么政治制度这里不必详述。不过，它可以用几句话来概括说明。无论是朝廷的事，国家民族的事，甚至州府衙门的事，民众是无权过问的。朝廷大官或地方官吏握有判决大权，对于他们的判决是不容申诉的。他们的话就是法律，他们可以完全不负责任地、无限制地施行诡计，每个官员可以逃避制裁为所欲为地中饱私

囊。官僚的抢夺勒索已成惯例，而这种恶行是他们任职的保障；只有当敲诈勒索者是一个笨拙的蠢材时，政府才会假借仁慈地介入以改变这种状况，但这时往往已经到了完全损耗枯竭的地步了。

英国读者可能想象不到中国地方官员的俸禄是多么的微薄。他们几乎不相信治理一个人口比全英国人口还要多的区域的两广总督①，他一年的俸禄总额只有微不足道的60英镑而已；因此为了生活和维持他的官职，为了积攒巨额资金，他只有靠敲诈勒索，出卖公正与良心。所谓科举考试就是通往仕途的一种手段。②假定一个青年学子取得功名③，他想继续寻求公职，那就还需行贿于北京当局，这样才可望谋得一个官位。一旦获得，由于他的俸禄并不足够维持生活，或许他还要为了保住自己的职位每年需付出许多钱财，因此压榨勒索畅行无阻是必然的结果，况且人一定不会真的蠢笨到连政府支持的事都不会做的地步，这样几年之后，他就使自己富裕到足以买一个较高的职位了。随着职位的升高，政府给予的特权也随之增加，压榨敛财的本事也不断提高，因此这个精明的"压榨者"最终又能以充足之钱财买到一个更高的官职。

被自己的生活方式扭曲了心灵的这种官贼，最终掌握了全社会的、政治的和刑事上的权力。这是一个封建制度，一个专制极权统治，一个非正义的独裁政体，它是靠自身的腐败而生存发展的。但是这个在公众的要害上——出卖权力——发展的体制，是满清王朝继续存在的主要手段。在这个以使腐败合法化为最终目的的政权下，谁还能怀疑一股强大的不满情绪的潜流存在于民众之中呢？

---

① 两广总督，英文原著为"Viceroy of, Canton"，直译应为"广东的总督"或"广州的总督"。

② 此句原文是："So-called education and the results of examinations are the one means of obtaining official notice."直译是："所谓的教育和考试成绩（结果）都是为了取得官方重视的一种手段。"

③ 原文为"a young scholar gains distinction"，可直译为"一个青年学子获得荣誉"。

中国民众，尽管官方让他们保持在对周围世界茫然无知的愚昧状态之中，但他们绝不是愚蠢的人。所有欧洲当局都认为中国人潜在的才能是非常巨大的，许多方面甚至超过了任何其他国家，包括欧洲或亚洲人。凡政治上的书籍是不许阅读的；日报在中国是被禁止的；周围世界，各国的人民和政治，都被拒之门外；清朝七品以下的官吏没有一个被允许阅读中国地理，更别说外国的了。现有王朝的法律，不是公众所考虑的，他们仅为高级官员所掌握。有关军事方面的书籍和其他被禁内容的书同样不仅被禁止，而且一旦违禁甚至可以处以死刑。不许任何人搞发明创造，也不许谁去挖掘、了解新的事物，违者必死无疑。这样，人们就一直被禁锢在暗无天日的生活中，尽管政府也施舍他们一点过时失效的消息，但这也是按当局所需而为的。

所谓中国的"文人"仅允许研读中国经典及其注释，即由古代哲学思想家编纂的作品，如孔夫子和其他作家的著作。[1]但是甚至这些作品，如对高级官员有不利之处，也是要注意删节，而仅仅这些部分作为公共读物刊印时，服从当局意志仍是重要的一点。中国就是这样统治的，或者说得更确切一点，就是在施行恶政，就是利用现在的法律和礼制在强制民众盲目地服从。

保持民众处于愚昧状态是中国统治者竭力坚持不变的。因此近来日本侵犯中国，除了在战役区中居住的那部分人以外，其他的中国人竟然完全不知道发生了战事。那些远离内地的民众不仅从未听说过战争，甚至连称为日本人的这样一种人都没有听说过；即使有点传闻，他们私下议论时也不过认为那只是"洋人""造反"而已。

中国梦魇般的精神包袱如此之沉重，改革的希望除了寄托于皇上[2]，别无其他选择；而促使皇上修改于国于民不利的条例，是"中

---

① 指四书五经等。

② 皇上，指光绪皇帝。尽管孙中山所发动的是旨在推翻清朝政权的革命运动，但是直至后来辛亥革命爆发后，孙中山谈到光绪皇帝时仍然充分肯定其历史作用："革命运动取得最大的发展，是在我们领受已故光绪帝的恩典的时期。在他未遭慈禧太后幽禁之前，曾有好几千名中国青年获准出国，周游世界，考察欧洲的制

〔转下页〕

国少年会"所制订的方案。希望北京当局通过近年来广泛地与外国外交官的接触能学到一些宪法上的规章和条例，这样同时也可能帮助中国人摆脱可悲的愚昧。为了中国的福祉，我大胆地和几位朋友去接近某些有关人士并恳求他们，以十分谦恭的态度周旋于这些人中间。然而这些请愿遭到的是严厉的打击。我们曾抓住时机，那时日本人正威胁北京，而皇帝担心过于严厉对待改革者会失掉人心，所以暂时采取不予追究的态度，直到议和成功。[1]随后下诏书，除对请愿人严加谴责外，并勒令立即中止一切改革建议。

温和手段之门已经关闭，我们越来越明确自己的意图和要求，同时逐渐地认识到施以一定的高压是必要的。[2]而且在各军营中我们发现也有不少拥护我们的人。但上层社会人士对军界十分不满，并知道海陆军人

光绪皇帝与康有为（右）、梁启超（左）

度习俗。在他们当中，有九成人感染了革命思想。无论我去到哪里，都会遇到许多这样的人。他们对我并不陌生，都急于要和我交换意见。当他们回国以后，不久就开始在全国各地发挥了酵母作用。"（《我的回忆——与伦敦〈滨海杂志〉记者的谈话（一九一一年十一月中旬）》，《孙中山全集》第1卷，第557页）

[1] 议和成功 1895年4月清政府与日本签订《马关条约》，即日本所谓"媾和条约"。此句原文为"peace was assured"，意即：和平有了保障。

[2] 甲午（1894年）中日之战，孙中山闻北洋海军败绩，叹曰："知和平方法无可复施。然望治之心愈坚，要求之念愈切，积渐而知和平之手段，不得不稍易以强迫。"（吴相湘：《孙逸仙先生传》，转引自罗刚编著《中华民国国父实录》，台北正中书局1988年版，第271页）

腐败贪婪，恶习养成，这是他们失败的原因。这种激愤的情绪已不限于一个地区，而是在广泛蔓延和加剧，预期的形势已经酿成，即将演变为坚决的行动。

"中国少年会"总部设于上海，①但实际行动安排在广州。在此会发展过程中出现的一些形势对它帮助很大。首先是那些心怀不满的军人的存在。在1895年北方战事停息后，四分之三的广东队伍被遣散了。被遣散的许多人无所事事、无法无天；留在军队中的一小部分他们的战友并不比那些被解散的痛快。他们哭喊：要解散则全体解散，要留则全体留。然而当局对他们的抗议充耳不闻。改革党即急起招募这些同情他们事业的人，于是改革党的兵力、物力都大有增强。

同时发生的另一事件促使形势加速发展。由于某种原因，一群警察脱下他们的制服，在省城某区进行抢劫掠夺。一两小时后，居民愤起将这些本来是警察的闹事者制伏并将为首的若干人关禁在同业会馆。警察局局长派出一队武装进入会馆放掉了被关禁的掳掠者，接着将会馆洗劫一空。居民当即开会，组成1000人的代表团至巡抚②府邸对警察的行动提出申诉。然而，当局斥责代表团这样的行动是造反，他们无权威胁政府。于是逮捕了代表团的首领，其余的人被驱散，并威吓他们不要多管闲事。③于是不满的情绪很快变成反叛情绪，就在此时，"中国少年会"向他们提出建议，他们即欣然加入到改革者中。

还有第三和第四件事，促进壮大了他们的队伍。总督李瀚章（著

---

①　这里实指兴中会。1894年11月，孙中山在檀香山成立反清秘密组织兴中会，1895年初在香港设立兴中会总部，并开始策划在广州发动起义。

②　巡抚，原文为"Governor"，也可译为总督。

③　关于此次警察骚乱，孙中山在《我的回忆》中是这样说的："此外，在广州的一帮巡勇中还出现了骚动不安，他们由于领不到薪饷而开始在市区劫掠财物。居民为此举行了一个群众大会，公推五百多人作为代表，前往巡抚衙门提出申诉。'这是造反！'巡抚吼叫着，并立即下令逮捕为首分子。我逃脱了。这是我第一次脱逃，后来我又有多次类似的险遇。"（见《孙中山全集》第1卷，第549页）

李瀚章（右）、李鸿章兄弟（摄于1896年）

名的李总督之兄）①制定了一个按照官员职位纳税的价目表，②这项措施贯彻于他管治的两省——广东和广西。这是又一项进一步压榨人民的新发明，当然官僚们会让人民补偿他们这笔额外的支付。第四件事是一次最为典型的敲诈人民事件——总督过生日。两省的官员联合给他们的主人一份生日贺礼，共100万两白银（约合200,000英镑），当然这笔钱是从富商那里用惯常使用的威胁、许诺等敲诈勒索手段得来的。李瀚章的属下一个名叫陈发农③的，由于出售科名，进一步激怒了所有的"文人学士"，因只要能支付3000两白银（约合500英镑）的人就可买到一张毕业文凭。因此富人和"文人"都怨愤，这一批人也

① 即两广总督李瀚章与直隶总督李鸿章。

② 孙中山此期间在伦敦写的另一英文论著 *China's present and Future: The Reform Party's Plea for British Benevolent Neutrality* （《中国的现在和未来——革新党呼吁英国保持善意的中立》，1897年3月）里提到此事："在最近以前还没有为出卖官职而制定一个固定的价目表的事情，现在当局的大官变得这样无耻，就是前任总督李瀚章——李鸿章的兄弟——对于两广（广西、广东）的每个官职曾定下一个正规的价格表。"（《孙中山全集》第1卷，第105页）当年李瀚章即因腐败被弹劾，于1895年4月以病免职回籍。

③ 陈发农，其人不详，其名照读音译出。

愿意与"中国少年会"共命运。

由于改革派的力量进一步加强和统一，影响更广，事变很快进入高潮，于是策划夺取广州①，废除当局，使其猝不及防；但要保证安全，一切尽可能在平静中进行，无论如何要避免流血屠杀。为确保成功发动军事政变，必须要有压倒一切的武装力量，因此决定招募两支队伍，一从汕头招募，一从西江沿岸招募。在这些地方选择汕头人，是因为汕头人完全不懂广州话。汕头在广州北面②，相距仅180英里，两地语言差异之大相当于英语之不同于意大利语。用一支陌生队伍进攻广州是明智的，他们对于事业可能更忠诚，因为他们无法与外面沟通，因此也就不可能受到广州人的干扰。但这也不会保证安然无事，因为他们可能解散或逃跑，会被看出是外来生人。这次动乱之后，如果他们在广州被发现，嫌疑将会立刻集中到他们身上。

起义已定于1895年10月某日发动③，起义队伍将越野进军，一队由西南，一队由东北，同时向广州进发。一切筹备工作令人十分满意，部队也开始向前推进。改革委员会④频繁召开会议，同时军械、弹药及炸药都囤积于总部。为了进一步加强正在前进的部队的力量，又从香港开来400人增援。等到集合的那天，南边的人仅4小时的行程即可抵达省城。还派有警卫队100人，全副武装在委员会周围巡视；又特派遣约30名信使紧急通知城里那些反政府的人准备第二天早晨同时起事。一切均已就绪，正当改革者静候大厅之时，突然收到一封急电，大意谓两军前进中受阻，⑤改革运动陡然遭受挫折。但是派出去的信使已经不可能召回，其他的人又没有谁知道那些反政府的人住在何

---

① 原文为"the city of Canton"，直译应为广东的城市，指广东省城广州。
② 汕头应是广州东边沿海城市。
③ 指定于九月九日重阳节（阳历10月26日）在广州起义。
④ 改革委员会，指兴中会广州起义领导机关。
⑤ 据孙中山《我的回忆》："一切似乎都在顺利进行，却突然来了一声晴天霹雳。这是汕头方面领导人拍给我的一份电报：'官军戒备，无法前进。'"（《孙中山全集》第1卷，第549页）

广州起义失败后流亡日本的孙中山（中）、陈少白（左）、郑士良（右）

兴中会广州分会旧址王氏书舍

孙中山1898年在横滨。孙中山（二排中）、杨衢云（前座左二），后立者宫崎寅藏

孙中山在澳门时的码头景象

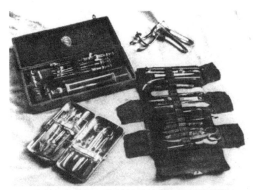

孙中山在澳门、广州行医时使用的医疗器械　　香港起义总部领导人杨衢云

处。进一步的消息证实继续前进已完全不可能，于是出现了"逃命"[①]的喊叫声。随后是军队的总溃退；烧文档、藏武器，并发电至香港，令特遣队停止出发。可是，发给香港代理的电报[②]，在所有人员都上了一条轮船之后才到达他手里，船上还装运了许多桶左轮手枪[③]。他并没有按照应该做的那样遣散队伍，反而命令他们继续开拔。当他们抵达广

①　"逃命"，原文为法语"sauve qui peut"，"四散逃生"、"大溃退"之意。

②　实际情况是广州起义计划败露之前，香港指挥部领导人杨衢云即因调遣失当，错失了军机，他于10月26日急电广州起义总指挥说"货不能来"，孙中山只得通知各路人马停止发动，并立即复电："货不要来，以待后命。"（参阅陈少白《兴中会革命史要》，孙中山复电转引自《孙中山集外集·复杨衢云电（一八九五年十月二十六日）》，上海人民出版社1992年印本）

③　"许多桶左轮手枪"　原文为"many barrels of revolvers"，本篇初译稿在期刊上发表时译为"许多左轮手枪"，因"barrels"这个词还可理解为枪管的意思；《孙文学说》第八章"有志竟成"中说："乃以运械不慎，致海关搜获手枪六百馀杆，事机乃泄……"（《孙中山全集》第6卷，第230页）但孙中山在《我的回忆》一文中明确说："但是来不及了，一支四百多人的特遣队已经带着十箱左轮手枪乘轮船出发。"（《孙中山全集》第1卷，第549页）冯自由《革命逸史·兴中会组织史》据史料记载："至八月间，各方运动渐臻成熟，香港总部遂定期于九月重阳日举事。预定由主要党员率领香港会党三千人，于是月初八晚乘夜轮进省，并木桶装载短枪，充作胶坭，瞒报税关。初九晨抵省垣时，齐用刀斧劈开木桶取出枪械，首先向各重要衙署进攻；……"（《革命逸史》（中），新星出版社2009年版，第653页）因此原文中"many barrels of revolvers"即订正译为"许多桶左轮手枪"。

州的码头后万没料到已自投罗网全部被俘获。①广州的领导纷纷各自逃跑。我自己，经过了多次死里逃生之后，终于登上一条小汽艇驶抵澳门，②在那里仅仅停留了24小时即前往香港。在香港拜访了几个朋友，见到了我的老师和朋友杰姆斯·康德黎③先生，告诉他我正在麻烦中，因为获罪于广东当局，恐怕我会被逮捕并押回广州施行处决。他劝我咨询一位律师，我立即照办了。

---

① 此句《孙中山全集》刊本译为："于是该党员及其部众尽投于罗网矣。"原著说明了该党员因违背电令，致使革命党遭受重大损失，但是文中并无该领导人被捕或赴难牺牲之意。孙中山于1897年在东京与宫崎寅藏谈话时说："当时弟已领千二百壮士进了内城（九月一日），已足发手。后有人止之，谓此数不足弹压乱民，恐有劫掠之虞。后再向潮州调潮人三千名为弹压地方，候初九仍未见到。各人会议，定策改期。是午后二时发电下港，止二队人不来。不料该头目无决断，至四时仍任六百之众赴夜船而来。我在城之众于九日午已散入内地，而港队于十日早到城，已两不相值，遂被擒五十余人。……其失则全在香港之队之来，使有证据，而其不来则无据可执也。因当日已合全省绅民反案，因佐证确实，遂不能移。"（《与宫崎寅藏等笔谈》，《孙中山全集》第1卷，第185页）又，据陈少白回忆："陈问：先生同杨衢云在房内的情形，说了什么话？孙说：我当时真恨极了，我责问他当日的事情。我说：'……你为什么到了时期，你自己不来，那还罢了，随后我打电〔报〕止你不来，隔一日，你又不多不少派了六百人来，把事情闹糟了，消息泄漏，人又被杀。你得了消息，便一个人拼命跑掉，这算是什么把戏？你好好把你的理由说来；不然，我是不能放过你的。'杨衢云俯首无词，最后他便说：'以前的事，是我一人之错，现下闻得你筹得大款，从新干起，故此赶来，请你恕我前过，容我再来效力。'"（《孙中山集外集·与陈少白的谈话（一八九八年三月下旬）》）

② 《我的回忆》："我潜逃到珠江三角洲海盗经常出没的河网地区，躲藏了几昼夜，终于登上一艘熟人的小汽船。刚一抵达澳门，我就荣幸地看到了一份悬赏一万两银子通缉孙文（即本人）的告示，而且听人说，一股巡勇截获那艘香港轮船，并立即逮捕了船上所有的人。一八九五年广州之役就这样结束了。"（《孙中山全集》第1卷，第549—550页）

③ 杰姆斯·康德黎（James Cantlie, 1851—1926），英国外科医生。1889—1896年任香港西医书院教务长。孙中山在香港西医书院（College of Medicine for Chinese, Hong Kong）学习时的医学教授。孙中山在伦敦遭阴谋绑架后，得到了这位老师的全力营救。后来康德黎写有《孙逸仙和中国的觉醒》（Sun Yat Sen and the Awakening of China，1912）一书。

杰姆斯·康德黎、谢尔顿·琼斯著《孙逸仙
与中国的觉醒》

康德黎等著《孙逸仙与中国的觉醒》平
装本

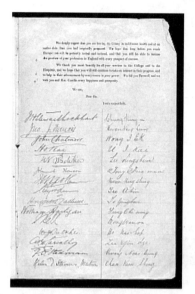

西医书院同人为感谢康德黎教授对学校作出的贡献所写的感谢函签名

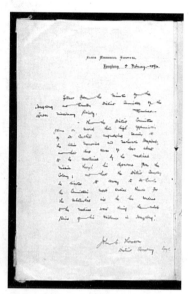

西医书院同仁致康德黎教授感谢函（1896.2.5）

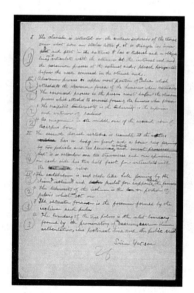

孙中山解剖学考试答题卷（1887.9）

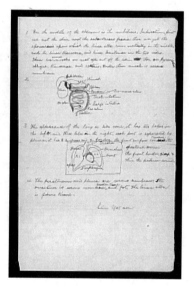

孙中山答题卷之二

第二章 被捕

我被我的"同伴"一边一个地夹着以半开玩笑半执意，又似朋友一般地强行推了进去。当前门匆促关上，并随即上了闩时，我大为惊讶，突然我脑中一闪，这房子一定就是中国公使馆。

我没有再去看康德黎先生，依照邓尼思先生①的指示，我被迫马上离开。

两天后我便搭上日本轮船去了神户，在那里停留几天后即前往横滨。在那里我改变了我的中国装束，换了一身日本式的欧洲服装；剪掉了辫子，让头发成自然状态，并且蓄了八字须。几天后又从横滨去到夏威夷群岛，居住在火奴鲁鲁②，在那里我有很多亲戚和朋友，还有很多怀有良好愿望的人。我所到之处，无论是日本、火奴鲁鲁或者美国，我发现一切有才智的中国人都充满了改革精神，都渴望祖国能创行代议政体。

我在火奴鲁鲁街上遇到了康德黎先生和康德黎夫人及其家属。③当时他们正在去英国的途中，他们一时没有认出我，因为我着的欧洲服

---

① 邓尼思先生　孙中山听从康德黎先生的意见去咨询的一位律师。《我的回忆》："在香港，我的安全并不更有保障。听从康德黎博士的建议，我去请教一位律师达尼思先生。他告诉我，最有效的安全措施是马上远走高飞。""'北京的臂膀虽然弱，但仍然是长的，'他说，'不论你走到世界哪个角落，都必须留心总理衙门的耳目。'"（《孙中山全集》第1卷，第550页）后来果然不出所料，清吏密探发现孙的行踪后就一直从日本跟踪至美国和英国。

② 火奴鲁鲁，原为夏威夷王国都城。1893年岛国的王权被推翻，建立夏威夷共和国临时政府；1898年夏威夷群岛正式并入美国版图，以后成为美国夏威夷州，火奴鲁鲁即为夏威夷州首府。火奴鲁鲁，夏威夷语指"屏蔽之湾"、"屏蔽之地"，是夏威夷群岛上的海港城市。19世纪初因当地檀香木贸易兴盛，华人即称火奴鲁鲁为檀香山。

③ 孙中山后来提到此次极其偶然而又万幸地遇见恩师之事甚为感慨："予到檀岛后，复集合同志以推广兴中会……行有日矣，一日散步市外，忽有驰车迎面而来者，乃吾师康德黎与其夫人也。予遂一跃登车，彼夫妇不胜诧异，几疑为暴客，盖彼已改装易服，彼不认识也。予乃曰：'我孙逸仙也。'遂相笑握手。问以何为而至此，曰：'回国道经此地，舟停而登岸浏览风光也。'予乃趁车同游，为之指导。游毕登舟，予乃告以予将作环绕地球之游，不日将由此赴美，随将到英，相见不远也。遂欢握而别。""故于甫抵伦敦之时，即遭使馆之陷，几致不测。幸得吾师康德黎竭力营救，始能脱险。此则檀岛之邂逅，真有天幸存焉。否则予尚无由知彼之归国，彼亦无由知吾之来伦敦也。"（《孙文学说》第八章"有志竟成"，《孙中山全集》第6卷，第230—232页）

清政府驻美国华盛顿公使馆（1900年前）

装，他们的日本佣人用日语和我讲话，她误认我是日本同乡。这样的
情况经常发生，每到一处，日本人起先总把我当做他们的同乡，直到
说话时，才知道是错了。

　　1896年6月，我离开火奴鲁鲁到旧金山，向东行之前，在旧金山
住了一个月。[①]在那里，我见到了许多同乡，他们盛情地接待了我。
在美国3个月后，我便乘梅杰斯蒂克号轮船去英国的利物浦。我在纽约
时，友人都忠告我，要谨防中国驻美国公使，他是满洲人[②]，对汉人

　　① 孙中山在《向英国律师卡夫所作的陈述词（一八九六年十一月四日）》里
说："我在纽约逗留了约一个月，在旧金山两个月。"（《孙中山全集》第1卷，
第37页）
　　② 当时中国驻美国公使杨儒（？—1902），系汉军正红旗人，光绪十八年
（1892）任驻美公使。

本无同情，尤其对一个改革者就更加敌视了。

1896年10月1日，我抵达伦敦，①住在斯屈朗路的赫胥旅馆。第二天我去了康德黎先生家，他家在波特兰区德文榭街②46号，在他家我受到了老朋友和他的妻子极为热情的接待。他们为我另租了一个房间，在格瑞法学院坊③8号，霍尔班格瑞小旅馆。此后我就安顿下来

伦敦格瑞法学院坊（Gray's Inn Place）8号霍尔班格瑞小旅馆（孙中山1896年曾居住于此）

并享受旅居伦敦之乐。在这个世界的最中心，我开始去了解游览许多名胜、博物馆和历史遗迹。作为一个中国人，使我印象最深的是这里庞大的车辆交通，川流不息的公共马车、出租马车、客车和货车以及街上到处推着车子的谦和的送货人，令人惊叹的是警察对这样繁忙的交通指挥控制得竟如此从容得当，同时人们心境平和、幽默诙谐。步行的游客也很多，但是并不感到像中国街道那样拥挤。因为一来我们

① 根据司赖特侦探所（Slateis Detective Agency）跟踪秘密报告，孙中山于9月30日夜9时50分抵达伦敦，抵达当晚临时在一家旅馆住下，第二天即10月1日去康德黎家。

② 德文榭街（Devonshire Street）一译德文郡街；旧译本作覃文省街。

③ 格瑞法学院坊（Gray's Inn Place），旧译作葛兰旅店（Gray's Inn）。据台湾出版《国父年谱（增订本）》考订："康氏夫妇招待甚殷，并为觅居附近之葛兰法学协会场（Gray's Inn Place）八号宝勒特小姐（Miss Pollard）开设之私人公寓（Boarding Home）。翌日，携先生迁往。"

伦敦孙中山故居纪念牌

的街道十分窄狭，实际上仅是小街小巷；再者我们运送货物，全靠扁担肩挑，甚至在街道宽敞的香港，步行的游人旅客来来往往也非常拥挤。

就在我刚刚知道从斯屈朗区到霍尔班区，从皮卡迪利广场到牛津广场这两个地方的时候，我被剥夺了自由。这场轰动一时的事件，由国家公众媒体做了详尽的报道。

我经常到康德黎先生家去，事实上是差不多每天都去，而且大部分时间是在他的书房里度过。一天在午餐时，他提到中国使馆就在这附近，并开玩笑地建议我去周围走走或者去访问一下；随即他的夫人却说，"你最好不要去，不要走近那儿，他们会抓你并把你送回中国去。"我们边说边大笑她说的话，一点也没想到这位妇女的直觉是多么的正确，很快我们就经历了这个现实。有天晚上到孟生①博士家晚餐，我们也是在香港认识的，当时他是我的医学老师，他也开玩笑地劝我，不要接近中国公使馆。我再次得到好友的告诫，但当时我不知道公使馆在哪里，所以朋友的劝告没有起到作用。我只知道要到德文榭街就必须在牛津广场下车，在那里一直向北走是一条宽敞的街道，直到我看到德文榭街的街名，在转弯处就可找到康德黎先生的房子。这就是当时我所知道的街区的范围。

10月11日星期天上午大约10点半钟，我正向德文榭街走去，希望按时与博士②和他的家人一起去教堂。这时一个中国人鬼鬼祟祟地从我后面走过来，靠近我，用英语问我是中国人还是日本人，我回答说，"我是中国人"。接着他又问我是哪一省的，当我告诉他我是广东人后，他说，"我们是同乡，讲一样的话；我是广东人。"他说的是"洋泾浜"英语③，即"商业"英语，那是来自不同地区的中国商人之间所说的共同语言。汕头和广州的商人，虽然他们的城市相距只有180英里（比伦敦到利物浦的距离还近），但他们所说的话彼此听不懂。全中国的书面语言是相同的，但书写和口语完全不同，口语有很多种。所以汕头和广州的商人在香港做生意时讲的是英语，而写的是共同的中国文字。以上这个话题很好解释，比如日本的书面语言中使用了中国字，所以中国人和日本人相会时，虽然没有共同的口语，但他们能够在地上或用纸笔互相以汉字表达意思，并可以常常用一只手的食指在另一只手上描绘出想象中的图形来互相了解。

---

① 孟生（Patrick Manson，1844—1922），英国医生，香港西医书院首任教务长，孙中山在该院学习时的医学教授。伦敦绑架事件发生后，他与康德黎一起积极参加营救。

② 博士（doctor），指康德黎先生。

③ 原文为"English or 'Pidgin'"，即英语混杂语言（pidgin English）。这里是指Chinese pidgin English，这是19世纪中叶出现于中国沿海通商口岸的一种极不规范的汉语式混合英语，一般称之为"洋泾浜英语"。

我的所谓中国朋友在他没有发现我的方言之前，一直用英语和我交谈。之后，我们就用广东方言谈话。我们沿着街慢步向前，边走边说，不久又来了一个中国人，于是我的身边左右各有一个人了。他们力劝我去他们的"住所"抽烟，和他们聊天。我婉言推辞，我们停留在人行道边。这时第三个中国人出现了，而第一个认识我的那个人却离开了我们。这两个留下的人进一步逼我陪他们，他们表面上态度友好，把我渐渐地引到人行道边上，这时邻近的一所房子的门突然开了，我被我的同伴一边一个地夹着以半开玩笑半执意、又似朋友一般地强行推了进去。我没有怀疑什么，因为我不知道进的是什么房子，我只是迟疑着，心里想着要按时赶到康德黎先生家与他们一同去教堂，如果再耽搁，就会太迟了。然而，实实在在我是进去了，当前门匆促关上，并随即上了闩时，我大为惊讶，突然我脑中一闪，这房子一定就是中国公使馆。房子里有几个穿官员制服的中国人，同时房子又那么宽敞，这足以说明问题。这时，我想起来了，中国公使就住在德文榭街附近某处，这是我以前经常路过的地方。

　　我被带到底层的一间房子，有一两个人和我说了几句话，他们也互相说说话。随后把我带上楼，我身旁一边一人半带强制性地逼我上去。接着我被带到三楼^①的一间屋子，并告诉我就留在这里。然而，这个房间看上去不能使绑架者们满意，不久就又把我关到另一间在四楼上的一个窗户上有栅栏的房间，窗外就是屋子后面。这时一位满头白发、留有胡须的老绅士进屋来，神态颇为高傲地说："对于你来说这里就是中国；你现在是在中国。"

　　他坐下后，继续审问我。

　　问我姓什么，我回答"孙"。

　　"你的名字，"他说，"是孙文；我们收到中国驻美国公使来

---

　　① 原文是"on the second floor"，字面上的意思是"在二楼"，但英国语言习惯一般理解为"在三楼"（地下底层为一楼），下文的"on the third floor"为"在四楼"。

清政府驻英国伦敦公使馆

电，通知我们说你已乘'梅杰斯蒂克'号轮船抵达这个国家；公使要
求我逮捕你。"①

---

　　① 孙中山抵达旧金山（San Francisco）时，清政府驻旧金山总领事冯咏蘅向
驻美公使杨儒密报："孙文……年约三十左右，身材短小，面黑微须，剪发洋装，
由檀香山行抵金山。同伴有二洋人：一名卑涉，亦美国金山人，素任檀岛银行副买
办；一名威陆，亦美国人，向在檀岛服官，前次创议废主，因其未隶檀籍，所谋不
遂。均挟厚资，居檀年久，是否孙同党，尚难臆断，唯见同船偕来，交情甚洽。孙
文借寓金山沙加冕度街第七百零六号门牌华商联胜杂货铺内。闻不日往施家谷转纽
约，前赴英法，再到新加坡。并闻有沿途联络各会党，购买军火，欲图报复之说。
该犯随身携带私刊书册两本，虽无悖逆实迹，检其上李傅相书，确有该犯之名，显
系孙文无疑。现将原书设法觅取寄呈，俟访明该犯赴纽行期，再行电禀。"（1896
年6月27日）杨儒得密报后即电报清廷，总理衙门电示："铣电悉。孙文将往欧洲
何国？偕行洋人系何国人？附搭某船？希确查密电龚使酌办。英能援香港、缅甸交
犯约代拿固妙；否则该匪若由新加坡潜结恶党内渡，应先电粤督预防，新加坡领事
亦应饬其认真查访。"1896年7月18日，清廷驻美公使致函驻英公使曰："弟因中

（转下页）

"为什么逮捕我？"我问。

对此，他回答：

"你曾为改革呈上一份请愿书到北京总理衙门①，要求把它呈递皇上。②这可能是一份很好的请愿书；只是现在总理衙门需要你，所以扣留你在这里，直到皇上令下我们即照旨办理。"

"可否让我的朋友知道我在这里？"我问。

"不行，"他回答，"但是你可以写信到旅馆把你的行李送给你。"

我表示想写封信给孟生博士，他提供了笔、墨水和纸。我致信孟生博士，告诉他我被监禁在中国公使馆，并要他告诉康德黎先生把我的行李送给我。这个老绅士——我后来才知道他是哈里代·马卡尼③先生——反对我使用"监禁"一词，并要我换一个词语。于是

美交犯另约，迄无成绪，此间无从措手，总署深知，故有转电尊处援约代拿，并饬新嘉坡领事认真查访之议。" 9月25日，杨儒密电龚照瑗："现据纽约总领事施肇曾探悉，孙文于九月二十三号礼拜三搭White Star Line Majestic轮船至英国黎花埠登岸。"10月2日，龚照瑗电报北京总理衙门："接杨使函电悉。饬拿粤犯孙文，该犯现由美到英，改洋装无辫，外部以无在英交犯约，不能代拿。现派人密尾行踪。瑗。寝。"并于10月10日复电驻美公使："密。孙文已到英，外部以此间无交犯约，不能代拿。闻将往法，现派人密尾。瑗。支。"（清廷追踪孙中山有关密件，见吴宗濂《随轺笔记》卷二《记事》，吴当年为清使馆法文翻译；参见《中华民国开国五十年文献》第1编第10册，台北正中书局1961年版）

① 北京总理衙门，即总理各国事务衙门，简称"总理衙门"、"总署"及"译署"。这是清政府于1861年设立的办理洋务及外交事务的最高决策机构。

② 关于请愿事，孙中山在《我的回忆》里说："传来的消息说，光绪皇帝已从梦中醒悟，不顾慈禧太后态度如何，有心赞助我们的革新。我立即草拟了一份请愿书，征集到数以百计的签名后，把它呈送到北京。"（见《孙中山全集》第1卷，第548页）

③ 哈里代·马卡尼（Macartney Halliday，1833—1906），旧译马凯尼。中文名马格里，字清臣，清廷驻英国公使馆英籍参赞。早年曾为英国军医，咸丰八年（1858）随英军来华。曾任李鸿章淮军教习，先后主持苏州洋炮局和金陵制造局（兵工厂），后因发生试放大炮爆炸事故被撤职。光绪二年（1876）经李鸿章等荐举随郭嵩焘出使英国，以三品衔候选道充任三等翻译官，协助设立驻英中国公使馆。后升任驻英中国公使馆二等参赞。

清政府缉拿钦犯孙中山出具的悬赏领款密件

清政府负责办理洋务与外交的机构——总理各国事务衙门

我写道："我在中国公使馆；请告诉康德黎先生把我的行李送到这里来。"①

之后他又说不要我写信给我的朋友，只要我写信到我住的旅馆。我告诉他我不是住在旅馆里，只有康德黎先生知道我住在哪儿。很明显，这是审讯者耍的狡猾的花招，他们想搜寻到我随身的物品，特别是我的文件，希望发现我的信件，借此查明谁是我的中国同犯或者通信人。②我把写给孟生博士的信交他过目，他读后交还给我，说："这很好。"于是我把信装进信封交给了哈里代·马卡尼先生，完全相信他会把信送出去。

①《向英国律师卡夫所作的陈述词》："我写的是：'我被监禁（confined）在中国使馆里。'他说：'我不喜欢"监禁"这个字眼。'我说：'那我该怎么写？'他说：'简单地写上"把我的行李送来"。'我说：'他们不知道我在什么地方，是不会把行李送来的。'第二封信我是这样写的：'我在中国使馆，请将我的行李送来。'他说：'发出这信之前，我必须请示公使。'他拿着信走了。以后直到我离开使馆时，再也没有见过他。"（《孙中山全集》第1卷，第40页）

② 虽然清廷驻英使馆所雇侦探早已跟踪侦察到孙所住之旅馆，但因没有住客本人亲笔委托，任何人无权检查住店客人的行李。

第三章 监禁

在我被监禁的第四天，一个所谓邓先生的来看我。他一来我就认出他就是绑架我的那个人。他说："这是皇帝的命令，他不惜任何代价，只要抓住你，死的活的都可以。"

孙中山囚禁室一角

　　哈里代先生离开房间后，把门关上并上了锁，我成了在押的囚
犯。过后不久，我房间门外响起了木匠活的声音使我烦躁不安。他们
在门上又安了一把锁，还在门外派了两名看守，其中一个是欧洲人；
有时还加到三个看守。在最初24小时，门外两个中国看守常进室内来
用他们的家乡话与我交谈，我完全懂他们的方言。他们没有告诉我有关
我被关押的事，我也不问他们什么——不过他们曾告诉我，把我关押到
这里来的就是这个老绅士，他叫哈里代·马卡尼，他们称他马大人[①]
：马代替"马卡尼"，"大人"相当于"阁下"。这就如同对中国公使的
称呼，比如龚大人[②]。龚是他的家族名，即姓氏[③]；大人表示对他的
尊称，意思就是"阁下"。他在公众面前从不说自己的真名，因此使
得每一个外国人都不自觉地称他为"阁下"。我真想知道，他和英国

---

　　① 原文为"Ma-Ta-Yen"，这是广东话"马大人"的英文拼音。《孙中山全
集》刊本误译为"马大爷"，因此下文对于"大爷"的解释："大爷者，官场通俗
之尊称"，也是误译。（《孙中山全集》第1卷，第58页）

　　② 龚大人指驻英公使龚照瑗。龚于1893年至1896年任驻英公使。孙中山被绑
架时他的任期已满，应于8月卸职；但此时新任公使尚未任命，仍由他继续履行职
务。

　　③ 原文为"family name or surname"，即：家族（家庭）名，即姓氏。

政府里的官员交往时，是否也只用姓；如果是这样，那就有贬低和轻视的意思了。中国官场及外交礼仪是很微妙的，在和外国人交往时，语调和词义上细微的差别都足以把尊敬变为侮辱。外国人要想理解中国文字语言上的变化，即由尊敬变为侮辱，一定要对中国文化有颇深的研究才能做到。中国外交家喜欢愚弄外国高级官员，当对方受到侮辱后便沾

哈里代·马卡尼（1833—1906），英国人，清政府驻英国公使馆洋参赞

沾自喜地对周围人炫耀自己了不得，表明外国"恶魔"——洋鬼子是如何甘拜下风的。

　　我被监禁几个小时之后，一个守卫进到房里来对我说，哈里代·马卡尼先生令他来搜查我。他搜出了我的钥匙、铅笔和小刀，没有发现我装有几张钞票的那个口袋，只拿走了我的几张无关紧要的文件。他们问我要吃什么，照我的要求他们拿了点牛奶给我喝。

　　白天两个英国仆人带了煤进来生火并打扫房间，我要求第一个来的人替我送封信出去，他答应了，于是我写了张便条给德文榭街46号的康德黎先生。第二个仆人进来时我请他代办了同样的事情。当然我一直不知道信的下落如何，但他们两人都说信已经送出去了。（星期天）晚上一个英国妇女进来铺床。[①]我没有委托她什么。这晚我和衣而睡，然而通宵未眠。

　　第二天——星期一，10月12日——这两名英国仆人又来到我的房里，带来煤、水和食物。一个对我说托他送的便条已经送出去了，而另一个叫科尔的，说他不能出去送信。我想，我的信绝不可能送到了。

————————

　　① 后来研究者认为这位进来铺床的英国妇女就是暗中给康德黎先生写密信的霍维太太，科尔就是在她的鼓励下才决定为囚禁者秘密送信的。

窗户钉有栅栏的囚禁室

13日，星期二，我再一次问这个年纪较轻的男仆——不是科尔——他是否把我的信送出去了，是否见到了康德黎先生。他说他送去了；他见我仍有怀疑，便发誓他见到了康德黎先生，说他收信时说，"一切知道了！"我没有纸了，就用铅笔写在小手巾的角上，再次请他送给我的朋友，同时把一枚半镑金币①放在他手中。我尽量往好处想，但我对他的诚实仍有所怀疑。之后我的怀疑得到了证实，他当时就已把我的信交给了他的主人，把一切都揭露了。

在我被监禁的第四天，一个所谓邓先生的②来看我。他一来我就认出他就是绑架我的那个人。他坐下来后开始与我谈话。

"我上次见到你，"他开始说，"并把你带到这里，这样做是履行我的职务。我现在是作为一个朋友来和你谈话。你最好承认你就是孙文；你否认是无用的，因为所有的事都已决定了。"他以一种伪君子的奉承却又刻薄的语调继续说："你在中国已很出名，皇帝和总理衙门都非常了解你的历史；你的名声已很卓著，即使现在死去，也是值得的。"（这是东方人具有的一种谄媚相，而西方人很少有，或者不欣赏甚至反对这种态度；但是在中国如何死和在什么名声下死被认为是至关重要的）"现在你在这里，"他继续说，"意味着生或死。你知道吗？"

---

① a half-sovereign，一枚半镑金币（《孙中山全集》刊本作："小金钱一枚"）。当时英国硬币，1金镑合20先令；半镑即10先令金币。
② 原文作"Mr. Tang"，《孙中山全集》刊本译为"唐先生"；但此人实指清使馆译员邓廷铿（字琴斋，广东三水人），"Tang"系广东话"邓"的英文拼音（第一个字母应读浊辅音），即普通话拼音"Deng"。

"为什么？"我问，"这是英国，不是中国。你们打算对我怎样？假如你们想引渡我，你们必须让英国政府知道我被关押的事；同时我不相信这个国家的政府会抛弃我。"

"我们并不打算按正式手续引渡你，"他回答说，"一切准备停当；轮船已经预订好；你会从这里被押上船同时会堵塞住你的嘴，所以不会受到骚扰；并且你会被安置在船上十分严密的地方。在香港港口外有炮舰等着你，你被换到舰艇上后直接驶向广州，在那里，你将受到审讯并会被处决。"

我指出，这是冒险行动，我可能在航行途中有机会和英国人交谈。对此，邓断言不可能，他说："你会被极为严密地看管起来，如同在此地一样，所以一切逃跑的可能都会被切断。"但是我认为在船上的官吏不可能都和我的逮捕者一样，他们中可能有同情我并愿意帮助我的。

"该轮船公司的人，"邓说，"是哈里代·马卡尼先生的朋友，他们一定会按照所吩咐的去做。"

在回答我的提问时他告诉我，我会被带上格伦公司的轮船，但是这周不能动身（这是10月14号），因为公使不愿花钱专门租一条轮船，他想租赁运货物的船，可先把货物运上船，这样就只付旅客的票钱。①

"下星期某天，"他补充说，"货物装船后，你就可上船了。"

我指出这个计划是很难执行的。他仅仅说："我们并不担心这点，我们可以在这里杀你，因为这是中国，在使馆里没有人能干涉

----

① 邓廷铿说将雇船秘密押运孙回国是事实。1896年10月16日清公使得总理衙门电示："庚电悉。购商船径解粤系上策，即照行。七千镑不足惜，即在汇丰暂拨，本署再与划扣。惟登舟便应镽，管解亦须加慎，望茇筹周备。起解电闻，以便电粤。"（见《中华民国开国五十年文献》第1编第10册，第192页；《中华民国国父实录》第1册，第363页）

我们。"①

　　为了教训我并稳定我的情绪，他引述了高丽一爱国者的事件，这位爱国者从高丽逃往日本，被一同乡引诱到上海，在上海被处死于英租界。他的尸体由华人送回高丽，为了惩罚他，尸体运达后，高丽政府砍掉他的头示众，而对谋杀者则授予了极高职位作为奖赏。很明显，邓愚蠢地相信因逮捕我并将我置于死地，他将同样会得到政府的提拔。

　　我问他为何如此残忍，他回答说：

　　"这是皇帝的命令，他不惜任何代价，只要抓住你，死的活的都可以。"

　　我强调说，高丽事件②是引起中日战争的原因之一，而我的被捕和处决可能会引起进一步的麻烦和更大的混乱。

　　"英国政府，"我说，"会要求处罚公使馆所有的人员；而你，作为我的同乡，竟如此对待我，我的广东同胞会为我报仇的，惩罚你和你的家庭。"

　　这时他改变了语调，收起了他傲慢无礼的话语，并且说他所做的都是按照公使馆的指示，他不过是在我处于困境时作友好的劝告。

---

　　① 孙中山脱险后当日在答记者问和在伦敦警察厅作陈述时都特别说到这一点，他曾问邓："如果不能把我运走，他们下一步将会怎么办。他说，就在使馆里杀死我，将尸体加以防腐，再送回中国执行死刑。我问，他们为什么要这般残忍，他说，政府不惜以任何代价捉拿你，不论是死是活。"（《在伦敦苏格兰场的陈述词（一八九六年十月二十三日）》，《孙中山全集》第1卷，第34页）

　　② 1894年（甲午）朝鲜政府为镇压东学党起义，请求清政府出兵协助镇压，日本乘机入侵朝鲜，并挑起发动甲午中日战争。

第四章　为生存恳求看守

我完全绝望了，唯一能做的只有祷告上帝以求得些许的安慰。我向科尔提出恳求，请他帮助我。完全可以想象我是多么渴望知道他的决定。

当晚12点，邓又来到我的房间重新开始这一话题。①我问他，如果他真是我的朋友，那他打算怎样帮我。

"我就是为此再来的，"他回答说，"我要做我所能做的一切，让你很快就能出去，同时，"他继续说，"我叫锁匠复制了两把钥匙，一把开你的房门，另一把开使馆大门。"

邓说他不得不这样做，因为钥匙是由最受公使信任的仆人管着，是总不离身的。

我问什么时候可以出去，他说要到明天，可能安排在星期五凌晨两点。

在他离开房间时，他嘱咐我做好星期五出去的准备。

他离开后，我写了几个字打算请英仆送交康德黎先生。

第二天（10月15日，星期四）上午，我把字条交给英仆；不料，这天下午邓告诉我那张字条已由该英仆上交使馆当局了。

邓说，他营救我的全部计划已被我的行动搞砸了，并且哈里代·马卡尼先生大骂他把怎样处置我的事情告诉了我。

我立刻问他是否还有一线希望，他回答：

"有，还有很大希望；但是你必须按照我说的去做。"

他建议我写一封信给公使请求宽恕。我同意这样做，于是要笔、墨和纸。邓吩咐科尔取来给我。

然而，我要求换中国墨和纸，我认为不应用英文写信给中国公使。

对此邓答道：

"呵，用英语最好，因为公使只不过是一个挂名的头头；每一件事情都掌握在马卡尼手里，所以你最好写信给他。"

我问应该写什么时，他说：

---

① 孙中山在囚禁中的这次谈话，参见本书编入的文献资料《清政府驻英公使馆整理的〈孙中山与邓廷铿的谈话〉》。

"你一定要否认你曾经参与广东阴谋事件①，表明你受到朝廷官员的错误指控，而你到公使馆来是要求纠正的。"

我按照邓的口授当场写了一封这样内容的长信。②在折好的信上写上致哈里代·马卡尼先生（他的名字是邓告诉我拼写的，因为我不知道如何拼写），我把信交给邓，他把信在身上藏好之后就出去了，此后我再也没有见过这个阴谋者。

毫无疑问，我做了一件非常愚蠢的事，这意味着我给敌人提供了字据，证明我是自动到公使馆来的。不过一个将死的人是任何机会都想抓住的，所以我，处于危难中的我，就轻易地受骗了。

邓告诉我，我所写的短信字条都由英仆交给了使馆，所以不曾有任何东西送出去交给我外面的朋友。这样我失去了一切希望，以为只有面对死亡了。

在这一星期中，我偶尔得到一点纸片就写了我的困境投于窗外。起初我请英仆替我投出去，因我的窗户不临街；但是所有的字条都被扣留下了。于是我试图自己投到窗外，希望能侥幸落到隔壁房屋后面的铅皮房檐上。

---

① 广东阴谋事件，指1895年10月孙中山所策划的广州起义。详情见本书第一章。

② 孙中山获释后在与英国律师卡夫谈话时说："他要我首先说明，我与广州谋反一事无关；说我参加谋反是不真实的。他说，最后一件事是'你亲身前来这里，打算请求公使帮助，使你的名字在国内不受牵连'。我把这些话写了下来。我这样做，因为我考虑到这是我得以离开那里的唯一途径。""我所写的那份书面报告是不真实的。我之所以这样做，是因为邓说过，如果我写下那些话，他就可以设法帮助我出去。那些话是他吩咐我写上的。他要我这样说，我从中国逃了出来，打算拜见任何一位中国驻外使节，请求他们为我解脱嫌疑。他要我写这报告，说如果按这个方式写好，他可以帮助我脱险。当时，我没有别的指望，所以就照他的吩咐做了。他对我说，我是从美国来，并要我写上我曾经到过中国驻美使馆，为着去见那里的公使。我在报告中写了这些内容，还写上驻美公使不愿倾听我的意见，所以我来到英国向这里的中国公使提出请求。"（《向英国律师卡夫所作的陈述词》，《孙中山全集》第1卷，第42、44页）

公使馆三楼孙中山蒙难室外观

为了使纸团掷得更远，我包了几个铜币增加重量，而当这些用尽后，就包两个先令，这些硬币，是在搜查时我设法藏在身上的。我希望这些纸团落于邻居家，能侥幸被邻家拾到。有一纸团击中了一根绳子，径直掉在了我的窗外。我请一佣人——不是科尔——去捡来给我；但他不但未去捡，反而告诉了中国守卫，他们把它捡走了。

他们搜寻周围，落在隔壁铅皮房檐上的一个纸团引起了他们的注意，于是他们爬上去，把那一纸团捡了下来，我的这一线希望也失去了。他们把这些便条都交给了他们的主人。

我现在的困境大大地超过了以往，他们用螺丝钉钉死了我的窗户，我和外面联系的唯一途径也没有了。

我完全绝望了，唯一能做的只有祷告上帝以求得些许的安慰。寂静阴沉的白昼过去，继之而来的是令人更为忧伤的黑夜。日日夜夜就这样缓慢地流逝，若非祷告给予安慰，我已经发疯。我获释之后曾对康德黎先生叙述，祷告是如何给了我希望，同时告诉他我无论如何绝不会忘记这种好似占据了我整个心灵的感觉。在10月16日（星期五）早晨，当我跪着做完祷告站起来时，一种平静的感觉，使我充满了希望和信心，我的祷告上帝是听到了的，我充满希望，一切会好的。所以我决定加倍努力，并决定向科尔提出恳求，请他帮助我。

当他进来时我问他："你能帮我做些事情吗？"

他的回答却是问我一个问题："你是什么人？"

"从中国来的一个政治避难者。"我告诉他。

他好像不十分理解我的意思，我于是问他是否听说过亚美尼亚人。他说他听说过，我便抓住这一线索，告诉他这正如土耳其的苏丹想要杀死所有的亚美尼亚基督徒一样，中国的皇帝想杀死我，因为我是一个基督徒，同时是一个为中国争取建立一个良好的政府而努力奋斗的政党成员。

"所有的英国人民，"我说，"都同情亚美尼亚人，同时我一点也不怀疑，如果他们知道我的处境，他们一定会以同样的感情对待我。"

他说他不知道英国政府会不会帮助我，我告诉他英国政府肯定会帮助我，要不然中国公使就不会如此严密地监禁我，就会公开地要求英国政府合法地引渡我。

"我的生命，"我对他说，"是在你手中。假若你把这里的情况让外人知道，我就可得救；不然，我就一定会被处死。是救一个人的命好，还是让他去死好呢？或者你认为是尽职于上帝更为重要，还是服务于你的主人更为重要呢？——或认为是应该尊敬公正的英国政府呢，还是要去偏袒腐败的中国的政府？"

我请求他仔细想一想我所说的，下次来时给我一个答复，并请据实相告，他能不能帮助我。

他走了，直到第二天早晨我才见到他。完全可以想象我是多么渴望知道他的决定。在他忙着替我换煤时，他指了指他放在煤桶上那张纸。我的生命好像系在这张纸的内容上。它是希望之使者，还是希望之门再次在我面前被关上？他离开房间后，我立刻把纸捡起来看：

"我会试着为你送封信给你的朋友。但你一定不要在桌上写信，因为门外的守卫经常在锁孔中窥探你，你应该在床上写。"

于是我躺卧在床上，面对墙壁，在一张名片上写信给康德黎先生。中午科尔再来，我示意便条所在。他走时把名片字条收好，同时我给了他20英镑，这是我仅有的一点钱了。康德黎先生的回条仍由科尔置于煤桶带回，科尔有意味地瞥了一眼暗示我煤桶里有什么东西。他出去后，我焦急地捡起纸条，读后大喜："振作起来！政府正在为你的权利进行交涉。不日你即将自由。"[1]由此我知道，上帝已回答

---

① 科尔这一次带回的康德黎的密信显然不是最初的一次回信，因为信中有这样的话"政府正在为你的事情努力"，而此时英国政府尚未介入此事。孙中山在获

（转下页）

了我的祈祷了。

在这一段期间，我一直没有脱过衣服，睡眠也很少，常常片刻即醒，这是十分麻烦的。在接到朋友的令我振奋的消息以前，我一直装作在真正休息的样子。

最令我担心的是这种灾祸会降临在我为之斗争的大事业上，假若我被押解回中国并被杀害，这一后果就会发生。一旦我被囚运回国，他们一定会向海外公布我是被英政府通过合法手续移交的，这样其他的政治犯在英国就没有避难之地了。这会使党人想起太平天国起义，由于英国的干涉，这个伟大的民族的和基督徒的革命①被扑灭了。如果我被遣回中国并被杀害，人们会再一次相信这次革命斗争的失败又是由于英国的帮助所导致，这样我们的革命将没有希望了。②

假使这次中国公使馆从我的住处得到了我的文件，事情将会更加复杂化，将会使更多的朋友遭受危害。幸好这个危险已经彻底消除，

释之后接受英国律师的调查访问时，回忆说："我得到答复，收到康德黎博士一张名片，上面并有孟生博士的签名。这时我的心情愉快一些，但仍有些怀疑。接到这张名片后，我又收到了康德黎博士的几张名片，都是科尔送来的。孟生博士的签名不能使我完全振作起来，我考虑到，他们可以随便从什么地方弄到康德黎博士的名片，因此，我要求科尔去请康德黎博士写几个字给我。于是，康德黎博士在一张小纸条上写了几句话给我。"（《向英国律师卡夫所作的陈述词》，《孙中山全集》第1卷，第43页）这个回忆是准确的，第一次只是让科尔带回一张签名的名片，表示已收到从公使馆里传出来的密信，再回信时显然营救工作已经取得进展了。

① 伟大的民族的和基督徒的革命（great national and Christian revolution），指太平天国运动，它既是反对清王朝的民族革命，同时又是以基督教名义创立的"拜上帝会"（又称"拜上帝教"、"太平基督教"）所发动的农民起义。

② 辛亥革命爆发之后，孙中山在伦敦与记者谈话时，对于个人的安危作出了解释："有人问我为什么竟然在伦敦随意走动而不加戒备。我的回答是，我的生命现已无足轻重，因为已经有许多人可以接替我的位置。十年前，如果我被暗杀，或者被解回中国处决，事业就会遭到危害。但现在，我付出多年努力所缔造的组织已经很完善了。"（《我的回忆》，《孙中山全集》第1卷，第554页）

太平天国运动是以基督教名义创立的"拜上帝会"所发动的农民起义。图为天王玉玺

康德黎夫人

一位十分细心的夫人早作了提防。康德黎夫人，由于她的责任心，在知道我被关押后几个小时之内就赶到我的旅馆仔细收拾我的文件和信函并全部销毁。假如世界各地的我的一些朋友没有收到回信，想必他们会怪这位考虑周到、明智而果断地采取了措施的夫人，却会原谅我没有回信给他们，因为我失掉了他们的地址，在许多情况下，我甚至不知道他们的名字。假如中国当局再诱捕我，他们已没有文件可找了，那他们还能靠什么知道我的同伙呢？

我幸亏没有觉得给我的食物中会有毒，但我的心境是如此恶劣以至于很厌食。我只能喝点流质食品，如牛奶和茶，有时吃一个鸡蛋。但在我收到朋友的信之后，我的饮食和睡眠都大有改善了。

伦敦蒙难记
Kidnapped in London

第五章　朋友们的营救

科尔离开孟生家，带回来了两位朋友给我的一张签了名的名片，这一是希望能给我安慰，减轻我的恐惧，二是证实科尔确已为营救我尽了力。两位博士前往伦敦警察厅试看有无效果，准备再次向警方提出要求。

公使馆外面正在发生的事情，我当然一点也不知道。我所有的求援字条、所有的碎纸片都丢到窗外去了，所有的信件我都已正式递交给了哈里代·马卡尼先生和邓，我知道这都没有用，然而更糟的是，他们对我施行了更为严密的看守，这样我和朋友的联系就越来越不可能了。

不过，在10月16日，星期五的早晨，我最后的恳求起作用了，就在那天之后，科尔即开始关注我的事情。科尔的妻子积极主动地做了大量的工作，1896年10月17日（星期六）给康德黎先生的信就是科尔妻子写的，由此营救工作开始启动。这封信到达德文榭街已是晚上11点了，可以想象博士读到下面这封信的心情：

"从上星期天起你的一位朋友就被关押在中国公使馆。他们打算把他送到中国去，在那儿他一定会被绞死。这个可怜的人是多么的悲哀，如果不马上采取行动，他将被送走，而且没有人会知道这件事。我虽不敢签上我的名字，但这是事实，请相信我所说的。无论如何你一定要立刻采取行动，不然就太迟了。我想，他的名字叫林音仙。"①

---

① 此信后来证实为清使馆中另一同情者所写。据吴相湘《海外新见中国现代史史料》："据上述档卷中是年十月二十二日（孙尚未获释）康德黎在高等法庭（High Court of Justice）证词：十月十五日，康遇孙所居留之葛兰旅店之波奈尔女士（Miss Pollard）言：孙自十一日来，四日未回旅店不知去向，即已关切之至；至十六日夜，康家信箱内忽有一未签名信言其中国友人被禁清使馆，康乃报警。……据档卷中柯尔证词：孙被禁后，马格里即嘱其小心看管，如孙托其传递任何消息，应即报告，每次必予奖金一镑。柯尔均遵行，故孙两次托致信康，柯尔均呈马而获奖金，嗣经孙苦求，十月十六日，柯尔偶与女管家霍维太太言及，霍维太太极力鼓励其传信，柯尔之意乃决。翌日遂将孙之名片递送康家。但当晚康家却发现有一未签名之信函报告此事。柯尔证词说：他不能确知更不能确言此信是否即霍维太太所寄发。这是柯尔宣誓不能作伪证的负责话，但以今论霍太太寄发的可能性很大，因为当时他只和她谈及此。并且不论如何，柯尔之心意由遵守马格里之吩咐转变至不听吩咐而为孙传递消息，霍维太太的影响力最大，这是柯尔证词承认的。"

另据《国父年谱》（增订本）："唯关于作书与递书之女子，据罗家伦最近在英文《康德黎爵士传》中所发现（此书为康氏之子Neil Cantlie与George Seaver合著，原名'Sir James Cantlie'，一九三九年伦敦出版，系根据康氏档写成），谓'柯尔以此事告知英籍女管家霍维太太（The English housekeeper. Mrs. Howe），霍太太对被囚者同情，乃作此函，于十月十六日间十一时投至康寓'。"当时孙中山在书中没有披露霍维太太的帮助，显然是考虑她仍在中国公使馆服务，以免她受到牵连。

显然一刻也不能耽误了。在打听到哈里代·马卡尼先生的住址后，天已经很晚了，康德黎先生立刻动身去找他。他一点也不知道马卡尼就是直接操纵那个无耻行动的主谋。对我而言这是福还是祸，没有人知道。他找到了哈利区3号这间房子，但门是关着的。那时已是星期六晚上11点15分，梅尔蓬路一个执勤巡警看见他从围墙内的大院出来时感到很奇怪。这个巡警告诉他，这房子已关闭6个月，这家人已下乡了。康德黎先生问他怎么知道的，巡警对他说，三天前的夜晚有一盗贼企图破门，这事引起警方仔细调查，看是谁住在这里，因此知道了这些情况，即房主很明显已经6个月不在这里了。康德黎先生紧接着驱车至梅里尔本路警察所，把案件提交值班警员。他接着又到伦敦警察厅要求警官接见。一位侦探长在他的私人房间

康德黎博士（1851—1926）

孟生博士（1844—1922）

接见了他，并表示将记下证词。这事很难使人相信，因为它不像是会发生的事。侦探长彬彬有礼地听完这个令人惊奇的案件，但是声明伦敦警察厅不可能积极主动地去办理这件事。康德黎先生离开警察厅独自走在街上时已是凌晨1点钟了，而事情的艰难于他动身时未有丝毫改变。

第二天早晨，康德黎先生去肯辛顿和他的朋友商量，不管是否有效，他想请驻伦敦的中国海关的一个头头去与公使馆私下疏通，劝说他们重新考虑他们的轻率行为和愚蠢的步骤。

但这办法并未得到支持，他只好再去哈利区3号，希望至少有

一个看管房屋的人住在屋里，这样起码可以打听在哪里能够找到哈里代·马卡尼先生或者得到他的通信地址。但除了看到盗贼撬门用的"短撬棍"证实巡警所说的窃贼企图破门的事情属实外，无丝毫线索可以找到这个狡猾的东方化了的施展圆滑外交手腕的人的踪迹。

之后康德黎先生去孟生博士家，到了那里，在前门看见一个人，这人就是科尔，使馆里的侍者。这个瘦弱的人最后鼓起勇气透露了我被关押的秘密。他找到康德黎先生家时，曾害怕得发抖；当得知康德黎先生已去孟生博士家，他立即赶到那儿并见到了两位博士。科尔当时把我写给康德黎先生的两张名片交给他们，名片上写道：

"上星期天我被两个中国人绑架，并被强行带进中国公使馆。我被关押起来，而且在一两天内将被遣送去中国，关在专门包租的一条船上。我肯定会被砍头。唉！我真是不幸。"①

---

① 此信与原始文件的文字略有不同，这里据名片原件翻译如下：

礼拜天我被绑架到中国公使馆，并将从英格兰偷运回中国去处死。恳求赶快救救我！为了遣送我回中国，中使馆早已包租了一条船，并且整个航程我将被关锁起来，与任何人不能联系。哎！我多么不幸！（现在请替我照顾这个人。他很穷，而且为了给我做事，他将会丢掉自己的工作）

科尔送的这封信虽比康德黎从邮箱里收到霍维太太的信要晚，但这是孙中山的亲笔，绑架事件确凿无疑。孙中山被囚禁在清使馆时还写了第二封密信："十月十一日，星期天，我在离中国公使馆门口不远的街上，被两个中国人拉入使馆。还没有进去之前，他们各在左右夹住我的一只手，竭力怂恿我入内和他们谈谈。当我进入后，他们把正门锁上，并强迫我上楼，推进一个房间，从那天起便将我关锁起来。如果他们做得到，就打算将我从英国偷偷运走；不然的话，也会在使馆里用别的方法杀害我。我出生于香港，四五岁时才回到中国内地。把我当作一名合法的英国臣民，你能不能用这种方法来使我脱险？"（《致康德黎简（一八九六年十月十九日）》，《孙中山全集》第1卷，第30页）

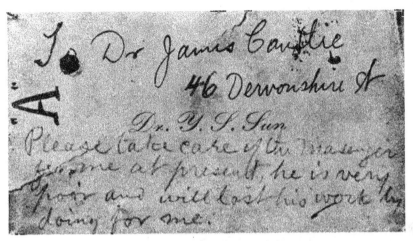

孙中山在关押中写给康德黎的密函名片A正面

孙中山在关押中写给康德黎的密函名片A背面

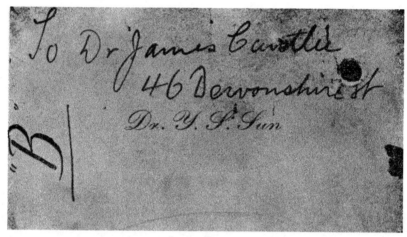

To Dr James Cantlie
46 Devonshire St
Dr. Y. S. Sun

B/

孙中山写给康德黎的密函名片B正面

a ship is already charter
by the C.L. for the service
to take me to China and I
shall be locked up all the
way without communication
to any body. O! Woe to me!

孙中山写给康德黎的密函名片B背面

19世纪的苏格兰场（伦敦警察厅）

　　孟生博士热忱地与他的朋友共同试图营救我，他们继续问科尔。康德黎先生说：

　　"哦，假若哈里代·马卡尼先生就住在城里，那就好了。很可惜他已离开。我们在哪儿可以找到他呢？"

　　科尔立刻回答：

　　"哈利代先生在城里，他每天来使馆；就是哈里代先生把孙锁在房子里的，还派我看管，并命令在门外严密监视，这样他就完全没有办法逃跑了。"

　　这个消息令人吃惊，释放更为困难，因为已处于一个更加不可预测的危险境地。因此诉讼行动应该极其小心进行，同时必须呼吁最高当局介入，这些狡诈和专横的人才能被制伏。

　　科尔继续回答他们的询问，告诉他们在使馆我被说成是一个疯子；在下星期二我会被送往中国（那只有两天了）；他不知道遣送我的船是哪条航线，但是城里有一个名叫麦其谷的人，他一定与此事有关。这星期又有两三名身着中国水手服的士兵来公使馆，科尔认为他们与我的被遣送有关，这几个人以前在使馆里是从没有见过的。

科尔离开孟生家，带回来了两位朋友给我的一张签了名的名片，这一是希望能给我安慰，减轻我的恐惧，二是证实科尔确已为营救我尽了力。两位博士前往伦敦警察厅试看有无效果，准备再次向警方提出要求。值日警察说："你们凌晨12点半来过，现在这么快又来，我看恐怕是没有用的。"当时最紧迫的是要知道到何处去诉说这个事实：一个人的生命已在危险中；国家的法律已被践踏；而这个人实际上将会在英帝国的京城被人谋杀。

离开警察厅后他们商量，决定去外交部。外交部常务秘书约定下午5点接见他们。他们按时被接见，这位谦恭有礼的官员耐心地听了他们所讲述的这个离奇的故事。可是当天是星期天，不能进一步办理，不过他向他们表示，明天将呈报一位高级负责人处理。但是时间是紧迫的，下一步怎么办呢？晚上可能悲剧就会发生：犯人被转移上船，开往中国；最可怕的是挑选的是外国船，在外国旗帜的掩护下，英国当局是不可能上去搜查的。最后的希望是，假若解押我的船是英国的，即使在船开离伦敦之前未及时检查，也可在苏伊士运河令其停下进行检查；①但若遣送我的船插的不是英国国旗，这一希望就将成为泡影。想到这点，两人决定到公使馆去，告诉他们中国人已经知道孙是他们手中的囚徒，英国政府和伦敦警察厅已经知道他们的目的是要把他遣送回中国处死。孟生博士决定单独前往，因为公使馆知道康德黎先生和孙氏是很熟悉的。

于是孟生博士即单独去访问了波特兰区49号。他要守门的那个油头粉面的男仆去叫一名能讲英语的中国人来。一会儿，一个讲英语的华人，就是捕捉我和折磨我的人，邓本人，出现了。孟生博士说他要求见孙逸仙。一种迷惑的表情掠过邓的脸庞，好像在慢慢想这个名

---

① 1875年10月，英国从埃及购得苏伊士运河股份，因而获得大部分控股权，此航线属英国管辖。

字，"Sun！—Sun！这里没有这个人。"孟生博士告诉他，他非常清楚地知道孙在这里；他想通知公使馆，英国外交部已经了解到事实；伦敦警察厅已将孙某被拘留之事公之于众。但这个中国外交官是一个很有说谎本领的人，且说谎之时总能迎合东方人所喜欢的角色。邓以他虚伪的言行向问话者保证，一切纯属讹传，使馆这里根本无此人。他的"坦率诚实"在一定程度上动摇了孟生博士对我被关押消息的确信，当他回到康德黎先生

1883年清驻英公使曾纪泽摄于英国伦敦

家时仍对邓看似真实的说法留有深刻的印象，邓甚至说我被拘押的事可能是我为了某种目的自己捏造出来的骗局，但不知其目的是什么。我的同乡邓的说谎本领甚至动摇了像孟生博士这样的人，后者居住在中国22年，能说一口流利的厦门方言，[①]对于中国人和他们的习俗的了解超过绝大部分远东人。不过，邓必须消除这种想法，以为诡计总不会被揭穿。邓将来肯定能够成为统治阶级的上层人物；一个像他这样的骗子，一定可以从依赖这种东西而存在和繁盛的政府里得到报偿。

直到星期天的晚上7点，两位博士才分手，他们对当天所做的事很不满意，仍很担心我的安全。危险的是我很可能在当天夜里很晚的时候被押走，特别是公使馆知道了英国政府已经了解这个事实，假如不能够立即上船，换一个关押受害者的住处是会被考虑的。这确实是很可能采取的一步，如果这样，毫无疑问他们将达到目的。幸亏，那位被称为

---

① 孟生博士于1866年起即由教会资助在台湾和厦门行医。1887年香港雅丽氏医院附设西医书院建立后即聘请孟生博士担任教务长。1889年，孟生辞去香港西医书院教务长职务，由康德黎继任。

曾侯^①的，不久前已离开伦敦回国，因而已经退了他的房子，否则的话，转移到他的住所对于我聪明的同乡来说就是一个非常可行的方案了，而一旦改换关押地点，他们便可依赖英国人的信任和友谊，请求他们检查房子。这个诡计没有实现；但押解至码头是完全可能的。上船日期定在星期二，到时押送之船必须先停在码头。没有比晚上押解这个"疯子"^②上船更能避免街头骚动和交通的嘈杂了。

---

① 曾侯 《孙中山全集》刊本关于"曾侯"有译者按："即曾纪泽，龚使之前任也。"此注不确。曾纪泽早在10年前已经卸任回国，6年以前（1890年）即已去世；龚照瑗之前任为薛福成，薛也早在3年前于1893年卸任回国，不久即在上海病故。文中所说不过为当时的传闻而已。

② 经伦敦警方调查证实，10月14日马卡尼曾约格伦轮船公司麦克格雷戈商谈将押送一个"疯子"回中国之事。（参阅陈锡祺主编《孙中山年谱长编》上册，第119页）

伦敦蒙难记
Kidnapped in London

第六章 寻求侦探

直到凌晨两点，康德黎博士才睡觉。这一天，他所做的事情是：禀报政府，向警察机关报案，提供消息给报纸，雇私人侦探晚上守候在公使馆门外。这天的工作完成了，实际上我的生命也就得救了，虽然当时我并不知道。

康德黎先生再次起程，这所有的事都装在他的脑海里，这时他想到了雇人监视公使馆的一些办法。他问了一个朋友打听到伦敦市区的一家斯雷特私人侦探公司的地址。他赶往那里，但斯雷特侦探所已关门。

　　看起来星期日好像是不需要侦探的。在英国难道星期天就不会发生麻烦事了吗？一定要记住这一点，把一个月分成几个星期只不过是人为的应世俗之便罢了，而犯案者是不会总让自己去适应这种奇异的日历的。然而，斯雷特侦探所关门了，这是个麻烦事。无论如何大声呼喊，按铃或者捶门，在贝津洛街的这栋花岗岩石建筑里面都无半点回音。

　　康德黎先生在马路上与一个警察，还有一个好心的马车夫商量，这个车夫把他送到秘密关押我的地方，停在附近的一个警察所。在那里，博士须将案情再陈述一遍，然而在对他的精神和神智等怀疑彻底

1890年代的苏格兰场（伦敦警察厅）

消除之前，一切都不可能继续进行。①

"你所要侦查的案件在何处？"

"在西区波特兰区。"

"啊！来这儿不对，你必须回伦敦西区办理此案；我们属于市警察局。"

博士心里明白，不管是东区警察还是西区警察，二者都无任何用处。

"无论如何，"他坚持要求，"能不能够派一名侦探去监视那栋房子？"

"不行。干涉伦敦西区的工作，这已超出了市警察局的权力。"

"能不能够找位老警察，一个后备人员，愿意做点这类的事，而他自己也可得点报酬？"康德黎先生问。

"好吧，这倒可能——让我们想想。"

于是这里的一些人便马上热心地商量，他们尽量回忆。啊，有了，他们觉得某某人可以。

"他住在哪儿？"

"哦！他住在莱顿斯通。你今晚找不到他了。你知道，今天是星期天。"

我知道是星期天，但是我的头恐怕保不住了！他们商量了很久之后推荐了一个人，终于打发走了这位固执的博士。这人住在伊斯灵顿的吉勃斯屯街区。

但是在动身去那里之前，康德黎先生心想应该把整个事情提供给

---

① 因所陈述的案情难以使人相信，当时警察怀疑报案者的精神不正常。孙中山在获释之后写给他的国学老师区凤墀的信里说："他等一闻此事，着力异常，即报捕房，即禀外部。而初时尚无人信，捕房以此二人为癫狂者，使馆全推并无其事。"

报纸，因此他乘车去《泰晤士报》①求见夜间编辑②。报社要求填写访问事由，于是他写道：

"中国公使馆绑架案件！"

这时是晚上9点，他被告知直到晚上10点以前都没有人。

于是他又往伊斯灵顿去找警方介绍给他的那个人。寻找一阵后，找到了一个灯光暗淡的街区，找到门牌号后，走进楼里。但是失望又接踵而来，因为"他不能去，但他知道有一个人可以去"。那么，对此事他帮不上忙，但他介绍的那个人又住在哪里呢？这真是一个奇怪的家伙，写有此人地址的卡片找不着了，他楼上楼下到处寻找：抽屉和箱子，一大捆旧信和已不穿的西服背心，都翻出来检查，终于找出来了。可是，他马上了解到，这个人已不住在家里，而是在伦敦市区看管一家酒店。

这不要紧，即便这样也是可以解决的，于是博士建议让那群挤在客厅里的孩子中的一个送一张便条到侦探家里，而请孩子的父亲陪同博士一起到伦敦市区某酒店去找那个看守人。终于乘坐的双座马车到达离酒店不远的地方，酒店在巴毕干附近，于是他们在这个地方寻找。但是在周围都未找到这个看守人，其实这样寻找是徒劳的：因为那个酒店要一直到11点钟关门的时候才需要看守，不过此时很可能这人就要来了。于是康德黎先生让他的这位朋友在酒店外等候，自己再去《泰晤士报》社。在那里他作为"读者"被接待，并且他的陈述被记录下来，至于发表与否要由《泰晤士报》慎重考虑后决定。这时已是星期天晚上11点30分，心情不安的博士最后只好回到了家里。他颇有些懊恼，他发现已经午夜12点了，他所盼望的侦探仍未出现。但是，他并不气馁，他打算亲自去守候。他与夫人道过晚安，即动身去监视使馆，如果必要的话准备积极主动进行干涉。

---

① 《泰晤士报》，Times（《时报》）的音译，创办于1785年。

② 原文为"sub-editor"，这里指夜间编辑，《孙中山全集》刊本译为"副主笔"不准确。

不过，当他怀着勇敢的意念大踏步地向公使馆走去时，意外地在街上遇到了他期待的那个人，他立刻布置了任务。这就是吉勒斯屯街区那位可靠的朋友送来的他的替代者。这时已经很晚了——已是晚上12点过后，但公使馆的窗子里仍灯光明亮，说明里面一定乱哄哄的，这无疑是孟生博士给他们的警告导致的，他们的邪恶行径不再不为人知晓。这位侦探坐在两轮双座轻便马车上，在威墨氏街南边房屋的暗处，就在波特兰区与波特兰路之间。那是一个美丽的月光如水的晚上，公使馆两处出口都清楚可见。这辆双座小马车是看守执勤时所必需的，我想，如果我从这座房子里被急匆匆押出，横过人行道，上了马车，几分钟我就将被运到步行无法追及的地方。出租车在清晨不可能随时雇到，所以侦探必须选择一个适当的位置，必要的话，便可以随时追踪。报纸上已登载了这件事，当营救小组把我救出时，马车会把我送走，但这是我后面将要叙述的故事的另一情况。①

直到凌晨两点，康德黎博士才睡觉。这一天，他所做的事情是：禀报政府，向警察机关报案，提供消息给报纸，雇私人侦探晚上守候在公使馆门外。这天的工作完成了，实际上我的生命也就得救了，虽然当时我并不知道。

---

① 详见第七章"营救方案之一"一节中所摘引报纸新闻。

第七章 政府干预

在被问及外交部刚刚发表的，大意是说索尔兹伯里勋爵照会中国公使要求释放囚徒的公告时，哈里代先生承认这是事实；但是在回答更进一步的问题如关于要求放人的结果如何时，答复是："此人将被释放，但应保证公使馆的有关权利不受到损害。"

10月19日，星期一，康德黎先生在斯雷特侦探所又雇请了私人侦探，并且在他们来后，就向他们布置了日夜监视公使馆的任务。

中午12点，康德黎先生按约定到了英国外交部，呈上他写的案情书。英国外交部显然急切想用某种非官方释放的办法，这样将比他们主动干涉要妥当，希望避免可能发生的国际纠纷。

此外，我被拘押的证据还仅仅是传闻，而且以一份似乎不可靠的报告为根据提出交涉是不明智的。为取得证据，第一步即去查询"格伦"航运公司，当发现公使馆已经雇了这条航线的轮船，政府才掌握了这个直接证据，查明这个案情不仅真实，而且实际执行的步骤已经作了精心的安排。从此时起，这一事件就移交到政府手里，而我的朋友也就卸除了他的负担了。

政府派了6名侦探在公使馆外执勤，并通知附近对案情有所了解的警察须提高警惕。

此外，警方得到了我的照片，我在美国拍摄的一张穿欧洲礼服的照片。对于那些从未到中国旅游过的外国人，所有华人看上去都是一模一样的，所以这张平时所摄的照片对于他们去辨认我是没有多大帮助的；而且这张照片中我留了胡须，发型也是"欧人式样"。①

中国人是要到了做祖父的辈分时才有资格留须的，但即使在一个早婚的国家里，我，当时还未到30岁，怎能渴求得到这种"优待"呢？

10月22日，星期四，一份针对公使馆或哈里代·马卡尼先生的"人身保护法"令状②已经提出，我不知道这件事，但伦敦中央刑事

---

① 孙中山流亡海外时因已剪掉辫子，身着西服，已无传统中国人的特殊标志，所以这里说凭照片不易辨认。

② "人身保护法"令状（A writ of *Habeas Corpus*）、"人身保护法"（"人权保护法"）源于12世纪的英格兰，由英王签发；至17世纪开始确立为由法庭实施的保护人身不遭侵害的法令。此法令由法庭法官签发，指令施行拘押的人将被拘押人送交法庭，以对所施行之拘押的合法性进行司法调查，并直接纠正羁押者对于人身自由造成的侵犯。"人身保护法"可由受害人本人或其代理人以及知情者向法院申诉申请；法院可针对政府或个人签发令状。

孙逸仙

Photo Taber, San Francisco.

1896年孙中山摄于美国旧金山（photo Taber, San Francisco）。他在《伦敦蒙难记》中说："警方得到了我的照片，我在美国拍摄的一张穿欧洲礼服的照片"，即指此照。

最早披露孙中山伦敦蒙难消息的英国《环球报》

法院的法官没有同意这一行动，因而此事未能实现。①

当天下午，《环球报》②的一位特派记者在康德黎先生家进行了采访，询问他是否知道关于一个华人被中国公使馆绑架的全部案情。他想了一想之后即把知道的都告诉了他。那么关于这个案件《环球报》已经了解到了些什么呢？博士说，在五天以前，10月18日（星期天）已把资料送给《泰晤士报》了，并于10月19日（星期一）又把补充的附加资料送去了，他想《泰晤士报》理应首先发表这些消息。康德黎先生说："不过我可看看你写的有关事情，我可告诉你所写的是否正确。"《环球报》所写的报道经过核实，得到博士的认可，但他要求报道中不要提到他的姓名。

实际上，在案情刊布很久之前就有很多人知道了这些事。在星

---

① 当时康德黎先生和孟生博士试图利用"人身保护法"营救他们的朋友，曾于10月22日向高等法院申请保护人权令，但因此令不能行使于外国使馆被法院拒绝（参见陈锡祺主编《孙中山年谱长编》上册，第122页）。伦敦中央刑事法院，原文为Old Bailey，因该院位于伦敦老贝利街（Old Bailey Street），即俗称老贝利。

② 《环球报》，Globe，一译为《地球报》。10月22日，该报当晚以"可惊可叹之新闻"、"革命家被诱于伦敦"、"公使馆之拘囚"等为标题报道了中国公使馆绑架事件，并于第二天重刊此一事件的新闻报道。

期二早上就大约有两三百人知道我遭监禁的事情了，使人感到奇怪的是，那些非常热心的记者在星期四下午之前还不知道这件事，不过一旦风闻，这事就不能平息了。自从《环球报》揭载了此一惊人消息之后，德文榭街46号就再也没有安静之日了。

《环球报》第五版发表此消息后不到两个小时，中央新闻社和《每日邮报》①的记者都采访了康德黎先生。他太过于沉默的态度令来访者不甚愉快，不过他仍把主要情节概括地告诉了他们。

两位采访者知道真相后即去中国公使馆要求见孙氏。接见他们的是那个十分警觉、善于狡辩的邓。他否认所有关于此人的消息。当记者在邓面前展示《环球报》的报道时，他莞尔一笑，并宣称所刊新闻乃是弥天大谎。不过，中央新闻社记者说，不管怎样，否认这件事是没有好处的，假如孙不被放出，他料想明天早晨就会有上万人被引到这个地方来找他的麻烦。然而无济于事，邓仍不为所动，说谎比以前更加厉害。

随后两名记者在米德兰旅馆找到了哈里代·马卡尼先生并作了采访。他的讲话这里主要摘自各报的报道。

采访哈里代·马卡尼先生

中国公使馆参赞哈里代·马卡尼先生，昨日下午3点半钟到了外交部。在和一位新闻界代表谈话时，哈里代先生说："我无法向你提供任何关于这个人被扣留在公使馆的信息，除了报刊上已经公布的以外。"在被问及外交部刚刚发表的，大意是说索尔兹

---

① 《每日邮报》，*Daily Mail*，1896年创办于伦敦。

A CHINESE DOCTOR KIDNAPPED.

To be Sent Back to China to be Tried for Treason.

LONDON, Oct. 22.—A great sensation was created this afternoon by the publication in The Globe of a story that detectives, at the instance of the Foreign Office, have been watching the Chinese Embassy here for some days past, in consequence of two Chinese officials having seized and kidnapped a Chinese physician named Sun Yat Sen, belonging to Hongkong, as he was passing the Chinese Embassy on Oct. 17, the kidnapped man having been detained in the embassy ever since.

《纽约时报》报道孙中山被捕的消息

罗伯特·盖斯科因-塞西尔，第三代索尔兹伯里侯爵，时任英国首相兼外相

伯里勋爵①照会中国公使要求释放囚徒的公告时，哈里代先生承认这是事实；②但是在回答更进一步的问题如关于要求放人的结果如何时，答复是："此人将被释放，但应保证公使馆的有关权利不受到损害。"

在此后与新闻记者的一次谈话中，哈里代·马卡尼先生说："我们拘留在楼上的这个人的名字不是孙逸仙。我们并不怀疑他的真实身份，他一到英

---

① 索尔兹伯里勋爵，即第三代索尔兹伯里侯爵（Robert Arthur Talbot Gascoyne-Cecil，3rd Marquess of Salisbury，1830—1903），旧译沙力斯伯里侯爵，简称沙侯。他曾三任英国首相。孙中山流亡英伦时他正担任首相兼外相。原文称Lord Salisbury，勋爵（Lord）这里只是一种敬称，等于"阁下"。

② 1896年10月22日，英国外交部次长山德森（T. H. Sanderson）致函马卡尼召其谒见索尔兹伯里首相（兼外相）。马卡尼只得如实向英国政府通报。英政府促其立刻放人（参阅《中华民国史事纪要》，台湾"中华民国史料研究中心"1961年版；罗刚编著《中华民国国父实录》第1册，第366页）。

国，他的一举一动我们都时刻注意到了。①他来公使馆完全出自他的自愿，并不是绑架、强迫或者引诱到这个屋子里的。一个华人初来伦敦，感到孤独寂寞，来找使馆问问或者和同乡聊聊，这是很平常的事。看来对这位奇怪的客人产生怀疑是有理由的，他仗着使馆无人认识他，即带着窥伺我们并要获得什么信息的目的而来。使馆没有谁见过他。他来访时是和我们的一个职员进行交

---

① 马卡尼雇用的英国私人侦探在孙中山抵达伦敦之后即对其行踪进行了严密监视，以下是侦探所写的跟踪报告之一：

马格里爵士

波德兰

关于孙文事件

爵士：

关于我们十月一日通信上所提的事，我们现在报告你。我们在赫胥旅馆方面，作有系统的监视。在一日那天，就是星期四，此人于下午四点半钟外出，沿着斯屈朗走，经过佛立特街（Fleet Street），到露揭特场（Ludgate Circus），看看商店的玻璃窗子，以后又回到旅馆。那时候是下午六点三十分。以后就没有看见他出来了。

在二日星期五那天，他于上午十点三十分离开赫胥旅馆，雇了一个一〇八五〇号四轮马车装行李，坐到葛兰旅店街八号，将行李运入，该人亦进去。

他在该处到上午十一点三十分才出来，步行到牛津街（Oxford street），看看商店的玻璃窗子，于是走进上霍尔庞（High Holborn）——九号（文具店），再进加快食堂（Express Dairy Co.），吃了中饭，于下午一点四十五分回到葛兰旅店街八号。

下午六点四十五分他再出来，走到霍尔庞的一个饭馆里停留了三刻钟，再回到葛兰旅店街八号的时候，已经八点三十分钟，就不再看见他了。

以后每天都有人监视他，但是没有什么重要的事情发生。此人常在主要的街道上散步，四周顾望。他不在家里吃饭，到各种饭馆去吃。

提起你电报里所说的一层，我们可以说在监视期间，他不曾见过什么中国人。在利物浦听说有几个在"Majestic"和他同船的人，答应到伦敦来看他。

讲到照相这个问题，我们恐怕非等到天气好些，不能办到。

无论如何，我们对于这点总是尽力注意。

你忠实的，司赖特侦探社（签名）

（伦敦中国使馆英文档）

（引自罗家伦《中山先生伦敦被难史料考订》，商务印书馆1930年版）

谈，之后介绍给我。我们闲谈了片刻，他所说的话使我怀疑他就是我们所注意的那个人。这些怀疑得到了证实，他就是此人，第二天他再来时即拘留了他，并且现在仍在拘留中，在等待中国政府的指令。"

在谈到国际方面的问题时，哈里代先生说："这个人不是英国人，而是属于中国的一个臣民。我们认为中国公使馆就是中国的领土，在这里唯有中国公使具有裁判权。假如一个中国人自愿到这里来，并且如果对他提出指控或者对他有所怀疑，我们认为拘留他，外界是无任何权力干涉的。①如果他在公使馆外面，那情况就不同了，因为那是英国领土，而且我们没有逮捕证不能拘留他。"

在回答记者的追问时，哈里代先生提到并未把这个人当囚犯对待，而是处处考虑到他的舒适。哈里代先生讥笑外面传言说某人在此受到折磨或非法逼供。他补充说明，已经收到一封英国外交部关于这个问题的查询信函，将会予以及时关注。

中央新闻社称：哈里代·马卡尼先生从外交部回到中国公使馆后，即到公使龚大人病床边，②对他说明索尔兹伯里阁下坚持要求释放孙逸仙之理由。

至于哈里代·马卡尼先生之行为，我不作评论；这让公众舆论

---

① 参阅第四章邓翻译与孙中山的谈话。这是清使馆所设圈套，事后孙中山意识到："毫无疑问我做了一件非常愚蠢的事，这意味着我给敌人提供了字据，证明我是自动到公使馆来的。不过一个将死的人是任何机会都想抓住的，这样，我在危难中就轻易地受骗了。"清政府驻英国公使馆即据邓翻译编撰的谈话记录整理备案，证明在公使馆内拘留孙是自己国家的权力，并不违反国际法。这种曲解国际公法的说法完全是为了逃脱制裁，欺骗公众舆论。正因为清使馆滥施外交特权，英政府才可能采取坚决行动进行干预。

② 当时驻英公使龚照瑗正因病卧床，同时他的任期已满，在等待总署调令。在此期间，公使馆涉外具体事务多由马卡尼参赞处理。11月23日，清廷任命罗丰禄为驻英公使，此时孙中山已经获释。

去评说并让其自问良心。在他自己脑子里，我毫不怀疑，他认为他的行为有理；其实他的言行和正常人几乎完全是不相符的，更不用说他是位身居要职的人。我认为邓已把他的地位表达得很正确，他曾告诉我，"在这里公使只是一个挂名头头，马卡尼是统治者"。

关于营救计划的各种各样的报道也在报纸上悄然出现。下面举一例。

营救方案之一

有关孙逸仙被逮捕之事，现已证实他的朋友已经策划了一个实现成功营救的大胆计划。假若外交部和伦敦警察厅不能确保他将不会受到任何伤害，他们就会从波特兰区51号鲍尔斯考特子爵住宅的屋顶翻越到公使馆，打破他房间的窗户将他救出。他的朋友已及时地把准备实施的计划通知了他，尽管后来有消息说孙逸仙已被戴上了手铐，但仍表示从里面帮助把窗子打开配合实现朋友的计划。的确，到目前为止，这个计划是成熟的，载送孙逸仙去朋友家的马车都已准备好。囚犯的朋友们宣称这个计划还需费思量，公使馆的那个口头翻译是个中国人，事实上就是他引诱孙落入公使馆的，尽管后来他一直矢口否认在公使馆这座院墙内曾经有过这样一个人。他的朋友说孙是穿过英国服装的，当他穿上西装时，总被误认是英国人，但实际上他的本质仍是典型的东方人。在香港，他被公认是一个性情温和、具有无比良好天性的人，并且他在各地行医，由于他娴熟的医术以及对于穷人的行善使他获得了声誉。这时他已在广东阴谋集团的爪牙的重重包围中，然而他毫不犹豫地谴责两广总督政府的残酷压迫。据说他为了全社会的利益已走遍了整个广东，这是被认为自当今皇帝开始统治①以来影

① 光绪皇帝（1871—1908）于1887年（光绪十三年）16岁时亲政，但仍由太后训政；两年之后慈禧太后结束训政，但她仍然大权在握。

光绪皇帝（1871—1908）

响最大，最令人生畏的一片地区。

实际情况是这样的。1896年10月19日科尔把下面的消息送给康德黎先生："在今晚我有一个好机会能让孙先生出来，把他带到波特兰区隔壁房子的屋顶上。假若你认为可行的话，可征得房主的同意，派人到那里等候接他。是否可以，请想法告诉我。"①康德黎先生把信交给伦敦警察厅并要求派一名警察和他一起在房子的屋顶上接应；但是伦敦警察厅当局认为这是不严肃的举动，劝阻他们打消这个意图，同时要他们坚信在一两天内我将从前门出去。

① 此信的真实性存疑，似系报纸传闻之"营救方案"内容。

第八章 释 放

从英国的角度来看这件事，我被释放一事完全是出于对我的关照；但对中国人而言，我的释放方式抹去了英方通过外交手段所取得的所有胜利。所以双方无疑都感到同样的满意。自我被释放后，我有了很多朋友，有了许多的聚餐和宴席，更有全伦敦为我祈祷的人给予我的永久的爱。

10月22日，科尔示意我注意煤桶。他离开房间后，我捡起了从报上剪下来的一份新闻，原来是《环球报》。我读了有关拘留我的报道，标题是："骇人听闻的故事！革命家被绑架于伦敦！关押在中国大使馆！"①随后是一份长而详细的对我的状况的报道。终于新闻界

① 原文标题使用醒目的字体。"中国大使馆"（Chinese Embassy）系报纸上所称，应为"中国公使馆"（Chinese Legation）。10月22日《环球报》出版晚报特刊，报道了此案：

在过去的几天里，流传着中国政府驻伦敦公使馆绑架和监禁一位中国名人的令人惊异的传闻。但是，就在今天下午，我们已能够确定这些传闻，并且收集到与此有关的一些事实。

大概在去年11月，中国政府获悉有人密谋攻占广州总督府，其最终目的是推翻满族或鞑靼王朝。密谋者宣称：过去的四五百年间，中国在它的统治之下显然日益恶化，除非推翻这个王朝，否则不能指望国家事务得以改善。

密谋者把逮捕总督作为实现革命目标的第一步。据说为了达到上述目的，从香港派遣四百名苦力到广州。这批人的到来似乎太早，引起官府怀疑，使秘密泄露，结果大约十五名领导人被逮捕斩首。

其他人看来逃脱了厄运。一位香港名医，名叫孙逸仙的绅士设法到了美国，随后又来到伦敦，投宿于格兰法学院路附近。

上星期六他出门后未返回旅馆，据传他被绑架到中国公使馆；另一种说法是他自认为在伦敦的大街上不会被逮捕，因而当他经过中国公使馆时，突然被两个中国人抓住，并被推进那所目前仍被拘押其中的楼里。

然而，绑架虽然得逞，被囚禁者却想方设法将自己被扣押的事实通知一些英国朋友。这些在香港时的旧友立即为他采取行动。外交部和苏格兰场都得到了关于此案事实的报告。开始人们对此事抱有疑问，但现在我们了解到，苏格兰场的侦探正在监视公使馆，以防将他运走。

被囚禁者的朋友们甚至断言，为了将他运出英国，已经做了最周密的准备，为此还专门租了一条船。据说他们已向法官申请人权保护令；但在授予这种法令权利方面似乎有困难，因为还不清楚英国司法当局究竟能对一个外国公使馆行使权力到何种程度。

此事最令人不可思议的是，使馆官员们回答孙的朋友们的询问时，竟矢口否认他被囚于此。然而孙的朋友们掌握了确凿的证据，证明这种否认纯属谎言。

（转引自《孙中山年谱长编》上册，第122—123页）

第二天（23日）《环球报》全文重刊这篇新闻，编者按语说："我们重印昨晚《地球报》发表的关于此案报道的特辑。"

出面干涉了，我感到我是真的平安了。消息之传来，就像一个被判死刑的人得到暂时缓刑，我的内心充满了感激之情。

10月23日，星期五，天大亮，时间在逐渐消逝，而我仍在监禁中。下午4点30分，终于，就在这天，我的英国的和中国的守卫来到房中并说"马卡尼在楼下要见你"，并告我要带上靴子、帽子和大衣。我照做了，但不知道到何处去。我走下楼梯，被带到地下室，心想是要把我藏在一个地窖里，

康德黎先生及夫人（1911）。康德黎上校是红十字会英国伦敦支队创始人

因为警方正在执行英国政府搜查房子的命令。我并没有被告知已经获释，我又认为是要将我带到另一关押的地方受处罚。我简直不能相信这是真的，我真的被释放了。然而的确，一会儿康德黎先生和另外两位一起出现在这一场景中，一位是伦敦警察厅的督察员贾维斯，另一位老人，是外交部的信使。

当时，哈里代·马卡尼先生在这些绅士们面前，把从我这里拿去的东西都还给了我，同时向政府官员讲了下面意思的话："我把这个人交给你们，我的要求是：公使馆特权及外交上之权利均不受干涉"，或说了诸如此类的话。我当时太激动，没有记住他所说的话，但是他们在我看来，就如他们现在所做的，既愚蠢又可笑。

以上会见是在公使馆地下室的走廊上进行的，同时告诉我我已经是一个自由人了。然后哈里代先生和我们一一握手——一种犹大式的致意。随后我们从一个侧门出来，被带到地下室天井。从那里我们上了天井的台阶，从公使馆后门出去，上了威墨斯街。

这可能是为了避免被人看到，也是让人忘却我们是从公使馆后门

被送出的这样一类小事情。

事实是营救的全部重要措施都已在这一小队在场的英国人的脑子里；这绝对与我狡诈的同乡，特别是与哈里代·马卡尼先生，那个腐朽落后的东方主义的化身无关。

英国政府的代表像下等人一样被人从后门送出，这一事实将影响首相及其内阁成员的声誉。实际上那是有意的怠慢和侮辱，而执行者则是一个十分精通中国人和外国人交往规矩的人。毫无疑问，这样做的借口是大厅挤满了记者；大楼外面街上也聚集了一大群人；外交部迫切希望此案在暗中了结，不引发示威集会等事情。无疑，这些理由是那些满洲的恶棍和他们的代理人马卡尼早就想好了的。

从英国的角度来看这件事，我被释放一事完全是出于对我的关照；但对中国人而言，我的释放方式抹去了英方通过外交手段所取得的所有胜利。所以双方无疑都感到同样的满意。

在10月份的那个星期五下午，一行并不引人注目的有关方面人士来到中国公使馆；而他们当中的一员，一位令人尊敬的外交部的老信使，有一份似乎承担着重大使命的小小的照会深藏在他的大衣口袋里。它一定是简明扼要的，因为仅仅两三秒钟，马卡尼就掌握了它的内容。它尽管是简短的，但是它承载了使我恢复自由的令人愉快的消息，同时让我逃脱了死亡，尤其是令人恐怖、极其残忍的对政治犯逼供交代中国同案犯姓名的酷刑。①

在威墨斯街挤满了人，一直守候着的新闻记者试图诱我当场无保

---

① 当时孙中山已做好了最坏结局的思想准备，他在《中国之司法改革》一文中说："当我被囚禁在波德兰区中国公使馆而不能与外界联系时，我一点也没想到我有可能获释。我已完全决定采取什么措施，我下定决心尽一切努力跳下船去，葬身于英吉利海峡、地中海、印度洋或中国海。如果这些试图不成功，不幸抵达目的地广州，我决定立即招认以免遭受头一轮毒打。即使如此，这种事我还是要受很多罪，因为他们会对我进行最惨毒的严刑拷打，逼我出卖同志。这，我是宁愿坚持到最后也绝对不会做的。"（《中国之司法改革》，*Judicial Reform in China*，1897年7月伦敦《东亚季刊》第1卷第1号。见《孙中山集外集》）

Penang, November 24, 1910.

My dear Mrs Cantlie:—

I have posted a letter to you just a few days ago, then I had not the least idea of coming to England so soon. But now I am wanting to go to England and America to do some business. I shall sail in a fortnight of time, and expect to see you soon in London. Please keep my coming secret from the Chinese Legation.

In case any one come to your house to enquire me in the name of Chungsan before my arrival that man will be a friend of mine you may treat him so.

With kindest regards to you and the doctor

Very truly yours

Y.S. Sun

孙中山致康德黎夫人信函手迹

留地提供一切。然而，我迅速地钻进了一辆四轮出租马车，同时，我的同伴康德黎先生、督察员贾维斯以及外交部信使，一同驱车至伦敦警察厅。在路上督察员贾维斯严肃地训斥我的过失 ①，并骂我是个坏小子，劝我今后再不要参加革命。车没有停在伦敦警察厅，而是停在官府大道 ② 一家饭店的门口，我们下车后站立在人行道上。记者们立即上来围住了我，他们从哪儿来的我不知道。我们在波特兰离开他们已1英里远，我的车一停，他们片刻就到了这里。此时不可能抑制住他们，其中一个人根本没有让我们知道，居然爬到驾驶旁边的位子上。他早就留在饭馆门口的车子里，他了解得很清楚，假若我到了警察厅，一时不能出来，他们就不可能立刻见到我了。如果不是有一些人在我的车顶上，我就不晓得他们是从哪儿突然出现的。我被人群从人

———————

① 过失，原文是delinquencies。警察当时认为孙中山所犯属于一般少年犯罪案而被公使馆拘留，所以训斥他是个"坏小子"（scolded me as a bad boy）。

② 官府大道 Whitehall，指英国政府，一译为白厅；也指伦敦官府大道，为英国政府机关所在地。

行道推搡进饭店屋子的后面，拥挤的力量比当时我被绑架到公使馆时还要强烈得多，他们渴望得到消息的心情和当时我的同乡渴望得到我的头颅一样急切。①记者们是用象形文字书写的，我十分惊异，我以前没有见过象形文字的写法，那时我也不知道英语可以用楔形文字书写。之后我才发现他们使用的是速记书写法。

对于记者我是有问必答，直至我无可奉告时，康德黎先生大声呼喊："先生们！时间到了！"这样我被强行从他们中救出，乘车前往伦敦警察厅。到达警察厅，显然我被他们看成是送过来的一个孩子，他们和贾维斯一样诚挚，凝神地注视着我。无论如何，困难的工作已经结束，在这里我可以自由地根据自己的实情进行表白。在那儿我花了一个小时叙述我被捕和被拘留的全部情况。我所谈的这些都做了记录并向我宣读了。②我签了名之后即与警察队的朋友们亲切友好地告别。康德黎先生和我赶路回家，我受到了殷勤的款待，并享受了一顿美味晚餐，大家热情地为我的"头颅"祝酒畅饮干杯！

晚上客人频繁来访，直到很晚，我才得休息。啊！这第一晚的睡眠！我会忘记吗？我持续睡了9个小时，我是被楼上几个小孩欢蹦乱跳的声音吵醒的。在他们激动兴奋的吵闹声中，我听出了缘由，我听到："柯林，你是扮的孙逸仙，尼尔，你扮哈里代·马卡尼先生，我营救孙。"接着一阵骚乱，马卡尼被打倒在地，随即发出一声猛烈的着地声，这时我感到我的小朋友尼尔不再做什么了，孙在胜利中被绮思救出，绮思是最大的孩子，于是在鼓声咚咚和刺耳的哨声中宣布大赦，接着合唱《不列颠掷弹兵》。这确实是一个安全的家；毫无疑问，我的少年朋友们为了我准备流下他们的最后一滴血。

---

① 孙中山从公使馆里被接出来之后在白厅区官府大道一家旅店向各报记者发表的谈话见《孙中山全集》第1卷《与伦敦各报记者的谈话》（一八九六年十月二十三日）。这个谈话首先就是驳斥马卡尼否认绑架的说法。

② 孙中山获释后在伦敦警察厅的谈话记录见《在伦敦苏格兰场的陈述词（一八九六年十月二十三日）》。

10月24日，星期六，我整天接受采访。第一个问题是"你如何让博士知道的？"同样的问题康德黎先生被问过许多次。[①]我们感觉舌头都僵了；在回答一个问题时，我们将会牵连某些人。在公使馆里，他们给予了我朋友般的帮助，他们将会失去他们的职务。不过，科尔决定辞去他的差事，这样可免去其他人受到怀疑，[②]谁是消息的传递者也就不必再隐瞒了。有一种很莫名其妙的说法，就是说我贿赂了他；这不是事实。他完全不懂得我所交给他的硬币是付给他的酬金；他认为我给他是要他为我保管；他告诉康德黎先生那天他得到20英镑，是我交给他请他保管的。我出来后，科尔把钱交还给我，我极力劝他把钱收下。我希望多给他一点，但这也是我仅有的了。[③]科尔这段时间受到不少恐吓，但是最大的恐吓是第一次去博士家。10月18日星期天下午，当他已经决心实际帮助我时，他把我的便笺放在口袋里，到德文榭街46号去交给康德黎先生。门开了，他走进厅里。博士不在家，于是他要求见他的夫人。当佣人去请女主人时，科尔意识到在大厅远端有一个中国人在注视他。他立刻怀疑他到这里来已被人跟踪，事情已被发觉，因为有一个中国人在这里，猪尾巴[④]以及……从墙壁的凹处认真仔细地察看他。康德黎夫人出来时，她注意到科尔害怕得在发抖，面色惨白，恐惧得说不出话来。这恐惧是由于那个十分逼真的中

---

　　① 记者们提问很多，很广泛，如10月24日《每日新闻》记者采访中写道："'你是白莲教的成员吗？''哦，不是。那是一个完全不同的团体，我们的运动是新的，限于受过教育的中国人，他们大部分住在国外。''你们的运动在战前开始了吗？''是的，战前不久。'"（《孙中山伦敦蒙难获释后与记者的两次谈话》，转引自《孙中山年谱长编》上册，第125页）

　　② 第一个写密信传递孙中山被囚禁信息的是清使馆的雇用人员霍维太太，孙中山在书中有意隐瞒了她的名字。详见第五章第48页注①。

　　③ 孙中山获释后曾向卡夫律师咨询酬谢科尔的方法。后来孙中山将在伦敦演讲所获数百英镑赠与科尔（《孙中山与中国革命的起源》，参阅《孙中山年谱长编》上册，第128页）。

　　④ 原文为pigtail，即辫子，这是一种形象或蔑视的说法；上文的Chinaman，是过去欧美人对中国人的一种带有歧视口吻的称谓，相当于"中国佬"的意思。

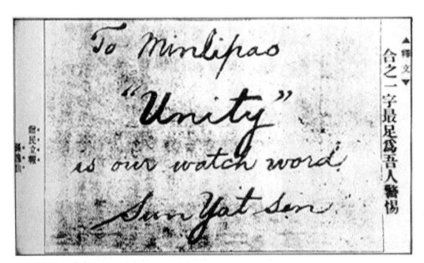

▲释文▼
合之一字最足爲吾人警惕

孙中山给《民立报》的英文题词

孙中山于1920年代为同乡陆兰谷亲笔题词

1893年康德黎教授在香港西医书院授课，所讲授学科有解剖学、骨学、初级实用外科

孟生博士（1844—1922）

国人雕塑的出现所引起的，这尊塑像是康德黎先生从香港带回家的一个古董。它已吓唬了很多来访者，科尔因为心里发虚比其他人更为恐惧，他那过度的紧张实际上使得那尊塑像更加异常的逼真。康德黎夫人消除了他的恐惧，并送他到孟生博士家找她的丈夫。我的这段经历快结束了；以后是否会出现与这件事有关的更加复杂的情况我就不知道了。迄今为止，未见其他英语国家的报纸讨论这个专题，同时议会也未召开，我不知道会有什么与此相关的事情即将发生。然而，自我被释放后，我有了很多朋友。在这个国家，我已进行了几次愉快的参观访问。我有了许多的聚餐和宴席，更有全伦敦为我祈祷的人给予我的永久的爱。

孙中山（前坐右二）与香港西医书院同仁

大總統誓詞

傾覆滿洲專制政府鞏固中華民國圖謀
民生幸福此國民之公意文實遵之以忠
於國為眾服務至專制政府既倒國內無變
亂民國卓立於世界為列邦公認斯時文
當解臨時大總統之職謹以此誓於國民

中華民國元年元旦
孫文

孙中山手书大总统誓言

附录 当时报纸的报道评论

译者说明： 以下"附录"文字系孙中山搜集当时报纸上刊载的有关孙中山遭绑架事件的各种评论编辑而成，因并非孙中山本人的著述，此处即照录商务印书馆的旧译，未另重新翻译，但在必要之处作了注释，特说明。

当时英国报纸关于此案之记载评论，谨择要附录于下。

其最先投函于伦敦《太晤士报》（今译为《泰晤士报》）者，为荷兰学士 Professor　Holland，文曰《孙逸仙案》：①

"记者足下：因孙逸仙案而发生之问题有二：一中国公使之拘留孙

---

① 此段引语为附录编者（孙中山）所写，原文是：

I append a few of the numerous articles called forth by my arrest. The first is a letter from Professor Holland to The Times,　and is headed：

THE CASE OF SUN YAT SEN.

To the Editor of THE TIMES.

中文意思是：

这里附我搜集的许多文章的一些评述。首先是郝兰德教授致《泰晤士报》的一封信，标题是：

孙逸仙案

致《泰晤士报》编辑

某，是否为违法举动？二设其为违法举动，而又不允释放，则宜用何种适当之方法，俾将孙某释出？

第一问题之答语，固毋庸远求。盖自一千六百又三年法国苏尔黎（Sully）为驻英公使时，虽有将某随员判定死罪移请伦敦市尹正法之事，然自是厥后，凡为公使者罕或行使其国内裁判权，即对于使馆中人亦久不行用此权。惟一千六百四十二年，葡萄牙驻荷公使蓝陶氏（Leitao）以见欺于马贩某，将该马贩拘禁于使馆，终至激起荷人之暴动，将公使馆搜劫一空。当时荷人威克福氏（Wicquefort）对于蓝陶此举深致评驳，盖蓝陶氏固尝在大庭广众中演说万国公法，非不知法律者也。今孙逸仙既在英国，自当受英国法律之保护，乃公使馆骤加拘禁，是其侵犯吾英国之主权者大矣。

第二问题虽不若第一问题之单简，然解决之方，要亦无甚困难。中国公使如不允将孙某释出，则英国借此理由，已足请该公使退出英国。如以事机急迫，恐饬令该公使回国之举或不免涉于迟缓，则以本案情节而论，即令伦敦警察入搜使馆，亦不必疑其无正当理由也。或谓使馆应享有治外法权，此治外法权一语过于简括，实则其意义不过谓使馆之于驻在国，为某种缘由之故，间有非该驻在国平常法权所能及耳。然此等享有权历来相习成风，业已限制甚严，且证诸成案，而于通行之享有权外，实不能复有所增益也。证诸一千七百十七年裘伦保（Gyllenburg）之案，可见使臣驻节于他国，苟犯有潜谋不利于该国之嫌疑，则该国政府得拘捕其人，搜检其使馆。又证诸一千八百二十七年茄赖丁（Mr. Gallatin）之御人一案，只需驻在国之政府以和平有礼之通牒报告使馆之后，即可遣派员警赴该使馆拘逮犯案之仆役。

曾任苏州洋炮局、金陵制造局总监的马格里，即哈里代·马卡尼

又除西班牙及南美洲各共和国之外，凡使馆已不复能藏匿犯人，即政事犯亦不得借此为逋逃薮，是又各国所公许者也。至于公使馆而擅行逮捕人犯，私加羁禁，则驻在国之地方警察惟有斟酌情势所需，为实力之干涉，以资解决而已。

今孙逸仙坚称被中国公使馆诱劫于道途，且将舁赴轮舟，以便解送至中国，是中国官场对于此案所负之责任，固无庸深诘。中国官场悍然出此，岂尚能有辩护之余地乎？万一诱劫之情果属

麦丁博士，中文名丁韪良（William Alexander Parsons Martin, 1827—1916）

非虚，押解之谋见诸实责，则此案之情之严重，不言可知。而其出于公使馆僚属之急于见功，亦可洞见麦丁博士（Dr. Martin）①在北京同文馆教授国际法有年，使臣在外应遵何道以行，中国政府岂犹茫然未之审也？——十月二十四日荷兰由奥克斯福发②。"

楷文狄虚（Mr. Cavendish）者，生平于国际交犯之法律最极研究有素者也，其语某君之语曰：

"孙逸仙一案，以予记忆所及，实无其他相同之例案可资引证。昔者桑西巴（Zanzibar，东非洲国名）③谋篡君位之人犯，系自行走

---

① 麦丁博士（William Alexander Parsons Martin, 1827—1916）即威廉·亚历山大·马丁教士。中文名丁韪良，美国传教士。1850年到中国传教。曾任北京同文馆、京师大学堂总教习，并曾担任清政府关于国际法方面顾问。所译《万国公法》（美国惠顿著《国际法原理》）于1864年在北京印行。

② 奥克斯福（Oxford）"牛津"的音译。此信写于牛津大学（或牛津市）。

③ 桑西巴（Zanzibar，东非洲国名）原非洲东部国家，今译桑给巴尔，1964年并入坦桑尼亚。

避于伦敦德国领事署，挟德政府相厚之情，冀为庇护；既而国际法之问题起，德人不允交出，遂移往欧洲大陆之德属境内。此与本案截然不同。盖孙逸仙系中国之籍民，其所入者系本国之使馆，其逮捕者系本国之使臣，其罪名则系谋覆本国之政府，凡此所述如悉系事实，则只须由英国外务部出而为外交上之陈辞，而无须为法律上之办理，盖按诸法律实无可引之条也。"

胡德氏（Mr. James G. Wood）为荷兰氏所建之议，亦投函《太晤士报》，为法律问题之讨论曰：

"荷兰学士所拟第二问题，虽揆诸情势，幸已无甚重要。然此端实大有足供研究者在。窃谓该学士所拟之答语，殊不足令人满意也。

该学士论及中国公使万一不肯将人犯释放条下，有云'以本案情节而论，即令伦敦警察入搜使馆，亦不必疑其无正当理由'云云。该学士既曰不必疑，则必有其可疑者可知；至于可疑者究竟何在，则该学士未之释明也。以该学士之所答，并不能谓为解决问题，只可谓之猜测而得一解决法耳。公使馆即或违法而拘留人犯，然伦敦警察并无入公使馆释放人犯之职权；万一有入公使馆而为此举动者，公使馆尽可以强力拒敌之，揆诸法律无不合也。以吾所闻，公使馆果有私拘人犯之事，则揆诸法律所可以行用之手续，惟有颁发交犯审讯之谕（Habeas Corpus，即保护人权之令，若被捕后不即交审，可发此谕交由公堂讯判，如无罪则二十四小时后即应保释）而已。顾事有难焉者，则此谕将交诸公使乎？抑交诸公使馆中之员役乎？设交诸公使或员役，而彼乃置诸不问，则可施以藐视公堂之处断乎？以予所知，实无成案可以援引也。

荷兰学士又谓公使之所居应享有治外法权，其实公使馆与轮舟不同，彼享有此权者乃公使之本身而非公使馆也。相传公使之本身及其家属随员等，于民事诉讼得享有完全蠲免权，是以此等问题者，乃个人问题，而非居处问题；乃若者可施若者不可施诸公使及其家属随员等之问题，而非若者可施若者不可施诸公使馆之问题也。惟其然也，故予所拟颁布交犯审讯令之办法，似不免牵涉而有碍于邦交也。

至引用成案，谓警察得持信票入公使馆拘捕在他处犯有罪案之人犯，如荷兰学士所谓'公使馆而擅行逮捕人犯，私加羁禁，则地方警察惟有为实力之干涉'云云。斯论也，实亦不足为万全之计，盖此等成案与孙逸仙案并无公同之点也。——十月二十七日胡德氏发。"

一千八百九十六年十二月三日香港《支那邮报》①有论云：

"孙逸仙者，即近日被逮于伦敦中国公使馆，拟置诸典刑，视同叛逆者也。顾此人他日似未必不为历史中之重大人物，然未经正当之法庭加以审讯，自不得谓为与会党有关，且不得谓该会党之举动确在倾覆中国朝廷也。彼以孙逸仙为叛逆者，仅出于伦敦中国使馆与夫广东官场之拟议耳。然孙君固非寻常人物，以开通之知识而目击中国数百兆人之流离困苦，彼一般华人之中，且有慨然动念、奋然思起者矣。据中国官场之宣告，谓此等华人曾于一千八百九十五年十月间起而图乱，其为之领袖者，则孙逸仙也。

中国之不免于变乱，夫人而能言之；而其变乱之期之迫于眉睫，则无论居于外国之外人不能知，即寓于远东之外人亦罕有能知之者也。迨广州之变既作，以事机不密，倏就倾覆，而当事者仍漠然不动于心，至堪齿冷。他日变起，其可危必更甚于昔之金田军②；盖其组织之新颖，基础之文明，较金田军尤数倍过之也。总之，领袖诸人以事机未熟，故暂图偃伏，非以偶然失败之故而遂尽弃其革命之计划也。

至革命派之缘起，虽无由追溯，而其大致要由不慊于满清之行

_____

① 香港《支那邮报》，*the China Mail*，Hong Kong，1845年在香港创办的英文报纸《中国邮报》，俗称《德臣西报》。该报经历了一百多年历史，于1974年停刊。

② 金田军　指太平天国金田起义军。

事。近中日一战，而此派遂崭然露其头角。孙逸仙博士辈之初意，原欲以和平之手段要求立宪政体之创行而已，迨至和平无效，始不得不出于强力。然历观中国历史中之崛起陇亩、谋覆旧朝者，其精神意气大都豪悍不驯；而孙氏则独不然，秉其坚毅之心志，不特欲调和中国各党派，且将使华人与西人、中国与外国亦得于权利之间悉泯冲突焉。然而事有至难解决者，则一举之后必有种种继起之困难，而此等困难最足使任事者穷于应付也。孙氏岂不知有大兴作，不得不借外国之国家与个人为之援助，然而中华全国方无处不为排外之精神所贯彻，是则欲泯除而开导之，固不能不有需乎时日也。总之此等事业，其性质至为宏硕，而其举措又至为艰难。惟孙氏则本其信心，谓他日欲救中国，势不能不出乎此；而目前则惟有黾勉以图，冀其终底于成功而已。

孙氏诞生于火纳鲁鲁，①受有英国完美之教育，且于欧美二洲游历甚广，其造诣亦至深。昔尝学医于天津，继复执业于香港。其躯干适中，肌肤瘦挺，容貌敏锐而爽直，举动之间毫无矫矜，而言语又极恳挚；至其知觉之敏捷，处事之果毅，尤足使人油然生信仰之心，是诚不可谓非汉族中之杰出者也。中国今日正与各国在专制时代无异，凡主张创行新政、革除腐败者，概被以叛逆之名，故有志之士欲传播其主义，势不得出以缜密。孙氏于千八百九十五年之始著有政治性质之文字，发行于香港，而传播于中国南省。其于良政府与恶政府描述极为尽致，两两相较，自足使人知所去取。然而措辞至为留意，虽以彼狠若狼虎、善于吹求之中国官吏，亦复未从而指摘之。中国人士得读此书，无不慨然动念。未几，遂有秘密会社之发生，则孙氏与焉。

当中日战事未起以前，中国水陆两军，以上官之遏抑，已多怀怨望；即文官亦非无表同意者。况中国伏莽遍地，响应尤易。其初次起事之期定于本年三月间，时则火纳鲁鲁、新嘉坡、澳洲等处，纷

---

① 流亡中的孙中山当时有意隐瞒国籍，假称自己是出生于夏威夷的美国人，所以当时报纸对他的报道即称其出生于火纳鲁鲁（即火奴鲁鲁，下同）。

纷输资回华。然人才尚形缺乏，军需亦未充足，遂改期至十月间。于时军械弹药陆续购备矣，香港之党人赴粤以攻广州矣，饷项亦甚形富足矣，外国之参谋官及军事家已延聘矣。日本政府虽无明白之答复，而党人则已请其援应矣。凡起事之谋，可谓应有尽有。不幸为奸人所算，泄其谋于当事，卒至全功尽覆。盖当时有侨寓香港之中国某富商，附和新党，知其集资购械等事可缘以为利，遂宛然以富商而为志士。既而知起事期迫，该商方为中日战事后某财政团之一，经营中国路矿等事，恐干戈一起则权利将受影响，遂不惜举党人之谋尽泄于粤官，而仍缘之以为利。党人之计既被所倾覆，孙氏即出奔于异国。此次以嫌疑被戮者凡四五十人，并悬赏以缉孙氏。

孙氏由香港至火纳鲁鲁，复由火纳鲁鲁至美国。驻美中国公使馆中人闻孙氏之绪论，颇有志于革新。既而赴伦敦，思欲以鼓吹驻美使馆者鼓吹驻英使馆。而不意美使馆有阳则赞成革命，阴则志香港富商之志，思缘以为利者，密白其事于驻英使馆。而孙逸仙被使馆诱劫之案，遂因以演成矣。此案虽由马凯尼一再辩护，而孙氏之始则被劫，继则羁禁，固已无可讳言。至孙氏之得脱于祸，实赖友人康德黎博士之力云。"

当时英人士讨论此案，多集矢于马凯尼，《太晤士报》最先著论抨击之，文曰：

"欧洲各国方以目前为邦交揖睦、彼此相安无事之时，而岂知伦敦中国公使馆突然发见一案，其以破坏法律及成例，而足以惹起国际之交涉者，关系固不浅哉！孙逸仙被幽于中国公使馆之中，幸其财力犹足以暗通消息，俾其英国友人得施营救之计。英警署既派遣侦探密伺于公使馆之外，俾该使馆无由将孙氏运解至船。而外务大臣萨里斯伯又要求该使馆期以立释。幸而此案早破，得以无事。否则孙氏既被递解，就刑戮于中国，英之外务部必且致责言于中国政府，而勒令将本案有关之人一一惩办，其损害于邦交固何如哉！孙氏既被诱劫入公使馆，即由马凯尼勋爵出见，旋即被锢一室，直至英外部出而干涉，始克见释。夫马凯尼，英人也，乃亦躬与于此案。此案之失败固可预料，即幸而获免，然他日与于此案者亦必同受巨创，马凯尼此举不亦可异乎？闻中国公使当释放孙氏之时，谓渠之释放此人，期无损于使臣应有之权利。噫！此等权利似决非文明国所欲享有者也，设竟或使用此等权利，则其为不可恕，又岂待言？昔者土耳其使臣在伦敦诱亚美尼亚人入使馆，意在絷其体，塞其口，而异送登舟，递解回国，冀为土耳其皇之牺牲。孙氏之案，毋乃类是乎？"

马凯尼睹是论，即复书该报曰：

"贵报评论向极公正，乃本日社论中评某华人被诱于中国使馆一案，词连于予，殊失贵报公正之素旨。彼华人之自称姓名甚多，而孙逸仙其一也。贵报既历叙使馆与孙逸仙所述之案情，而对于予之行为则颇致微词，是明明以孙逸仙之所言为可信，而以使馆之所言为不足据也。贵报引土耳其使臣在伦敦诱阿摩尼亚人事为佐证，殊不知本案并无所谓诱劫，彼原名孙文、伪名孙逸仙所供之辞，如谓被捕于道途、被挟入使馆等语，皆至不足信者也。孙逸仙之至使馆，系出己意，且为使馆中人所不料。其初次之来在礼拜六日，即十月十号。二次之来在礼拜日，即十月十一号。[1]治国际法学者对于孙逸仙被使馆

---

[1] 孙中山获释后在接受英国内务部调查时特别揭穿了马卡尼的谎言："我晓得马格里爵士曾投书报界，说我在星期六来过使馆。我可以肯定，不论是星期五或星期六我都没有到过那里。我以前也从不曾到过那里。""初到伦敦的那些天，我的时间主要是用于游览。我曾到南甘星敦博物院和大英博物馆，有一天还到过水晶宫。星期六，即十日，我到过摄政公园、动物园和植物园。我去那里时是上午十一二点钟，一直逗留到下午三点钟。然后，我去霍尔庞，四点钟左右返回寓所。从那以后，我除了只在附近进餐外，再没有外出。"（《向英国律师卡夫所作的陈述词（一八九六年十一月四日）》，《孙中山全集》第1卷，第40、38页）

拘留一节，无论作何评论，抱何见解，然必先知本案并无所谓诱骗，即其入使馆时亦并未尝施以强力或欺诈，此为本案之事实，而亦至可凭信者也。"

观马凯尼此书，其云孙逸仙姓名甚多，是明明将以此肆其污蔑，使外国知予非正人。而不知华人习俗，多有以一人而兼三、四名者，此在马凯尼要无不稔知之也。华人自有生以后，襁褓中父母所呼之名，一也；稍长从师，学塾中师长所授之名，二也；既而身入社会，则有所谓字者，有所谓号者，惟名字屡易，而姓则不变。彼马凯尼之在中国，有称为马大爷者，有称为马凯尼者，有称为马晋山者，以此例彼，其道一也。①

一千八百九十六年十月三十一日《斯比克报》(*The Speaker*) 亦刊有一论，其标题为《波德兰区之牢狱》，论曰：

"马凯尼者，役于中国公使馆者也。此公使馆之受役者，以不慊于《太晤士报》之评斥，而投函更正，是亦犹土耳其大僚胡资氏 (Woods Pasha) 为土政府辩护之故，而现身于英国之报纸也。然此事出诸真正之东方人，则不特为情理所宜然，而亦足征其性质之特别；若出诸假托之东方人，则适足以供嘲笑而已。马凯尼之布告天下，谓孙逸仙医士之入公使馆，并非由于诱劫；然使孙逸仙当时稔知彼延接者、招待者为何如人，孙氏固肯步入彼波德兰区之牢狱（以公使馆在伦敦之波德兰区，故名）而绝无赽趄瑟缩乎？马凯尼于此语乃不置一答辞，何也？况马凯尼既睹孙氏被捕，而乃绝不设法以冀省释，直待

---

① 此一段编者插语系孙中山所写，中文仅翻译了大意。这里作一点说明：原文中谈到一般中国人起码有四个名字，第四个名字是结婚时所取 (4th, the name he takes when he is married)，但此句中文省略未译。此外，中译中"有称为马大爷者"，原文 "Ma-Ta-Yen" 是广东话拼音，意为"马大人"，非"马大爷"；"有称为马晋山者"，马卡尼的中文名是马格里，表字清臣，原文 Ma-Tsing-Shan 是马清臣的广东话英文译音，旧译本误为"马晋山"。

李鸿章（1896）

外务部出而为坚毅之要求，始得出狱，又何故也？夫公使馆苟不欲解孙氏回国，何必系之于使馆中？马凯尼身在伦敦，且以迫于责任之故，遂不得不陷入此可怜之地位。若此剧而演于中国之广州，固不失为循法而行，至正至当也。马凯尼既遭失败，将使北京当道者病其无能，固应缄口结舌，自比于中国人之所为，而乃犹昂首伸眉，论列是非于伦敦《太晤士报》乎？

且使此次被劫者而为德国人或法国人，则事之严重将不可问，幸而其人籍隶中国，闻者不过一笑置之。而报纸之对于此事，亦仅如闻李鸿章之忽焉而界以相位，忽焉而以未奉召命擅自入宫，被太后之谴责而已。①然而自今以往，凡过波德兰区之牢狱者，不得不竦然以惧、哑然以笑也。（下略）"

予得释后，即投函各报馆，以谢英政府及英报纸相援之情，文曰：

"予此次被幽于中国公使馆，赖英政府之力，得蒙省释。并承报界共表同情，及时援助。予于英人之尚公德、好正义，素所钦仰，身受其惠，益堪征信。且予从此益知立宪政体及文明国人之真价值，敢不益竭其愚，以谋吾祖国之进步，并谋所以开通吾横被压抑之亲爱同胞乎！爰驰寸简，敬鸣谢忱。　　孙文缄于波德兰区覃文省街之四十六号"②

（录自上海商务印书馆1912年版译本《伦敦被难记·附录》）

---

①　"而报纸之对于此事，亦仅如闻李鸿章之忽焉而界以相位，忽焉而以未奉召命擅自入宫，被太后之谴责而已。"此事是指：光绪二十二年九月十八日（公元1896年10月24日）大学士李鸿章刚刚受命总理各国事务衙门行走，然同日又以擅入圆明园禁地游览，谕交吏部议处；二十四日部议革职，嗣后慈禧太后谕改罚俸一年。

②　有关"附录"末所附孙中山致新闻媒体的感谢信，参阅"译者前言"。

Kidnapped in London

一　清政府驻英公使馆整理的
《孙中山与邓廷铿的谈话》①

（1896年10月14日）

邓：我以公事扣你，若论私情，你我同乡，如有黑白不分，被人欺你之处，何妨将此事细微曲折，一一告我。倘有一线可原之路，我亦可念同乡之谊，代求钦差②为你申雪，你亦可回籍再谋生业。况广东近事③，我亦略知，且听你说，看与人言合否。

---

① 清使馆译员邓廷铿与囚禁中的孙中山的谈话，参阅《伦敦蒙难记》第三章"监禁"。本篇谈话虽已收入《孙中山全集》，但此文并非孙中山亲笔，系出自邓氏所整理呈报清廷之材料，并且此材料又由另一清吏、驻英使馆译员吴宗濂存录于所著笔记《随轺笔记四种》卷二《龚星使计擒孙文致总署总办公函》（光绪二十二年九月二十九日）之附录《邓翻译与孙文问答节略》一文之中，因此本文所录与实际谈话内容当有很大出入；此外，孙中山因身陷囹圄，企图蒙蔽官方，争取脱险，所谈内容多属编造，这份官方记录只能作为史料参考。

② 钦差，指清政府驻英国公使龚照瑗。

③ 广东近事，指1895年已遭镇压的广州起义。吴宗濂《随轺笔记》尚记有10月12日邓翻译与孙中山的第一次谈话内容，其中有一段谈到广州起义事："（邓）问：'你在广东谋反，因事不密，被人先觉，以致不成，是否属实？'孙答：'我虽有大志，而时尚未至。惟广东有一富人欲谋是事，被我阻之。'邓云：'何不同谋，反阻何故？'孙云：'他是为己，我是为民。'邓云：'请将为己为民四字，明白告我。'孙云：'他之为己，欲得天下自专其利。我之为民，不过设议院，变政治，但中国百姓不灵，时尚未至，故现在未便即行。盖该富人不知审时，我所以阻之也。我素重西学，深染洋习，欲将中国格外振兴，喜在广报上发议论，此我谋反之是非所由起也。'"（见《孙中山全集》第1卷第28页注①）

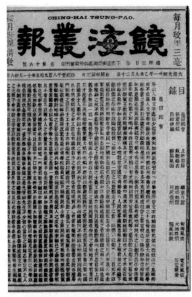

葡籍友人飞南第在澳门《镜海丛报》上刊载了广州起义的消息

孙：事可明言，但不知钦差愿意排解否？

邓：钦差最喜替人申冤，只要将实情说出，我必竭力代求。……

孙：我是孙文，非陈姓也。号逸仙。再号帝象，此号是母所名。因我母向日奉关帝象，生平信佛，取号"帝象"者，望我将来象关帝耳。"载之"二字，系由成语"文以载道"而来，并无别情。向在广东洗〔冼〕基设西医局，因治病有效，常与绅士来往。其时北京开强学会，我在省设农学会①，总会在厢〔双〕门底，分会在咸虾栏②。凡入会者，将姓名籍贯登簿，当发凭票一纸，交其人收执。曾托尚书罗椒生③之侄罗古香向前抚台马④说情，请其批准开办，因抚台病，后迁延未批。而农学会早先开办，不过教民种植，意欲开垦清远县之荒田。此田系会中所置，以为如有成效，即可将广东官地一并开垦。入会者有绅士、船主、同文馆学生等人。不料前年九月初八九左右，李家焯⑤忽然带勇前来，将总会、分会一概查封，在总会查出

———————

① 农学会 1895年10月6日（八月十八日）设农学会于广州王家祠，为起义军事总机关。

② 咸虾栏 农学会分会设于广州东门外咸虾栏张公馆，陆皓东常驻于此。

③ 罗椒生（1814—1874），名惇衍，字星斋，号椒生。广东顺德人。道光进士。曾任户部尚书，兼署工部。

④ 前抚台马 指1895年10月病故的广东巡抚马丕瑶（1831—1895）。马丕瑶因参劾两广总督李瀚章腐败问题受到朝廷表彰。

⑤ 李家焯 清廷广州缉捕委员。10月25日（九月初八日）兴中会会员朱淇之兄朱湘向李家焯告密，起义事泄。

广州起义领导人之一陆皓东烈士遗像　　　　少年时代的陆皓东

名册一本，分会查出铁锅二个、大斧多张，并拿去会友数名。其中有一姓陆者[①]，本系蚕师，过堂苦打，强逼成招，[②]已被正法，其馀尚在狱中。所可恨者，绅士如罗古香等则不敢拿。镇涛、广丙两船主[③]托人取保出去，而事亦了。同文馆学生因是旗籍，亦置不问。独以我为首，专意拿我。且三天之后，又闻有西门丁泥[④]六桶，内系洋枪，由香港

---

①　姓陆者，指陆皓东（1867—1895）。乙未广州起义被捕牺牲。

②　陆皓东被捕后，因事已败露，即自供举义不讳，其词慷慨激昂："与同乡孙文同愤异族政府之腐败专制，官吏之贪污庸懦，外人之阴谋窥伺，凭吊中原，荆榛满目，每一念及，真不知涕泪之何从也。居沪多年，碌碌无所就，乃由沪返粤，恰遇孙君，客寓过访。远别故人，风雨连床，畅谈竟夕。吾方以外患之日迫，欲治其标，孙则主满仇之必报，思治其本，连日辩驳，宗旨遂定，此为孙君与吾倡行排满之始。盖务求惊醒黄魂，光复汉族。""要知今日非废灭满清，决不足以光复汉族，非诛除汉奸，又不足以废灭满清。故吾等尤欲诛一二狗官，以为我汉人当头一棒。""今事虽不成，此心甚慰。但我可杀，而继我而起者不可尽杀！"（转引自陈锡祺主编《孙中山年谱长编》上册，第100页）对此供词，当时囚禁中的孙中山则随机应变，编造故事企图蒙混过关。

③　镇涛、广丙两船主　镇涛船主指广东水师镇涛舰管带程奎光，乙未广州起义被捕遇难。广丙船主系广东水师广丙舰管带程璧光（程奎光之兄），曾参加甲午海战，战败解职归乡；广州起义事泄旋逃南洋。

④　西门丁泥，水泥的旧译音，旧译又作士敏土。

付至农学会，亦被李家焯拿住，以为我谋反之据。又在火船拿获散勇五十馀名，作为我之党羽，后讯知是台湾散勇，因有二人因别案与陆姓同罪，其馀均由总督给资回籍，此非谋反之党羽可立明也。查香港买洋枪，非由的保不卖，若往香港，一查便知虚实，此系李家焯私买废枪以坐我罪也。且我暂避藩署，一经事发，方将托人与陆设法，不料他一见刑具即妄招认，无可挽回。① 倘有军火，何难电阻？三天后寄来，又谁收谁用耶？

邓：李家焯何故与你为仇？

孙：他之仇我，因机房之事也。缘他部下勇丁直入机房抢丝，被人捉住。李家焯得知，派勇夺回，随往抚辕控告，以不服稽查，挟制官长为辞。有人求我替机房定计，与李互讼。李知事败，以故仇我，即借农学会以控我，指为暗藏三合会②，有谋反之举。我之误处，误在专讲西学，即以西国之规行于中国，所有中国忌禁概不得知，故有今日之祸。

广丙鱼雷快艇

---

① 参见上页注②。
② 三合会，当时一种反清秘密会党组织。

邓：前日所说富人，何妨明说。

孙：谋反之事，我实无之。前日说有人商之于我，意图谋反，此人系广东大绅，曾中进士，并且大富，姓某名某是也（按：此人近颇为当道倚重，或系孙之妄扳，故删其姓名）①。我行医时，素与绅士往来，惟他尤为亲密。平时互发议论，以为即是国计民生之道，只知洋务亟宜讲求。所说之话，他甚为然，以我之才干，可当重任。故于中日相接莫解之时，专函请我回广东相商要事。

广东水师镇涛舰管带程奎光烈士遗像

我在香港得信即回见他，他曰："我有密事告你，万勿宣扬。"乃述其梦云："我身穿龙袍，位登九五，我弟叩头贺喜。故请你商量，何以助我？"我即问曰："你有钱多少？"他答曰："我本人有数百万两，且我承充闱姓，揭晓后始派彩红，现存我手将近千万，如立行谋事，此款可以动用，迟则失此机会。"我又问："有人马多少？"他云："我有法可招四万之众。"我答云："凡谋事者必要先通在上位之人，方得有济，尔于政府能通声气否？"他不能应。况他之品行最低，无事不作，声名狼藉，我早尽知。他之所谋，只知自利，并无为民之意，我故却之，决其不能成事也。他寄我之函，的系亲笔，虽未将谋反之言说出，其暗指此事可以意会之词，亦可为证。是欲谋反者是他，而非我也。乃李家焯故意张大其词，以重我罪，藩署官场中人及绅士等均有意替我申雪，因事关重大，不敢干预，即递公呈代办亦恐无济。其时制台②派兵搜查，我由藩署坐轿而出，直至火船，径赴香港，幸无人知。此我真有莫白之冤也。李家焯此次害我，不独家散

---

① 此处《孙中山全集》注为："此富绅指刘学询，原写上姓名，被删去。按语为邓廷铿所加。"（见《孙中山全集》第1卷第28页注②）

② 制台，指李瀚章被罢免后新调任的两广总督谭钟麟（1822—1905）。

人亡，我所有田地均已被封，不知尚能复见天日、得雪此恨否？况我曾上禀请设内河轮船公司，已蒙张香帅①批准，不遇此事，我早往上海开办矣。李家焯之害我，其毒无穷，自我避往香港之后，去年又造谣言，说我私买军火，在外国招募洋匠五千，进攻粤省。我不得已，潜往各国游历。及抵英国，我所往各处均系游玩之所，凡制造军火各厂我概未去，此亦可见我非有谋反之事也。万望钦差代为申雪，俾得回国，另谋事业，断不敢再行为乱。况中国近来颇讲洋务，我意中主意甚多，不难致富，又何必行险耶，你果念同乡之谊，还当代我力求钦差。

1892年孙中山设计建造的香山翠亨村新住宅

---

① 张香帅，即湖广总督张之洞（1837—1909），字孝达，号香涛。一度曾调署两江总督。

二 孙中山复翟理斯函①（附手迹）

（1896年10月）

比闻间师②盛称 足下深于中国文学，著述如林，近欲将仆生平事迹附入大作之内，并转示 瑶函，属为布复。拜读之下，愧不敢当。

夫仆也，半世无成，壮怀未已。生于晚世，目不得睹尧舜之风、先王之化，心伤鞑虏苛残、生民憔悴，遂甘赴汤火，不让当仁，纠合英雄，建旗倡义。拟驱除残贼，再造中华，以复三代之规，而

英国汉学家翟理斯像

步泰西之法，使万姓超甦，庶物昌运，此则应天顺人之作也。乃以人谋未臧，势偶不利，暂韬光锐，以待异时；来游上邦，以观隆治。不意清虏蓄此阴谋，肆其陷害，目无友邦，显违公法，暴虐无道，可见

---

① 翟理斯（Herbert Allen Giles，1845—1935），英国汉学家，曾任驻华外交官。当时他在伦敦编纂《中国名人辞典》（*Chinese Biographical Dictionary*，一八九八年出版时自译书名为《古今姓氏族谱》）。他闻知孙中山脱险之后，即通过康德黎先生函约孙中山撰写一篇生平简介。本篇是孙中山为编纂辞典之事给翟理斯的复函。

② 间，指间地利，即康德黎的粤语音译。

一斑。所赖贵国政仁法美，一夫不获，引以为辜。奸计不成，仆之幸也，抑亦中国四百兆生民之幸也。

足下昔游敝邦，潜心经史，当必能恍然于敝国古先圣贤王教化文明之盛也。乃自清虏入寇，明社丘墟，中国文明沦于蛮野，从来生民祸烈未有若斯之亟也。中华有志之士，无不握腕椎心！此仆所以出万死一生之计，以拯斯民于水火之中，而扶华夏于分崩之际也。独恐志愿宏奢，力有不逮耳。故久欲访求贵国士大夫之谙敝邦文献者，以资教益，并欲罗致贵国贤才奇杰，以助宏图。足下目睹中国之疮痍，民生之困楚，揆之胞与仁人义士，岂不同情？兹叨雅眷，思切倾葵，热血满腔，敢为一吐。更有恳者：仆等今欲除虏兴治，罚罪救民，步法泰西，揖睦邻国，通商惠工各等事端举措施行，尚无良策；足下高明，当有所见，幸为赐教，匡我缺失，是所祷冀。至于仆生平事迹，本无足纪，既承明问，用述以闻：

仆姓孙名文，字载之，号逸仙，藉[籍]隶广东广州府香山县，生于一千八百六十六年，华历十月十六日①。幼读儒书，十二岁毕经业。十三岁随母往夏威仁岛（Hawaiian Islands），始见轮舟之奇、沧海之阔，自是有慕西学之心，穷天地之想。是年母复回华，文遂留岛依兄，入英监督所掌之书院（Iolani College，Honolulu②）肄业英文。三年后，再入美人所设之书院（Oahu College，Honolulu③）肄业，此为岛中最高之书院。初拟在此满业，即往美国入大书院，肄习专门之学。后兄因其切慕耶稣之道，恐文进教为亲督责，着令回华，是十八岁时也。抵家后，亲亦无所督责，随其所慕。居乡数月，即往香港，

① 据广东翠亨孙中山故居纪念馆所藏《孙家列传祖生殁纪念部》（抄本），孙中山生于1866年阴历十月初六日，公历11月12日。

② Iolani College Honolulu，中译名：火奴鲁鲁意奥兰尼学校。孙中山于1879年9月入该校就读。1882年7月毕业，并获夏威夷国王颁发的英文文法奖赏。

③ Oahu College Honolulu，中译名：火奴鲁鲁奥阿厚书院。1882年孙中山从意奥兰尼学校毕业后即入该校就读。

火奴鲁鲁意奥兰尼学校，1879—1882年孙中山在这里读书

香港歌赋街44号，中央书院。1884—1886年孙中山在这里读书

再习英文，先入拔萃书室（Diucison [Diocesan] Home，HongKong）。数月之后，转入香港书院（Queen′s College①，H. K.）。又数月，因家事离院，再往夏岛（H. L.）。数月而回，自是停习英文，复治中国经史之学。②二十一岁改习西医，先入广东省城美教士所设之博济医院（Canton Hospita1）肄业；次年转入香港新创之西医书院（College of Medicine for Chinese，HongKong）。五年满业，考拔前茅，时二十六岁矣。此从师游学之大略也。

文早岁志窥远大，性慕新奇，故所学多博杂不纯。于中学则独好三代两汉之文，于西学则雅癖达文之道（Darwinism）③，而格致政事亦常浏览。至于教则崇耶稣，于人则仰中华之汤武暨美国华盛顿焉。

（见一八九六年十月二十六日《伦敦与中国电讯报》）④

原函刊佚名编《总理遗墨》

---

① Queen′s College，中译名：皇仁书院（直译当为：女王学院）。孙中山当时（1884年4月）就读于该校时名为"香港中央书院"（The Central School），入学学名为孙帝象。1889年该校改名为维多利亚书院（Victoria College）；1894年始称皇仁书院。

② 即从区凤墀补习国学。

③ 达文之道（Darwinism），达尔文主义，即进化论。

④ 原文落款："（See London, and China Telegraph, 26, Oct. 1896.）"，可知本篇作于孙中山获释后一两天。

孙中山复翟理斯函手迹

比間間師咸稱　足下深於中國文學著述

如林近欲將僕生平事跡附入大作之內亚轉

示　瑶函屬為布後拜讀之下愧不敢當

夫僕也半世無成壯懷未已生於晚世目不得

覩堯舜之風先王之化心傷難虜荼殘生

民悼（惟）遂甘赴湯火不讓當仁斜合英雄建

旗倡義擬驅除殘賊再造中華以後三代之

而步泰西之法使萬姓超越庶物昌運此

則應天順人之作也乃以人謀未臧勢乃偶

不利暫韜光銳以待異時來游上邦以觀

隆治不意清虜蓄此陰謀肆其陷害目

無友邦顯違公法暴虐無道可見一班所

賴貴國政仁法美一夫不獲引以為辜奸

計不成僕之幸也抑亦中國四百兆生民之

足下者游敕邦潛心經史當必能怵
然於敬國古先聖賢王教化文明之盛也
乃自清虜入冠明社坵墟中國文明淪於
蠻野從來生民禍烈未有若斯之甚也中
華有志之士無不握腕椎心此僕所以出萬
死一生之計以拯斯民於水火之中而扶華
夏於分崩之際也獨恐志願宏奢力有

幸也

不逮耳故久欲訪求賢國士大夫之誘敝
邦文獻者以資教益並欲羅致賢國賢
才奇傑以助宏圖　足下目覩中國之
瘡痍民生之困楚撲之胞與仁人義士
豈不同情藥叩　雅眷思切傾葵熱血
滿腔敢為一吐更有懇者供芻蕘今欲除虜
興治罰罪救民出湯泰西楫睦鄰國通

尚惠妥籌善後事舉措施行尚無良策

足下高明當有所見幸為賜教匡我

瞬失是所禱冀至於僕生平事跡本無

足紀既承 明問用述以聞

僕姓孫名文字載之號逸仙籍隸廣東

廣州府香山縣生於一千八百六十六年華

歷十月十六日幼讀儒書十二歲畢經業

十三歲隨世往夏威仁島始見輪舟之奇 *Honoruru Hawaiido*

滄海之闊自是有慕西學之心窮天地之

想是年母復回華文遂留島依兄入英監

督所掌之書院肄業英文三年後再入 *Iolani College, Honolulu*

美人所設之書院肄業此為島中最高 *Oahu College, Honolulu*

之書院初擬在此肄業即往美國入大

書院肄習專門之學後兄因其切慕

耶穌之道恐文進教為親督責著令

四華是十八歲時也抵家後親亦無所督

責隨其所慕居鄉數月郎徒香港再

習英文先入拔萃書室數月之後轉入

Queen's College in

Wilson Home Hospital

香港書院又數月因家事離院再往夏島

數月而回自是傳習英文後治中國經史之

學二十歲改習西醫先入廣東省城美教

設之博濟醫院肄業次年轉入香

港新創之西醫書院五年滿業考核

前茅時二十六歲矣此從師游學之大畧也

文旱歲志窺遠大性慕新奇故所學

多博雜不純於中學則獨好三代兩漢

之文於西學則雅廔達文之道兩格致政

事亦常流覽重於教則崇

耶穌於人

則仰中華之湯武暨美國華盛頓

三 孙中山致区凤墀函①（附手迹）

（1896年11月）

启者：弟被诱擒于伦顿，牢于清使馆十有馀日，拟将弟捆绑乘夜下船，私运出境，船已赁备，惟候机宜。初六七日内无人知觉，弟身在牢中，自分必死，无再生之望，穷则呼天，痛痒则呼父母，人之情也。弟此时惟有痛心忏悔，恳切祈祷而已。一连六七日，日夜不绝祈祷，愈祈愈切。至第七日，心中忽然安慰，全无忧色，不期然而然，自云此祈祷有应，蒙神施恩矣。然究在牢中，生死关头，尽在能传消息于外与否耳。但日夜三四人看守，窗户俱闭，严密异常，惟有洋役二人日入房中一二次，传递食物各件。然前已托之传书，已为所卖，将书交与衙内之人，秘事俱俾知之，防范更为加密。而可为我传消息者，终必赖其人。今既蒙上帝施恩，接我祈祷，使我安慰，当必能感动其人，使肯为我传书。次早他入房中，适防守偶疏，得乘间与他关说，果得允肯。然此时笔墨纸料俱被搜去，幸前时将名帖写定数言，未曾搜出，即交此传出外，与简地利、万臣两师②。他等一闻此事，着力异常，即报捕房，即禀外部。而初时尚无人信，捕房以此二人为癫狂者，使馆全推并无此事。他等初一二日，自出暗差，自出防守，

---

① 区凤墀（1847—1914），名逢时，字锡桐，号凤墀，广东南海人。基督教传教士，长期在香港和广州传教。曾任德国柏林大学中文教授。孙中山曾拜其为汉语教师，孙逸仙之名即为其所起。区本人也系兴中会会员。本篇是孙中山脱险后向其报告伦敦蒙难经过。原信见《孙中山先生遗墨之一》（上海真光杂志社1927年版）。

② 简地利、万臣两师，即孙中山香港西医书院老师康德黎先生和孟生博士。简地利、万臣是广东话读音。

恐溜夜运往别处。初报馆亦不甚信，迨后彼二人力证其事之不诬，报馆始为传扬，而全国震动，欧洲震动，天下各国亦然，想香港当时亦必传扬其事。伦顿几乎鼓噪，有街坊欲号召人拆平清使衙门者。沙侯[①]行文着即释放，不然则将使臣人等逐出英境，使馆始惧而放我。此十馀日间，使馆与北京电报来往不绝，我数十斤肉任彼千方百计而谋耳。幸天心有意，人谋不减，虽清虏阴谋，终无我何，适足以扬其无道残暴而已。虏朝之名，从兹尽丧矣！

弟现拟暂住数月，以交此地贤豪。弟遭此大故，如荡子还家，亡羊复获，此皆天父大恩。敬望先生进之以道，常赐教言，俾从神道而入治道，则弟幸甚，苍生幸甚。

致区凤墀函手迹细部

致区凤墀函手迹

---

① 沙侯，即英国首相兼外相索尔兹伯里侯爵（Robert Arthur Talbot Gascoyne-Cecil, 3rd Marquess of Salisbury），一译为沙利斯堡侯爵。参阅《伦敦蒙难记》第七章相关注解。

四　冯自由《革命逸史》中有关文献^①

孙总理被囚伦敦使馆之清吏笔记

冯自由像

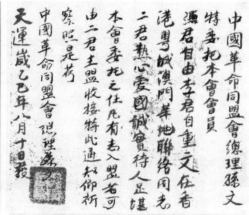

孙中山给冯自由、李自重的委任状

关于孙总理丙申（一八九六年）在伦敦清公使馆被囚一节，拙著《中华民国开国前革命史前编》已叙述綦详。查当日任驻英公使

---

①　《革命逸事》中有关文献，本书摘自新星出版社2009年版本。冯自由（1882—1958），原名懋龙，字健华，后改名自由。广东南海县人。1895年秋在日本横滨由孙中山介绍参加兴中会。民国后曾任临时政府稽勋局局长、立法委员、国民政府委员等职。长期从事民国史著述工作，著有《中华民国开国前革命史》、《革命逸史》、《华侨革命开国史》、《中国革命运动二十六年组织史》和《华侨革命组织史话》等。

清驻英公使馆随员龚心湛（1871—1943）

为皖人龚照瑷，使馆职员有龚心湛①（号仙舟，龚之侄也）、吴宗濂②（挹青，江苏嘉定人）、邓廷铿（琴斋，粤人）、王鹏九、车焕章、谢邦清及英人马格里诸人，均曾奔走于诱禁总理及预备雇船解送回国诸事。吴宗濂于民国后曾任驻荷兰公使。于清光绪二十五年己亥（一八九九年）著有《随轺笔记》一书，录载当时清吏对于此事之计划及一切布置，颇为详尽。余于民十七编著《开国前革命史》时，曾托友人但植之（焘）向吴宗濂借读，借供史料，顾久久未得，无从选录。近由他友多方觅得原书，特将书中关于此事之记事全文录出见赠，亦清代官样文章之一趣闻也。亟为照录如下：

光绪二十二年七月，准出使美日秘大臣杨子清星使函称，粤省要犯孙文谋乱发觉，潜逃赴美，奉总署电令，确查该犯行踪，并饬电知龚星使援香港缅甸交犯约，转恳英国代拿等因，并附节略，叙其面貌年岁籍贯。八月十九日复准通使电称，孙文于西九月二十三日（即华八月十七日）由纽约搭船至英国梨华埔海口登陆等语。时星使卧病已久，神志甚清，当遣参赞马格里（英人）

---

① 龚心湛（1871—1943），原名心瀛，号仙舟，安徽合肥人。时任清政府驻英国公使馆随员。民国后曾任汉口中国银行行长、安徽国税筹备处处长、财政厅厅长、安徽省省长。在北洋军阀政府段祺瑞内阁中任过财政总长、内务总长兼交通总长，还曾一度代理国务总理。

② 吴宗濂（1856—1933），字挹清，号景周，江苏嘉定人。时任清政府驻英、法公使馆法文翻译。民国后在北洋政府曾任安福国会参议员。著有《随轺笔记》，书中存有孙中山伦敦遭绑架事件的史料。

婉询英外部，拟援香港及缅甸交犯约，请拿该犯。外部答二约只能行于安南缅甸，不能施之他处，设竟代拿，必为刑司驳阻。星使之犹子仙舟司马心湛乃雇包探赴梨华埔守候。旋据该探密报，孙文剪发作洋装，于八月二十四日登陆，即日乘火车至伦敦，下榻客店，有二西人随行。九月初四日孙文行经使署之门，遇学生宋芝田（学生者使馆学生也），询其有无粤人在署，宋曰有之。孙即请见，乃进署门，入厅事，四等翻译官邓琴斋刺史廷铿，粤产也，遂与接谈。该犯以异地遇同乡，分外惬意。自言姓陈，号载之，继出金表以观时刻，刺史索观，则镌有英文拼切之孙字，刺史恍然。不动声色，约孙翌日再来，同赴海口探望粤商，刺史欣诺。孙既去，急密告仙舟，转禀星使，星使与马格里王鹏九两参赞密商办法。皆曰可拿。初五午前孙果贸贸然来，饭后，邓刺使请孙登楼，先至首层，观星宪之会客厅、签押室，继至二层，入李琴伯朋府盛钟卧室，坐谈良久。适马参赞到，刺史遂告孙曰，君能再上一层枉顾弟房乎？孙曰甚好。遂随刺史拾级而升。马参赞在前引导，先入预备之空房内，作开门侍客状。邓指曰，此即弟房，请君先进，孙刚涉足，错愕间，马参赞即将房门关闭，告曰，奉有总署及驻美杨子清星使密电，捉拿要犯孙文，尔即是也。既经到此，请暂留一日一夜，静候总署回电。孙见已识破，无可如何，唯唯应命，星使遂饬邓刺史武弁车焕章谢邦清造炮学生宋芝田及洋仆二名，日夜轮守。初七日接总署回电，力嘱慎密办理，不可为英所知，致被反噬，应如何措手，悉听主裁。初八日星使嘱宗濂代拟电稿，言惟有专雇一船径解粤省，否则只可释放，派探密跟，穷其所往，请示祗遵。此电去后，总署无复。十三日星使又发电云：释放宜早，免有痕迹，仍无复电。时署外已有人日夜守伺。十六日英国《格罗字报》忽刊其事，[①]不

---

① 《格罗字报》，即《环球报》（*Globe*），于1896年10月22日（阴历九月十六日）详细报道了清使馆非法绑架孙中山事件。

直使署所为，他报访事人接踪来访，邓刺史力辩其无，马参赞直认不讳。翌晨各报刊布，指为使署拐骗监禁，哗然四起，甚有以使署房屋绘为图画者，亦有以此事标题，特印大字告白，兜销报章者。使馆门口自朝至于日中戾，聚众至数百。英外部沙侯署闻消息，即柬请参赞去，①婉告曰，中英交犯约，曾经前大臣议而未成，刻既无约可援，如解犯潜过英地，殊与公例不符，宜将孙文即日开释。马参赞诺诺连声而退，急即回禀星使，不移时而外部总办及巡捕头果皆戾止，索领孙文。马参赞遂将孙文放出，交该总办及巡捕头，由后门坐车而去，盖避前门聚观之众也。是夜各报刊有孙文对答之辞，殊形荒谬。据谓邓星使告以拟将其装入箱中，运至船上，或先行毒死，解华戮尸，此皆该犯臆造，借以骇人听闻也。西国久无此等刑法，见此数语，益笑中国之教化毫无。十八日接总署复电，②内称雇船解粤甚是，电款六千余镑，即令汇丰拨解等因。惜其时孙文已为英廷索去，无可挽回，当即据实电复。十九日仙舟接短工洋仆查耳来信，内言孙文起初几次着伊送信，优给金钱，伊皆一律缴呈马格里参赞，未得分文奖赏。嗣孙复许酬金五百镑送一密信，并嘱其事后离开使署随孙度日，故伊甘冒不法，以洋信密报孙文坎特立门森两英医，两英医即在外设法，派人伺守，并报外部及巡捕房，各报闻之，遂亦附和作不平鸣，致贵署不能不将孙文释放，曷胜怅怅。马参赞当时恫吓，谓如有走漏风声，当送官严办，予是以照实供

---

① 英国首相兼外长沙力斯伯里侯爵（今译索尔兹伯里侯爵）早在《格罗字报》（《环球报》）报道绑架事件前三天，即10月19日（阴历九月十三日）就已电令外交部及内政部采取行动干预清使馆绑架事件，随后照会中国公使馆释放人犯。《随轺笔记》此处有意将时间颠倒，以表明英国政府的行动完全是受新闻舆论所惑。

② 总理衙门命令严密押运人犯的这封电报早在10月16日（阴历九月初十）孙中山被关押的第五天就已经收到，此时清使馆正积极密商偷运孙中山之法，直到关押的第十三天即10月23日（阴历九月十七日）孙中山才被释放。《随轺笔记》将总署电报发送时间移后，显系蓄意歪曲事实。

明，听候惩治云云。仙舟司马以此信示马参赞，马参赞无计可施，徒形愤愤，各报议论纷如，痛斥马参赞及中国使署者又数日，而孙则致函英报，遍谢英廷、英报、英民，文过饰非，倾动众听。英国议绅之不明事理者，且举以诘责政府，拟请转令使馆不得再用马格里。幸沙侯相顾全大体，片言解纷，星使又无所见闻，得以怡然养疴，更幸外部允照星使照会中所请各节，移知香港总督，严查不法，以戢乱谋，而杜后患。即日由星宪容报总署，此案遂结，然传递密信之奸仆，以孙文所酬止有英金二十五镑，控诸刑司，又不得直，至今迄不甘服。孙逆亦以港督悬有厉禁，不敢回华，以身试法，故辗转窜匿，遁迹东瀛。而我中国东南半壁，即借此得以谧安，则我星宪龚公之一纸公文，保全者诚大而远哉。粤民有知，尚其铸像以祝也可。时光绪二十五年八月嘉定吴宗濂追识于汉皋铁路局之牟隐庐。

按邓廷铿号琴斋，广东三水县人，乙未前孙总理在广州行医时尝与邓有一面之雅，故丙申远游伦敦，以他乡遇故，自容易受骗。邓后任广州某报记者，自称环球三周客，盖邓时以生平曾三度环游世界之经历炫耀人前也。辛亥革命后，邓于民元二月尝诣南京临时大总统府投刺求谒孙总理。总统府副官某等知其曾陷害总理，欲治以汉奸之罪，特向总理请示。总理曰，桀犬吠尧，各为其主，已过之事，毋庸深究，彼来求官，但不予之官足矣。即令副官护送邓出府，庶免发生危险，是可见总理器量之广，殊非常人所及也。

兴中会始创于檀香山之铁证

广州起义失败后流亡日本的陈少白

孙总理于民元前十八年甲午冬手创兴中会于檀香山，为当年兴中会员及今日一般国民党员周知之事实。而总理遗教中且有"乃赴檀岛美洲创立兴中会"之自述，则是檀香山之为兴中会发源地，可谓毫无疑义。余于民元前十七年乙未九月兴中会第一次在广州举义时，方十四岁。是年秋冬间，总理偕陈少白、郑士良两先生亡命至横滨，与吾父镜如公组织驻日兴中

檀香山兴中会旧址

分会，且同下榻于余家所设之山下町五十三番文经印刷店。余因是得与总理及陈、郑两先生朝夕亲炙，并熟聆兴中会先后创设于檀岛香港之故事，获益良多。民十七年及二十五年余著《中华民国开国前革命史》及《革命逸史》相继出版，二书均叙述檀香山为兴中会发源地，盖纪实也。近阅《中央周刊》第五卷第三十四期，始知有人主张兴中会于民前二十年创于澳门之新说，尤以吾友邹君海滨持之最力。是说倘能成立，诚不失为党史上之新发见，然而事实俱在，无可移易。余为兴中会员目前生存十数人中之一人，存真守璞，责无旁贷，谨抒管见，并提出物证人证为发生异议者一解释之。

考邹君海滨所主张"兴中会于民前二十年创于澳门"之说，其唯一之论据，为在伦敦出版之总理自著《伦敦被难记》一书，是书原本为英文，上海民智书局及其他书局多译出出售，惟译文各有不同。邹君所根据者，大概为民智书局或三民书局译本，其译文为："予在澳门，始知有一种政治运动，其宗旨改造中国，故名之曰兴中会"云云。然细观英文原文，则译文与原意义相差太远，且有画蛇添足之嫌，兹录载英文原句如下：

It was in Macao that I first learned of the existence of a political movement which I might best describe as the formation of a Young China Party.

此段英文原意，应译作"余早年在澳门，始知有一种政治运动革命之存在，此种政治运动大可名之曰少年中国党之形成"，方不失真。盖原文只称"少年中国党"，而并无兴中会三字，少年中国党与兴中会，有同风马牛，兴中会始终未闻有少年中国党之英文名称，固不得武断谓兴中会即《伦敦被难记》所谓少年中国党也。又英文原本并无"其宗旨在改造中国"一句，译本故意添入此语，尤为画蛇添足。各书局之译者以不解英文原意，勉强附会为兴中会以迎合潮流，可谓大误。而读译本者不知译本误译，竟从而错认"少年中国党"一语之普通名词为后二年产生之兴中会。则尤大误特误矣。故主张"兴中会于民前二十年创于澳门"之说者，如不能证明兴中会附有英语"少年中国党"之名称，及提出少年中国党即是兴中会之相当考证，则其说可谓根本不能成立，应自宣布取消其主张可也。

考《被难记》所述，"余早年在澳门知有一种政治运动之存在，大可名之曰少年中国党之产生"一语，实为总理当日对英人之外交措辞。盖香港乃清末四大寇多年放言无忌之政谈所，亦为兴中会本部之策源地，乙未九月广州一役虽经营失败，然党中潜势力犹密布于广惠各属，仍恃香港为卷土重来之出发点。香港既为英人殖民地，其官吏时有压迫党人以交欢清政府情事，总理为未来策动起见，不得不讳言香港二字，而以澳门代之。实则《被难记》所述"早年余在澳门"一段文字，澳门二字当作香港读之，始无悖于事实。在《孙文学说》第八章亦有"当时虽在英京，然亦事多忌讳"之自述，可知总理当日不便直承为兴中会首领，且讳香港为澳门，因别有苦衷也。

或疑《被难记》所称"少年中国党"为当时一种政治运动之固有团体，亦属大误。盖"少年某国某政团"一语，乃东西各国维新党之普通名词。自玛志尼创设"少年意大利"之后，他国改革政治之团体，以少年某国自称者，不一而足，少年土耳其即其一例。我国志士之自称"少年中国"者，尚在土耳其之先。民前十年壬寅秦毓鎏、程家柽、叶澜及余等在东京发起中国青年会（与耶教青年会性质不同），其英文名字即为Young China Association。同时梁启超在《新民丛报》之笔名，自号"少年中国之新民"。民前二三年己酉庚戌间旅美同盟会员李是男等组织"少年学社"及《少年中国报》于旧金山，其英文名字均称：Young China。此足证明"少年中国"之一名词，实为我国维新党之通称，且在民前十七八年以前我国稍具政治性质之团体，尚无革命立宪、排满保皇及急激和平之分。康有为所设南学会、强学会，杨衢云、谢缵泰等所设辅仁文社，尤列所设兴利蚕子公司，总理所设农学会，皆可以维新党称之，即名之曰少年中国党人之组织，亦无不可。就中总理之组织农学会于广州，其目的在于交结官绅以进行革命工作，时在澳门行医后二年，及檀香山兴中会成立后一年，实为兴中会之别动队。由上所述，可知总理所称“少年中国党”，乃当日一般维新志士之通称。在民前十八年甲午以前，吾国持激烈主义之志士尚无此种团体结合。康有为所设之南学会强学会，公然以请愿变法为号召，旗帜似较鲜明，特总理以康有为夜郎自大，目空一切，势难与之合作耳。

关于兴中会始创之地点及时期问题，当以民二十一年《陈君少白答复中央党史史料编纂委员会》一书为最有力之文证。在总理肄业香港雅丽士医校时期，及兴中会成立前后，诸同志中与总理关系密切者，以陈君为最，总理实不啻倚之为左右手，其言至有价值。今录原书于下，以供考证：

> 党史史料编纂委员会先生鉴：来示敬悉。承问兴中会创立年期。查逸公系于甲午夏威夷岛（檀香山）吹唱革命，此会实创于是时。是年底由檀返香港。翌年乙未正月僦屋士丹顿街，系继续开会而已。汉民君壬寅之说，去事实略远。
>
> 逸公毕业于壬辰之秋，旋问世于澳门，癸巳创东西药局于羊城，甲午去羊城而之上海，稍作逗留，遂往檀山。壬、癸两年并无开会立党之事。冯自由君乙未之说，应系指回国后而言，仍非事实也。（自由按：党史会去函似有误会，盖余所著《中华民国开国前革命史》系于民十七年出版，已明载兴中会于甲午冬创设于檀香山，而兴中会本部则于翌年乙未正月成立于香港矣）肃此。敬复著祺，陈少白拜启。二十一年十一月八日。

吾人只据陈君函中“壬、癸两年并无开会立党之事”一语，便足以打消“民元前二十年兴中会创设于澳门”之异说而有余。其他之研

宫崎滔天（后排中立者）与孙中山（二排左二）1897年秋在日本

1896年李鸿章（中坐者）出访欧洲，李右边站立者为罗丰禄（孙中山获释之后新上任的驻英公使）

讨，特无关宏旨之枝节问题耳。陈君谓总理于甲午夏从上海赴夏威夷一节，中间尚漏去"北上天津，上书李鸿章，条陈变法无效"等事。据陈君以前告余谓总理于甲午春因在广州药房业亏折，失意归乡，十余日后，忽来香港，持所撰《上李鸿章书》草稿相商，旋偕陆皓东赴上海，复北上至天津，由罗丰禄①介绍求谒李鸿章，条陈改革，以李拒绝延见，遂南下而之檀岛云云（事详余著《开国前革命史》）。证以陈君

1895年2月，孙中山在香港中环士丹顿街13号建立的兴中会总机关，对外以乾亨行作为掩护

此函，则总理是岁之旅程，可分五期：即春间从香港至上海，夏间从上海至天津，秋间从上海至檀岛，而抵达檀岛则已在秋冬间矣。嗣兴中会成立，遂于年底首途回香港，组织乾亨行为实行机关。故兴中会于甲午冬始创于檀岛之事实，洵为确凿不磨，毫无疑义。

此外尚有二种理由，足以证明兴中会创于澳门一说，为不足信。兴中会为反清复汉之革命团体。总理既联合同志结盟组党，其誓词曰"驱逐鞑虏，恢复中国，创立合众政府"，则是从兴中会成立之日

----

① 罗丰禄（1850—1901），字稷臣，福建闽县（今福州市）人。福州船政学堂出身。后官派留学英国，并兼任使馆翻译。回国后入李鸿章幕府，为李鸿章英文翻译及外交顾问。孙中山上书求谒李鸿章，当时即由罗氏接见。1896年11月，伦敦绑架事件之后因李鸿章力荐，清政府任命罗丰禄为驻英公使。

起，便与满清势无两立，决无再向满清督抚上书请愿改革朝政之理。由此可知总理北上求谒李鸿章之前，尚未有兴中会之组织彰彰明甚。又考总理在澳门行医，时期为民前二十年壬辰。主张兴中会于澳门之说者，殆谓兴中会之创设即在总理行医于澳门时期，其理由亦至薄弱。盖开会立党必须联合生平志同道合之密友，而后可以成立具体之组织；今乃并生平密友如所谓四大寇①者亦未参预，则此种团体之有无产生，更可知矣。以余所知，当日总理在澳门所结交者，仅有镜湖医院之少数绅商何穗田、吴节薇、陈庚如等，此辈徒知利禄，毫无国家思想，岂可与言排满复国。故主张兴中会创于澳门一说，即无异谓总理于民元前二十年脱离旧日同志，一人自创设兴中会于澳门，此必不可能之事也。稍明兴中会掌故者，当无不洞察其说之无以自圆矣。

要而言之，欲探求兴中会之掌故，首宜向旧日之兴中会员详征博引，乃可得其真相。若徒恃误译原文之译本而遽下断语，则犹隔靴搔痒耳。查现在生存之兴中会员尚有十余人，请试举其姓名地址，以供发生异议者之谘询可乎。计在檀香山入会者，有郑照、许直臣、钟宇、曾长福四人；郑、许、钟三人均于甲午冬加盟，曾君则于民前九年癸丑加盟，郑、钟、曾三君现在檀岛，许君则于前岁香港沦陷后由港移居澳门。在香港入会者，有余育之一人。余君系乙未春加盟，现在上海冠生园供职。在日本横滨入会者，有温炳臣、黄焯民及余三人，均于乙未冬加盟；温君现仍居横滨，黄君于抗战后归国，现居澳门。在南非州尊尼士堡埠入会者，有霍胜刚一人，现仍在香港经营萃文书店。其他硕果仅存可屈指数者，寥寥无几。则是目前生存之兴中会员，至多不过十数人而已。吾愿今之发生异议者，更向目前生存之兴中会员一一请益，自可获得无数兴中会成立前后之新资料，当较误读错译之《伦敦被难记》为优胜万万也。

此文乃应中央党史会之谘询而作，盖自邹君海滨对于总理所述

---

① 四大寇　当时革命党友人戏称孙中山、陈少白、尤列、杨鹤龄四人为四大寇。

"赴檀岛创立兴中会"之遗教发生异议后，党史会因之开会研究多次，对于兴中会首创之地点问题，迄未解决。迨余于去冬自香港脱险来渝。张君溥泉特访余征取意见，余即以上述理由分别答之。张君颇以为然。最近党史会为此问题，先后召集委员会及小组会，论讨此事，闻列席诸同志无有赞同兴中会创于澳门之主张者，足见此种异议已无成立之余地。余于党史会为纂修。于邹君为良友，抱残守缺，固属义不容辞，辩惑释疑，亦为势非得已。用是不得不根据事实，以阐明一切。倘邹君及二三发生异议者更能提供别项新证件，以自圆其说，则余极愿相与再事研讨，以重史信，是亦吾辈应有之责也。

1906年孙中山与冯自由（前左坐）等在新加坡

孙总理修正《伦敦被难记》第一章恭注

《伦敦被难记》英文本为孙总理于丙申年（民元前十六年）在伦敦清使馆被囚出险后所作。书中第一章叙述自身所经历之革命事由，甚为简略。馀文则记载被囚情形及师友营救出险经过。考其第一章全文所述，曾投身主张君主立宪之少年中国党及纠合全体党员向清廷联名上书请愿立宪，并在澳门入党，上海设总部等事。皆与总理生平言行完全不符。此种政治运动，亦向为总理所深恶痛绝，决无冒昧参加之理。此书在民元以前并无译本，故鲜为世人所注意。余于辛丑（民元前十一年）春始在横滨总理寓处见之。时余及粤籍留学生郑贯公、冯斯栾、李自重、王亮畴诸君方发起广东独立学会，日往还于东京横滨之间。常假前田桥一百二十一番地总理寓处为聚谈所。总理实赞助甚力。余获读此书第一章后，深为诧异，乃向总理请示如此措辞之理由。总理曰，英人最富于保守性质，世有约翰牛（John Bull）之称。其宪法号称不流血的和平宪法。若与之谈急激之革命手段，彼国人必不乐闻，故不得不从权以此立言。且香港为其殖民地，时有禁压党人行动以交欢清政府情事。吾党每次向粤进攻之出发点，始终不能离开香港，故亦不能坦白陈述，以妨碍进行，容日后至相当时期方可据实修正云云；余心为之释然。兹将民智书局出版之《伦敦被难记》第一章译文加以修正，其词句有与英文原本意义相差太远者，则为误译英文少年中国党（Young China Party）作兴中会一语。两者宗旨：一主张和平渐进之君主立宪，一主张激烈急进之革命排满，性质互异，有同冰炭，读者如不了解总理当日对外措辞之困难，而混为一谈，则离题万丈矣。译文录载如次：

孫文學說序

文奔走國事三十餘年畢生學力盡萃於斯精誠
無間百折不回滿清之威力所不能屈窮迫之困苦所不能
撓吾志所尚一往無前愈挫愈奮再接再厲用能鼓動風
潮造成時勢卒賴全國人心之傾向仁人志士之贊襄乃得

推覆專制創建共和本可德此繼進實行革命黨
所抱持之三民主義五權憲法以及革命方畧所規定
之種種建設宏模則必能乘時一躍而登中國於富
強之域躋斯民於安樂之天也不圖革命初成黨人則
起影□隨謂予所主張者理想太高不適中國之用眾

口鑠金一時風靡同志之士亦惑誠焉是予為民國總
統時之主張反不若為革命領袖時之有效而見之施
行矣此革命之建設所以無成而破壞之後國事更
因之以日非也夫去一滿洲之專制轉生出無數強盜之
專制其為毒較前尤甚於是而民愈不聊生矣

溯夫吾黨革命之初心本以救國救種為志欲出斯民
於水火之中而登之衽席之上也今乃反令之陷水益深
蹈火益熱與革命初衷大相違背者此固予之德薄
無以化格負儕能鮮不足駕馭羣眾有以致之歟吾
黨之士於革命宗旨革命方畧亦難免有信仰不

《〈孫文學說〉序》手稿

余早年在澳门始知有一种政治运动之存在。此种政治运动，大可以名之曰少年中国党（Young China Party）之形成。余以该党宗旨识见宏远，适合时势，深表同情，即报名入党。盖为国利民福计，极欲有所尽力耳。该党原有见于中国之政体不合于时势之所需，故欲以和平手段渐进方法请愿于朝廷，俾推行新政。其最要者，则在改行立宪政体，以代旧式专制及腐败的政治。中国睡梦至此，维新之机，苟非发之自上，殆无可望。此少年中国党所由设也。该党之所以偏重于请愿上书等方法，原冀皇帝之尊或一垂听，政府之散或可奋起。且近年以来，北京当道诸人与各国外交团接触较近，其于外国宪政当必略有所知。或能赞助人民此项运动。以是余及其他同志奋然本利国福民之诚意，会合全体，联名上书。但结果反令多人受严厉之惩罚。时则日本正以重兵进逼北京。在吾党固欲利用此时机，而在朝廷亦恐以惩治新党背全国人之心，遂暂搁不报。但中日战事既息，和议告成，而朝廷即悍然下诏，不特对于上书请愿者如此叱责，且云"此等陈请变法条陈，以后不得擅上"云云。吾党至是始知和平方法无可复施。……少年中国党总部确在上海设立。而其实行活动之地则在广州。

　　以上一段译文，凡稍读总理传记及革命史者，皆知为不符事实，而竟出于总理之著述，其为一种对外忌讳之措辞，不言可知。自民国建元后，中外文士以此向总理质疑者，大不乏人。总理久欲追述往事，据实修正，以释群疑。以劳于国事，无暇执笔。直至民国七年广东军政府改组赴沪闲居时，始抽暇撰成《孙文学说》一书。书中第八章首段即声明否认《伦敦被难记》第一章全文所述之革命事由，而加以郑重修正；次段乃追述其三十一年来所记忆之事实，如数家珍。及民国十二年一月复有《中国革命史》之作。文中所述革命之运动，（一）立党、（二）宣传、（三）起义三则，更足补《孙文学说》

孙中山题赠妻子宋庆龄及岳母的书《孙文学说》

第八章所未及。由是一部学者对于《伦敦被难记》发生之误解，一扫而空，无复有质疑者矣。兹录载《孙文学说》第八章《有志竟成》首段如左：

夫自民国建元以来，各国文人学士之对于中国革命之著作，不下千数百种。类多道听途说之辞，鲜能知革命之事实。而于革命之原起，更无从追述。故多有本予之《伦敦被难记》第一章之革命事由。该章所述本甚简略。且于二十余年前，革命之成否尚为问题。而当时虽在英京，然亦事多忌讳，故尚未敢自承兴中会为予所创设者；又未敢表示兴中会之宗旨为倾覆满清者。今于此特修正之，以辅事实也。

上文即总理对于《伦敦被难记》第一章之修正，且声明为全文之修正，而不止一字一句之修正。所云"今于此特修正之，以辅事实"，其意义至为明显。世有再援引总理久已根本取消之革命事由，而仍称之曰遗教，即无异强指总理为主张君宪之保皇党，诬蔑甚矣。《孙文学说》第八章首段既修正《伦敦被难记》所述革命事由后，同时于次段追述革命原起及三十年来所身历之革命事实。凡一万二千言，实为清季革命时代最正确之历史资料。兹更录载原文所述兴中会成立以前之革命事实一节如下。此即对于《伦敦被难记》第一章全文之修正辞也。

　　兹篇所述，皆就余三十年来所记忆之事实而追述之。由立志之日起，至同盟会成立之时，几为余一人之革命也。故事甚简单，而于赞襄之要人，皆能录之无遗。自同盟会成立以后，则事体日繁，附和日众，而海外热心华侨，内地忠烈志士，各重要人物，不能一一笔录于兹篇。当俟之修正革命史时，乃能全为补录也。予自乙酉中法战败之年，始决倾覆清廷创建民国之志，由是以学堂为鼓吹之地，借医术为人世之媒，十年如一日。当予肄业于广州博济医学校也，于同学中物色有郑士良号弼臣者。其为人豪侠尚义，广交游，所结纳皆江湖之士。同学中无有类之者。予一见则奇之。稍与相习，则与之谈革命，士良一闻之而悦服，并告以彼曾投入会党，如他日有事，彼可为我罗致会党，以听指挥云。予在广州学医甫一年。闻香港有英文医学校开设，予以其学课较优，而地较自由，可以鼓吹革命，故投香港学校肄业。数年之间，每于学课余暇，皆致力于革命之鼓吹。常往来于香港澳门之间，大放厥词，无所忌讳。时闻而附和者，在香港只陈少白、尤少纨、杨鹤龄三人。而上海归客，则陆皓东而已。

孙中山、宋庆龄结婚照（1915年于日本）

若其他之交游，闻吾言者，不以为大逆不道而避之，则以为中风病狂相视也。予与陈、尤、杨三人常住香港，昕夕往还。所谈者莫不为革命之言论。所怀者莫不为革命之思想。所研究者莫不为革命之问题。四人相依甚密，非谈革命，则无以为欢。数年如一日。故港澳间之戚友交游，皆呼予等为四大寇。此为革命言论之时代也。及予卒业之后，悬壶于澳门、羊城两地以问世。而实则为革命运动之开始也。时郑士良则结纳会党，联络防营，门径既通，端倪略备。予乃与陆皓东北游京津，以窥清廷之虚实，深入武汉，以观长江之形势。至甲午中东战起，以为时机可乘，乃赴檀岛创立兴中会，欲纠合海外华侨以收实效。不图风气未开，人心锢塞，在檀鼓吹数月，应者寥寥，仅得邓荫南与胞兄德彰二人愿倾家相助，及其他亲友数十人之赞同而已。时则清兵屡败，高丽既失，旅威继陷。京津亦岌岌可危。清廷之腐败尽露，人心愤激。上海同志宋耀如乃函促归国，美洲之行因而中止。遂与邓荫南及二三同志返国，以策进行，欲袭取广州以为根据。遂开乾亨行于香港为总部，设农学会于羊城为机关。当时赞襄干部事务者，有邓荫南、杨衢云、黄咏商、陈少白等。而运筹于羊城机关者，则陆皓东、郑士良，并欧美技师及将校数人也。（下略）

此外总理尚有民十二年一月所著《中国革命史》。其第一章叙述兴中会成立前后之革命事由，可与《孙文学说》第八章互相印证。就中列举"立党"一则，于兴中会创立之年代地点人数，尤为正确明白，毫无疑义。亦对于《伦敦被难记》第一章之修正辞也。兹更照录原文首段如下：

（一）立党乙酉以后，余持革命主义，能相喻者不过亲友数人而已。士大夫方醉心功名利禄。唯所称下流社会。原有三合会之组织，寓反清复明思想其中。虽时代湮远，几于数典忘祖。然苟与之言，较缙绅为易入。故余先从联络会党入手。甲午以后，赴檀岛美洲，纠合华侨，创立兴中会。此为以革命主义立党之始。然同志犹不过数十人耳。（下略）

1923年2月，孙中山与夫人在广州大元帅府

观上文所录，总理对于《伦敦被难记》第一章之修正辞，及前后追述兴中会成立以前之革命事由，即可证实《伦敦被难记》第一章所载"余在澳门"云云至"少年中国党总部设于上海"之全文约三百字为子虚乌有。更可证实甲午赴檀岛创立兴中会之前，并无以革命主义立党情事。事实彰彰。有目共睹。余前于所撰《兴中会始创于檀香山之铁证》一文，尝谓《伦敦被难记》第一章为总理当年对英人之外交措辞而并非事实，盖有所本也。然该章全文虽经总理郑重声明修正二十馀年，但逞奇立异，道听途说，仍援引该章全文之一二句语以颠倒事实者，至今尚有其人，似属骇人听闻。今再根据总理之修正辞，及先后追述之革命事实，不揣冒昧，谨分别列举定义五点，以供研究革命史者之参考。倘有同志能不逾越此定义之范围质疑问难，余固甚乐闻之。关于兴中会成立前之革命事由，应下定义五点如下：

（一）《伦敦被难记》第一章全文，已经总理于《孙文学说》第八章首段郑重修正，认为不符事实，应作根本取消，以后不得再为援引。

（二）根据总理修正文，在兴中会成立前，世间并无所谓"少年中国党"之存在。所称澳门云云及上海设总部，均属因时制宜，子虚乌有之谈。

（三）总理始终并无加入主张君主立宪和平改革之少年中国党情事。

（四）兴中会确于甲午年（民前十八年）在檀香山创立。一见于《孙文学说》第八章"甲午中东战起，以为时机可乘，乃赴檀岛创立兴中会"之自述，二见于《中国革命史》"立党"一节"甲午以后，赴檀岛美洲纠合华侨创立兴中会。此为以革命主义立党之始"之自述。三见于民国十二年一月一日总理所颁布之中国国民党宣言"溯自兴中会以至于今，垂三十年"一语（按甲午至民十二年，恰为三十年）。故兴中会于甲午创立于檀香山之事实，实为确凿不磨之遗教。以后不得再有异议。

（五）民智书局及坊间出售之《伦敦被难记》译本均错译英文Young China Party（少年中国党）为兴中会。凡稍解英文皆知其误。读者幸勿将错就错。

1897年秋孙中山与宫崎寅藏笔谈乙未广州起义之手迹

其书、其人、其事——《伦敦蒙难记》探析

周楠本

一

　　甲午战后所签订的不平等条约——马关条约，激起了强烈要求社会变革的民族自尊情绪，这集中反映在随后发生的两件大事上：第一件大事是1895年春康有为、梁启超发动当时全国各省在京应试的举人联名上书光绪皇帝，请愿变法，这就是近代历史上著名的"公车上书"；另一件大事，是同年10月以孙中山（孙逸仙）为首的兴中会革命党人密谋广州暴动，史称乙未广州起义。这两件事，在富国图强的目的上是相同的，在推进政治改革的意义上也有近似之处；但是此二事对于中国未来政治的影响根本不同，前者是维护和改造满族统治政权，后者是推翻、打倒它，因此这两件事的结果完全不一样。乙未广州起义因迅速遭镇压，在国内并未能激起大的波澜，远不及半年前京城发生的"公车上书"。由于维新思想不仅在知识界，而且在军界、工商界也有深远的影响，因此要求改良社会的新思维迅速波及各省。但是，遭到镇压的乙未广州起义并未灰飞烟灭，当时的国人没有意识到它已经为推翻满清王朝埋下了火种。研究中国近代历史的人不会低估当年逃亡海外的起义首领孙中山（孙逸仙）在英伦出版的《伦敦蒙难记》这本书，此书在欧美世界产生了轰动性效应，它为争取西方列

强关注中国社会改革产生了积极的催促作用。这本书不仅让它的作者作为东方的社会改革家走上了世界政治舞台，同时也促使西方政治家开始意识到，如要改变古老中国的蒙昧现状——用今天的话来说就是要使中国社会融入世界市场，能够与国际接轨——孙中山的改革道路势在必行。显然这本书的影响超出了已经夭折的广州起义本身，它预示着为建立民国而做的最初尝试，比预谋的武力夺取广东省城，其意义、目标要远大得多。

《伦敦蒙难记》的作者孙中山此时已清楚地认识到舆论准备的重要性。孙中山获释之后并没有急于逃离这一险些丧命之地，虽然他知道清政府的爪牙绝不会就此罢休，轻易放过他。两广总督与广东巡抚致电总理衙门称："……孙逆尚在英都，龚使自能设法解粤甚好。否则，重赏博浪沙壮士，不必令生还也。港督云：'派洋巡捕严查，来港即行驱逐，不准住界内。若在界外，听中国自拿。'该犯闻此信，恐不回港也。西贡新加坡无从办理耳。麟，祎，三十。"[1]此电系当年阴历十月三十日所发，即1896年12月4日发出的，此时孙中山已被释放一月有余。既然人已放掉，"自能设法解粤甚好"一句又从何说起呢？这个电报不仅说明清政府仍在千方百计设法捉拿捕杀"孙逆"，同时也可以看出，清政府的封疆大吏已经将此事视为畏途，他们建议总理衙门，既然驻英公使不能活捉"孙逆"，就应该就地暗杀，绝不能让他活着回广东；而且告知总理衙门，"孙逆"将不会回香港，港英当局也绝不会协助逮捕他，所以无从办理。颇有意思的是，两广总督电称的"重赏博浪沙壮士"这一刺杀行动的比喻真是耐人寻味，难道说孙中山在清廷封疆大吏的心目中是一个秦始皇一般的帝王人物吗？或许他们认为在英伦行刺，必须担当冒犯英国君王和触犯英国法律的风险，因此只得重托于舍生取义的"博浪沙壮士"了。

当年章太炎见到报载孙中山伦敦遭绑架事件之后曾与维新领袖

---

[1] 此电保存于清总理衙门的密电档中，转引自罗家伦《中山先生伦敦被难史料考订》，商务印书馆1930年版，第78—79页。

人物梁启超交换过意见。梁对孙中山的看法是："孙氏主张革命，陈胜、吴广流也。"梁氏虽屡次应试落第，然此时已声名鹊起，且尚未做流亡者，站在正统立场评价算是很客观的了。

不过当时他对孙中山的能量估计未免过低，所以章太炎答道："果主张革命，则不必论其人才之优劣也。"[①]章氏显然更欣赏孙中山的革命，虽然他对于孙的能量及政治素养也不了然。

知识界的精英对于反清起义也不过如此的评价认识。孙中山当然知道舆论准备以及理论建设的至关重要性，因此他出狱后在伦敦一边广交朋友，积极进行政治宣传活动，一边抽出许多时间泡在大英博物馆、图书馆阅览，深入思考中国问题。首先是集中精力撰写他的蒙难经历，即 *Kidnapped in London*（《伦敦蒙难记》）。仅两月余，此书就于1897年1月在英国首都伦敦和英格兰西南近海城市布里斯托尔出版发行。

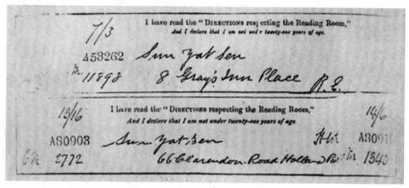

孙中山在大英博物馆阅览时的签名卡

孙中山撰写此书得到了康德黎先生（James Cantlie，1851—1926）的鼎力帮助。孙中山在序言中很坦率地承认在当时自己并无能力用英文完成这部专著，他是在一位好友的帮助下写成的。这话并非谦虚，当时孙中山的英文程度虽然已经不低——康德黎夫人日记里有这样的记录："孙医生预定月底在牛津大学演讲，他把自己写的讲稿拿给康

---

① 引自陈锡祺主编《孙中山年谱长编》上册，中华书局1991年版，第134页。

德黎看，非常好。"①——但是孙中山知道他的这一本书非同寻常，这是一部将要把他推向国际政治舞台，将会使他名扬英伦及欧美的著作，他必须精心精意地对待，这就必须求助于他的老师。从康德黎夫人日记里也反映出康德黎对于孙中山的这本书确实倾注了心力：11月19日"康德黎正在帮孙写他的传记"；12月21日"康德黎已经写完孙的传记并送交印刷"。②在康德黎夫人眼里，这就等于是她丈夫的著作。1897年1月20日："康德黎关于孙逸仙的书明天出版。"1月21日："关于孙的书今天出版。"③书出版当天，《泰晤士报》即登有《伦敦蒙难记》新书书讯。可以说这本英文著作是他们师生两人合著的。

康德黎由于在香港工作过多年，对于清政府的腐败无能十分了解，对于中国的现实、国情毫不隔膜，显然他是极其赞成自己的学生的政治改革事业的。早在香港西医书院时期，他就积极支持孙中山参与发起的教友少年会，这是兴中会成立前最早宣传改革思想的政治性团体，在《伦敦蒙难记》中称为中国少年会或中国少年党（"Young China" Party）。孙中山遭阴谋绑架，仍关押在清使馆里时，康德黎向英国《环球报》提供的新闻报道即证明他对于孙中山所发动的广州起义不仅持同情态度，而且是非常理解的，他对于当时中国的政局观察得很清楚。正因为具备这样的条件，康德黎才热情地参与撰述这本传播中国革命火种的著作。

《伦敦蒙难记》出版后不久，孙中山即在伦敦《双周论坛》（*Fortnightly Review*，1897.3.1）发表了一篇题为《中国的现在和未来——革新党呼吁英国保持善意的中立》（China's Present and Future: The Reform Party's Plea for British Benevolent Neutrality，1897）的论文，这是直接向英国当局呼吁，对于中国革命运动至少应该保持中立，不要支持满清政府，不要再像过去那样帮助清政府镇压太平天国。这对

---

① 转引自《孙中山年谱长编》上册，"1897年1月31日"条。
② 同上书，"1896年12月7日至31日"条。
③ 同上书，"1897年1月21日"条。

于孙中山的事业是至关重要的，如果英国能够接受他的呼吁，起码孙中山在香港就可以合法地从事改革运动，不至于遭到通缉、绑架。（广东当局就是唯恐孙中山返回香港，所以不满驻英公使的推诿责任，才有"孙逆尚在英都，龚使自能设法解粤甚好。否则，重赏博浪沙壮士……"这样的话。）虽然孙中山此时还没有成熟的建立民主国家的政治纲领，但社会哲学上的思考已经开始了。他在《孙文学说》里回忆说："伦敦脱险后，则暂留欧洲，以实行考察其政治风俗，并结交其朝野贤豪。两年之中，所见所闻，殊多心得。始知徒致国家富强、民权发达如欧洲列强者，犹未能登斯民于极乐之乡也；是以欧洲志士，犹有社会革命之运动也。予欲为一劳永逸之计，乃采取民生主义，以与民族、民权问题同时解决。此三民主义之主张所由完成也。"①也许这里孙中山将完成三民主义思想的时间提前了一些，但是至少说明孙中山的头脑中应该已经有了三民主义的雏形。

康德黎目睹了孙中山的研究工作，他在《孙逸仙与中国的觉醒》（*Sun Yat Sen and the Awakening of China*，1912）一书里说："和我们一起住在伦敦的时候，孙逸仙从不在玩乐上浪费时间，他总是不停地工作，阅读关于政治、外交、法律、陆海军等方面的书籍，矿山及开采、农业、畜牧、工程、政治经济学等也为他所注意。他坚持不懈地仔细加以研究。他所涉猎的知识领域很少有人达到。"②在伦敦绑架案之后逗留英国的这个时期，孙中山就已经观察和思考到这样一个问题：即使像欧洲强盛的民主制国家，都未能达到至善至美的理想社会，仍需发动社会革命运动；像中国如此腐败落后的积贫积弱的封建专制主义国家，更须全方位地解决民生、民族、民权问题。这一思考不仅大大超越了历代主张"中学为体，西学为用"的民族主义改革家，其难能可贵之处还在于他考察欧洲列强社会模式时，尽管也吸收

---

① 《建国方略·孙文学说》（第八章），《孙中山全集》第6卷，中华书局1985年版，第232页。

② 转引自《孙中山年谱长编》上册，第136—137页。

了西欧先进社会学说的养料，却没有迷惑于当时已盛行的空想社会主义，他所说的"是以欧洲志士，犹有社会革命之运动也"，其中的乌托邦运动他必定已注意到了。三民主义的形成证明他是一个极具独立精神和现实主义头脑的社会革命家。

在伦敦孙中山还翻译了一部医疗著作《红十字会救伤第一法》①，1897年6月出版。这是孙中山一生唯一的一本译著，却挑选了一本与社会科学毫无关系的著作。康德黎曾是香港红十字

孙中山获释后在伦敦翻译了《红十字会救伤第一法》，这是1907年民报社再版本，书名改为《赤十字会救伤第一法》。

会的组织者和负责人，而这一本书是他的同行、伦敦红十字医生柯士宾所著。康德黎鼓励刚获得自由的孙中山翻译这本著作是有其深意的。孙中山在译序中说："柯君道君主仁民爱物之量充溢两间，因属代译是书为华文，以呈君主，为祝六十年登极庆典之献。旋以奏闻，深蒙君主大加奖许，且云华人作桃源于英藩者以亿兆计，则是书之译，其有裨于寄英宇下之华民，良非浅鲜。柯君更拟印若干部发往南洋、香港各督，俾分派好善华人，以广英君主寿世寿民之意。"②由此可知，翻译这本医疗著作之前已奏明英国女王，并获得赞许。在英国女王的眼中，孙逸仙已属于"华人作桃源于英藩者"，其译著"有裨于寄英宇下之华民，良非浅鲜"。孙中山在大英博物馆结识的日本友人南方熊楠说："（下午）5时许，在博物馆遇见孙，赠我以他译的《红十字会救伤第一法》三本，田岛、镰田和我各一册。（另外，呈

---

① 此书后来孙中山进行了修订，再版时书名改为《赤十字会救伤第一法》。

② 《孙中山全集》第1卷，第108页。

送英国女王及沙利斯柏利爵士各一册。他说为了装订，每本花了五英镑）"①将这部译著赠送英国女王和英国首相大臣，可知其意义绝不止是为了将西医外科医疗技术以及人道主义思想传播到中国，更重要的是让英国以及英联邦的政治家们认识到中国革命领导人，也即正在被中国满清朝政府通缉追捕的"乱党"、"匪徒"，实际却是非常具有先进科学思想的、为"完全打倒目前极其腐败的传统而建立一个贤良政府"而不惜献身的政治精英，绝非是清政府当局指为谋反作乱的乱民歹徒，也绝非是中国以往的农民运动领袖可以相提并论的。

二

下面我们回到孙中山伦敦蒙难这一事件本身，谈一谈有关伦敦绑架案史实方面的问题。

1896年10月23日（伦敦时间，阴历为九月十七日），孙中山被释放的第二天（或当天），北京总理衙门收到驻英公使龚照瑗的密电：

清驻英公使龚照瑗

九月十八日（引者按，这里指北京时间，公历为10月24日）收出使龚大臣电称：察知孙文在英有党羽，扣留第三日，即来馆旁，日夜伺察，员弁出外，亦必尾追。置箱柜中，亦难送出，船购定退去。久羁恐生枝节，现与外部商允，如孙回香港，必由港督严察，并请瑗具文，以凭照办。惟有释放，仍派人密跟。瑗，篠。②

①《南方熊楠日记》2，（1897—1904），转引自《孙中山年谱长编》上册，第136页。

② 转引自罗家伦《中山先生伦敦被难史料考订》，第61—62页。

这是总理衙门密电档里保存的正式电文，而驻英清使馆档案里此电的存稿行文与此相比却颇有出入：

孙犯已在馆扣留十三日。有犯党在馆旁逻。馆中人出入，亦必尾随，日夜无间，竟无法送出。外间亦有风声，船行亦不敢送。只得将购定之船退去，与外部商允，如孙回香港，必由港督严察。并请具文，以凭饬港督照办等语。因将孙犯释放，仍派人密跟。瑗，篠。（九月十七日。）（伦敦中国使馆档。）①

此电原稿说得很明确："因将孙犯释放，仍派人密跟。"但正式发出的电文却改为"惟有释放，仍派人密跟"，这样语义就变得含糊了，像是建议释放而尚未释放，可见当时龚照瑗不敢承担先斩后奏、放走朝廷通缉要犯的责任。

清使馆所存此电的原稿说"孙犯已在馆扣留十三日，有犯党在馆旁逻"，正式呈报时则改为："察知孙文在英有党羽，扣留第三日，即来馆旁，日夜伺察"。清公使将走漏消息的原因归之为被孙中山的"党羽"发觉，并将被发觉的时间提前了十日，却只字不提因关押看管不严，竟让孙中山从牢里秘密传递出求救信之事。这样隐瞒谎报案情显然是为了开脱渎职之罪。从以上电文的对照可见，即使是原始档案材料，如清使馆档案也必须考订分析，否则就很有可能曲解历史。

给总理衙门电文中有"置箱柜中，亦难送出"一句，看一看《伦敦蒙难记》及孙中山获释后在伦敦警察厅的陈述就可以明白这话是什么意思了。《在伦敦苏格兰场的陈述词》里，孙中山讲到过：他向邓翻译表示，在押送他的时候他会叫喊呼救，清使馆翻译邓廷铿答道："会把你绑起来，堵住你的嘴，装入箱子或袋子里，在夜间运上船。""我又说，如果不能把我运走，他们下一步将会怎么办。他说，就在使馆里杀死我，将尸体加以防腐，再送回中国执行死刑。我

---

① 转引自《中山先生伦敦被难史料考订》，第62页。

问，他们为什么要这般残忍。他说，政府不惜以任何代价捉拿你，不论是死是活。"①"置箱柜中，亦难送出"这一句原电稿里本无，是正式电文里加上的，这是向总理衙门强调押运囚犯完全不可能，即使"置箱柜中"偷运尸首也难以执行。

龚照瑗呈总理衙门的密电还隐瞒了重要的一点，就是英国政府已派出警察监视公使馆，这就不仅是"有犯党在馆旁逻"，更有英国警察在馆旁逻。他不敢据实禀报，害怕总理衙门知道事情竟然弄到英国政府已经动用警力采取强力干预措施的糟糕地步了。

龚照瑗因不敢承担引起外交事端的责任，所以不仅要向朝廷隐瞒走漏消息的实情，而且还要极力否认强行绑架事件，一口咬定："按公法，使署即中国之地，彼既肆无忌惮"自入使馆，即予"暂行扣留"。

显然总理衙门对于龚照瑗的呈报不会再有兴趣。一个月之后，十月十九日（公历十一月二十三日）朝廷就改派罗丰禄为新任公使了。

关于绑架事件，清使馆洋参赞哈里代·马卡尼对报界是这样狡辩的："贵报引土耳其使臣在伦敦诱阿美尼亚人事为佐证，殊不知本案并无所谓诱劫，彼原名孙文、伪名孙逸仙所供之辞，如谓被捕于道途、被挟入使馆等语，皆至不足信者也。孙逸仙之至使馆，系出己意，且为使馆中人所不料。其初次之来在礼拜六日，即十月十号。二次之来在礼拜日，即十月十一号。治国际法学者对于孙逸仙被使馆拘留一节，无论作何评论，抱何见解，然必先知本案并无所谓诱骗，即其入使馆时亦并未尝施以强力或欺诈，此为本案之事实，而亦至可凭信者也。"②关于逮捕孙中山之事，无论是向总理衙门呈报，还是面对舆论界，清使馆官员都是按照自投罗网的口径严密保持一致，不留丝毫口实。即使在事隔三年之后，当年的阴谋参与者、清使馆法文翻译吴宗濂在其所著《随轺笔记·龚星宪计擒孙文致总署总办公函》及

① 《在伦敦苏格兰场的陈述词（一八九六年十月二十三日）》，《孙中山全集》第1卷，第34页。

② 参见《伦敦蒙难记·附录》。

《随轺笔记·龚星宪计擒粤犯孙文复行释放缘由》二文里依然按照这一口径作了歪曲史实的记载。

事实上这种作伪实属枉然，清使馆不仅越境偷运人犯违反国际公法、践踏驻在国的法律，即使在使馆地盘内捕人，也是滥施外交特权，绝非龚照瑗密电总理衙门所称"按公法，使馆即中国地"，"孙无忌惮，自来使馆"即可逮捕。龚照瑗在致总理衙门总办密函中提到："中英交犯约，经曾前大臣议而未成，刻下既无约可据，如解犯潜过友邦之地，殊与公例未符。"这里说的"曾前大臣"指的是曾纪泽，即清廷驻英第二任公使，兼任驻法国、俄国公使。《伦敦蒙难记》里提到了他。当时孙中山被囚禁时曾听到传闻，使馆可能将他转移到曾侯旧宅关押以躲避英国政府的检查。曾纪泽曾奉旨与俄国交涉引渡"逆酋"白彦虎（新疆叛乱分子）未成，曾氏是深知国际公法的，而且也深知驻外使节所享有的外交特权。关于此点他还特别在拟禀报朝廷的日记中写明："西人之俗，公使所寓，如其本国辖镜，不归主国地方官管理。馆中人役，亦不受主国官衙约束。有在外犯法者，询属某国人，即交其国公使讯治，主国不侵其权。然必确系寓居使馆、派有职事之人乃然，所谓公使应享之权利也。若其人不隶使馆，而为某国寄寓者，即仍由地方官管辖，……"①孙中山是旅居英伦的中国流亡者，并非"馆中人役"，更非"派有职事之人"，他只受英国地方官管辖，他的行为也只对英国地方官负责，按照公法和惯例，孙中山作为一个外国寄寓者，他的人身自由应当得到英国政府的保护。伦敦绑架事件结束之后，英国外交部次长柯申（Rt. Hon. George N. Curzon. MP.）就英国议会提出的质询作了如下几点回答：

（一）外交部于10月18日星期天首闻其事，马上展开调查。

获可靠证据后，沙侯立即照会清使，指出囚孙属妄用外交特权，

---

① 曾纪泽：《出使英法俄国日记》，光绪五年元月廿三日，见钟叔河编《走向世界丛书》，岳麓书社2008年版。

要求清使马上放人，该要求于10月23日获得满足。

（二）孙之被囚，既属违反国际法，亦属严重滥用外交特权。本国驻华公使已按此意照会满清政府，并要求该政府严厉约束其驻英公使，免其重蹈覆辙。

（三）该事为清使所作，责任亦由其承担。①

对于公使的外交权限，龚照瑗及哈里代·马卡尼参赞（他曾跟随曾纪泽七年）不会不清楚，即使是事先不知，事发后接到英政府照会也应该清楚；但是他们自信所有的阴谋谎言都是奉旨效忠，都是为了国家社稷的利益，因此他们自始至终坚持这种只能显示自己毫无外交常识的无知妄说以自欺欺人。可以说这种愚顽的封建统治意识在中国是源远流长，即使在满清王朝被推翻一百年之后也不容易消失。现在我们仍然还可以听到这种历史的回音："根据上面这些当时的原始文件（引者按：即指清使馆谎报案情的密电，以及清吏《随轺笔记》等），我们清楚地看到：当时直到十月十日为止，驻英中国使馆的人，都没有亲自捉拿孙中山的意思；直到十月十一日孙中山自己大意，'改装易姓'、'无忌惮，自来使馆'，他们才见人起意，觉得'使馆即中国地，自应扣留。'于是案情急转直下，好戏出场矣！"②这样的言论，不必说其历史观念，只说其外交、法律方面的知识，可以说是完全停留在一百多年前清朝官员的水平上；并且作为一个历史研究家，将一些并不能真实反映历史事实的原始文件以及阴谋绑架者所编造的材料当做史实铁证，这样的治学方法和思维逻辑，只能使人承认一个事实：封建专制思想遗留根深蒂固。

① 见《孙中山年谱长编》上册，1897年2月条，第132页。

② 李敖：《孙中山研究·孙中山向清吏下跪求饶——伦敦蒙难罗生门》，中国友谊出版公司2006年版。

三

哈里代·马卡尼指派执行绑架行动的负责人名叫邓廷铿。孙中山只知道是使馆里的一邓姓英语翻译，是他的广东同乡，讲一口洋泾浜英语。在清公使龚照瑗向总理衙门呈报孙中山落网的密电里称其为"看管之邓翻译"，即负责看管关押囚犯的邓姓译员。总理衙门"出使英国档"里所保存的驻英大臣龚照瑗于1896年3月15日呈报的中国使馆全体人员名单里有："学生：孙鸣皋、罗肇铨、张善庆、邓廷铿。"①罗家伦的史料考订里说："据吴宗濂的《随轺笔记》说，他是四等翻译。但是据龚照瑗于一八九六年三月十五日呈报总理衙门的驻英使馆人员名单，则在三月的时候，邓廷铿不过是一个使馆里的学生。想是到十月的时候，他升任了四等翻译，不过总理衙门无案可查。"②龚照瑗于这年八月公使任期即满，三月所呈报的名单已是销差前的定员名单，此时邓氏仍不过是一名学生。即将离任的公使有义务向总理衙门荐举贤能，但对于出使大臣呈报嘉奖和提升人员的呈文，总理衙门必定有批复，而且公使馆也必定有存档。既然总理衙门无案可查，看来邓廷铿当时很可能还只是一个使馆暂时留用做翻译的文科学生。因此龚照瑗致总署的正式函电里只能称他为"看管之邓翻译"（另致总署函里则称之为"看管委员邓翻译"）。如果这时邓氏已被正式任命为翻译官，就不会给他加上"看管"或"看管委员"这么一个临时设置的如押狱头目一类的职衔了。难怪此人对于这次秘密行动超乎异常的卖力，极想通过此次行动大显其能力和忠诚，争取转正为使馆四等翻译官。对于他诡辩谎言的本领，孙中山甚有体会，并且从谈话中看出此人急于想向朝廷报功请赏。孙中山很后悔当时抱着一线希望，误以为他的这位同乡可能出于恻隐之心，帮助他蒙混过关，救他出狱，居然按照这个看管委员邓翻译的意思写了一封承认是

---

① 见罗家伦《中山先生伦敦被难史料考订》，第89页。
② 同上书，第28—29页。

自己进入使馆特来恳求公使为他申冤的信函。孙中山在狱中写的这份材料，纯系编造之词，其目的就是否认自己与广东暴动事件有瓜葛。清使馆当然非常清楚这材料纯系一派胡言，但是他们并非是为了收集罪证，他们所需要的是可以否认非法绑架人犯的证据，是要这份囚徒本人的亲笔帮助他逃避国际公法的制裁。当时孙中山提出给中国公使写信应该用中文，要求换中国毛笔和墨汁时，这个关押看管委员竟以公使卧病不管事为由，指定用英文给洋人参赞马卡尼写信。一个被捉拿归案的中国囚犯，如果是为了获得他的口供，朝廷是绝不需要英文供词的，显然阴谋绑架者另有企图。

由于英国政府经过调查认定此次事件属于非法绑架，侵犯了英国的司法权，中国公使馆只得按照英国政府规定的时间释放囚犯，孙中山在牢中写的这份英文材料因此没有派上任何用场。事后清使馆没有将这份文件存档，也没有呈送总理衙门。本来它就毫无审案价值。并且，骗取的这个文件不仅没有提供革命党组织的丝毫信息，连发动起义的组织兴中会的名称、同党们的去向等，清使馆都毫无觉察，一无所得，反而满纸尽是囚犯极力为自己开脱的"狡辩"之词；如果这种供词保留存档将来只会证明审讯者愚蠢低能。不过清使馆利用这份材料整理编造出一份谈话录，这就是《邓翻译与孙文问答节略》。中华书局版《孙中山全集》按照清使馆整理的这份材料作为孙中山的著述予以收录，题为《与邓廷铿的谈话（一八九六年十月十四日）》，这是非常不妥当的。这个谈话是阴谋绑架策划者马卡尼为诱骗口供精心设计的圈套，而且谈话记录完全根据诱供者的意图剪辑、杜撰，这个谈话是没有让囚禁者本人过目审核签字的。《孙中山全集》此文的注释说："是日他再次找孙中山谈话，诱骗孙呈函使馆承认为自愿进入使馆，并许以在广州起义问题上帮助孙解脱责任……孙中山是在这种处境中向邓谈及广州起义情况的，谈话内容又为邓记录呈报，某些地方难免与事实有所出入。"[①]既然是"诱骗孙呈函"，"又为邓记录

① 见《孙中山全集》第1卷此篇题注，中华书局1981年版，1986年重印本。

呈报"，既为阴谋，那就绝不止是"某些地方难免与事实有所出入"了。同样的道理，孙中山的谈话也是利用对方，谎话连篇，毫无疑问也会存在与事实有所出入的问题。像这种带有相当程度捏造性质的材料，是绝不能视为孙中山的作品的，最多只能作为一种研究资料附录于孙中山著作里，并且对于研究资料不应作任何删节，只有保存其原貌，才具有真正的研究价值；但收入《孙中山全集》的这篇《与邓廷铿的谈话》将诋毁孙中山的文字均节略掉了，加之改换题目后，似乎就百分之百地成为孙中山的著述了。实际上这篇记录稿真正具有著作权的应该是诱供者邓廷铿，近似于现在常有的一种文体"访谈录"，访谈整理者是有著作权或编著权的。这样的话，我们总不能视为他们二人的合著吧。

孙中山从一被逮捕起就非常清楚他的身份已经完全暴露，马卡尼已明白地向他宣布是接到朝廷命令执行逮捕。但是毕竟当时他尚未被押运回中国，尚存一丝瞒骗逃脱的幻想，此时也只能依顺清使馆诱供的意图，采取死硬抵赖狡辩的办法，否认自己是逆党，与广州反叛事件没有任何关系。但是最难辩解的是面对已被清廷捕杀的陆皓东的"供词"。陆皓东被捕时因为知道孙中山已经脱逃，并且知道有叛徒出卖，孙中山的革命党身份也已经暴露，因此他在临刑时即毫不掩饰地阐述了自己的反清志向及与起义首领之间的关系："与同乡孙文同愤异族政府之腐败专制，官吏之贪污庸懦，外人之阴谋窥伺，凭吊中原，荆榛满目，每一念及，真不知涕泪之何从也。居沪多年，碌碌无所就，乃由沪返粤，恰遇孙君，客寓过访。远别故人，风雨连床，畅谈竟夕。吾方以外患之日迫，欲治其标，孙则主满仇之必报，思治其本，连日辩驳，宗旨遂定，此为孙君与吾倡行排满之始。盖务求惊醒黄魂，光复汉族。"[①]烈士的慷慨陈词对身陷图圄的孙中山来说是当头一棒。此时真是考验革命家头脑清醒镇定的程度以及紧急情况下随机应变的能力了。陆皓东已经牺牲，不存在任何危险了，当前最重

① 引自陈锡祺主编《孙中山年谱长编》上册，第100页。

要的无疑是保存自己和其他活下来的革命党人。面对陆皓东大义凛然的"供词"，当时孙中山只能硬着头皮继续演绎他所虚构的故事，胡乱编了一通陆皓东的经历。他表示陆不过是他所办的农学会的一个养蚕师，所供之词，是"过堂苦打，强逼成招"，因"一见刑具即妄招认，无可挽回"。从这个看管委员邓翻译所记录的谈话内容看，孙中山在此种情况下头脑仍然非常镇定，他没有因为自己已经暴露即放弃任何可能的机会，特别是没有泄露一点关于起义的真实情况。他完全否认陆皓东的"招认"；矢口否认已经被清廷破获了的从香港运军火及起义人员进省城参加暴动的事情，却反控广东缉捕统领李家焯私藏军火，因被告发，"李知事败，以故仇我"，即栽赃自己身上。虽然说这是极其幼稚的狡赖，并且孙中山也很快意识到让他作如此荒唐的"辩白"，不过是清使馆设下的圈套，只有这样他们才能骗取孙中山承认是自己自愿进入公使馆的，承认不存在强行绑架事情；然而这个与清吏谈话的记录，从另一方面来看，却又是一篇出色的戏弄朝廷的狡黠强辩文字，孙中山借这个谈话宣扬了他的政治主张："（邓）即问：'你在广东谋反，因事不密，被人先觉，以致不成，是否属实？'孙答：'我虽有大志，而时尚未至。惟广东有一富人欲谋是事，被我阻之。'邓云：'何不同谋，反阻何故？'孙云：'他是为己，我是为民。'邓云：'请将为己为民四字，明白告我。'孙云：'他之为己，欲得天下自专其利；我之为民，不过设议院，变政治。但中国百姓不灵，时尚未至，故现在未便即行。盖该富人不知审时，我所以阻止也。我素重西学，深染洋习，欲将中国格外振兴，喜在广报上发议论，此我谋反之是非所由起也。'"[①]问答中的这一段议论显然是根据孙中山写给马卡尼的英文信而编的，邓未必能觉察这一番议论的机敏之处：他否定了"自专其利"打江山得天下的思想，表达了谈话者真正的民主政治抱负；同时这番言论与洋务大臣们的观念意

---

① 《邓翻译与孙文问答节略》，见《随轺笔记》；转引自《中山先生伦敦被难史料考订》，第46页。

识或维新思想也并不太相悖逆。应该说"问答节略"中的这一节是孙中山研究的珍贵资料。

问答中最显聪敏的是，孙中山所指的那个欲串通他谋事而被他阻止了的广东富人却是当时甚有名望的豪绅刘学询，后来入了李鸿章的幕府。邓氏在整理材料时删掉了该人名字，并加按语："按：此人近颇为当道倚重，或系孙之妄扳，故删其姓名。"[1]"孙之妄扳"岂止此一人，上面所说广东缉捕统领李家焯私藏军火却栽赃于他，这些不都是孙之妄扳吗？而真正在逃的参加起义的兴中会同志以及流亡中所发展的革命党人如冯自由父子等，在邓氏整理的这份材料里却找不出一人。

据吴宗濂《随轺笔记》中所录，龚照瑗致总理衙门总办密函云："所有孙文与看管委员邓翻译廷铿问答节略，另录呈览。"但是在总理衙门档案卷里龚照瑗的密函以及这份"问答节略"均未存档，这不排除总理衙门案卷不全，保存不善所致；但也有可能是龚照瑗根本没有寄出此信及所附文件，因此现在我们也只能在吴著《随轺笔记》里看到这些材料了。

其实龚照瑗致总署总办密函所附录的这篇《邓翻译与孙文问答节略》不但没有为朝廷提供破获"匪党"组织的线索，反而依据这份露骨的诱导囚犯作伪的文件可以指证审讯者或诱供者有通匪的嫌疑。例如看管委员邓翻译说："我以公事扣你，若论私情，你我同乡，如有黑白不分，被人欺你之处，何妨将此事细微曲折，一一告我。倘有一线可原之路，我亦可念同乡之谊，代求钦差为你伸雪，你亦可回籍再谋生业。况广东近事，我亦略知，且听你说，看与人言合否？"又云："钦差最喜替人申冤，只要将实情说出，我必竭力代求。"披阅者必会注意，问话者所谓"只要将实情说出"，指的是"如有黑白不分，被人欺你之处，何妨将此事细微曲折，一一告我"，这就是告诉囚犯，只要好好辩解，"我必竭力代求"；尤其还说只要有"一线可原之路"，就会"代求钦差为你伸雪"，这岂不是极为露骨地串通犯

---

[1] 《与邓廷铿的谈话》，《孙中山全集》第1卷，第28页。

人胡编谎言蒙混过关吗？邓氏在总理衙门"出使英国档"花名册里仅仅是使馆里的一个学生，一名押狱看管有何资格这般大胆妄为地做出此种承诺。在这个看管委员邓翻译的全部问话里根本看不到让犯人交代秘密组织及同党的内容。《邓翻译与孙文问答节略》这个文件关于广州起义通篇是胡编乱造，比如谈话中囚犯这样"狡辩"：北京有强学会，他在广州所开的是农学会，"不过教民种植，意欲开垦清远县之荒田"；不料因与广东稽捕委员李家焯结有私仇，遭其诬陷，竟"借农学会以控我，指为暗藏三合会，有谋反之举"，实际是"李家焯私买废枪以坐我罪"；"李家焯此次害我，不独家散人亡，我所有田地均已被封，不知尚能复见天日、得雪此恨否？"这样一篇谈话记录，对于出使大臣和总理衙门，尤其是赞同强学会的洋务大臣们来说应当都是极其忌讳的，它不仅对龚照瑗不利，甚至还要连累广东当局，而对于革命党却毫无损害。

四

吴宗濂在所著《龚星宪计擒粤犯孙文复行释放缘由》一文中绘声绘色地描写了"计擒"过程：孙文肆无忌惮地进入使馆之后，"英文四等翻译官邓琴斋刺史廷铿，粤产也，遂与接谈。该犯以异地遇同乡，分外惬意。自言姓陈，号载之。即出金表，以觇时刻。刺史索观，则镌有英文拼切之孙字。刺史恍然，然不动声色。孙约翌日再来，同赴海口，探望粤商。刺史欣诺。孙既去，急密告仙舟，转禀星使。星使与马格里王鹏九两参赞，密商办法。皆曰可拿。初五日午前，孙果贸贸然来。饭后邓刺史请孙登楼。先至首层，观星宪之会客厅，签押房。继至二层，入李琴伯明府盛钟卧房，坐谈良久。适马参赞到，刺史遂告孙曰：'君能更上一层楼，往顾弟房呼？'孙曰：'甚好。'遂随刺史拾级而升。马参赞在前引导。先入预备之空房内，作开门待客状。邓指曰，此即弟房，请君先进。孙刚涉足错愕间，马参赞即将房门关闭。告曰：'奉有总署及驻美杨子通星使密电，捉拿要犯孙文，尔即是也。既经到此，请暂留一日一夜，静候总署回电。'"①

清吏笔记的漏洞、破绽其实并不难发现。该笔记为证明孙中山系自进使馆，于是编出一套故事，说孙中山肆无忌惮地两次自来使馆，但是真正的原始档案材料所显示的却不是这样。

1896年10月10日（九月初四）驻英国公使龚照瑗密电驻美国公使杨儒："孙文已到英，外部以此间无交犯约，不能代拿。闻将往法，现派人密尾。"如果这天孙中山到过使馆，这么重要的匪情动态，按理使馆是必定要向总理衙门呈报请示的，哪怕是连夜也得呈报，而不会仅仅向驻美公使通报"孙文已到英"，"闻将往法，现派人密尾"。次日，11日（九月初五）抓获孙中山后，龚照瑗立即电呈北京总署云："孙文到英，前已电达。顷该犯来使馆，洋装，改姓陈，按使馆即中国地，应即扣留，惟何时解回，约颇不易，当相机设法办理。"就是这封报告孙中山就擒的重要密电也没说孙中山日前曾自来使馆一事，说的仍是"孙文到英，前已电达"，与前一日致杨儒密电完全一致。这连着两日呈报总理衙门的电文显示，孙中山仅仅一次来到使馆，也就是被逮捕这一天被强行带进使馆的。而且前一天的密电里还称"闻将往法，现派人密尾"。这电报已经非常明白地证明公使馆早已有布置，绝非偶然发现。看管委员邓翻译所谓索观金表发现"镌有英文拼切之孙字"才恍然顿悟，等等，这简直是讲述传奇故事。如果真是前一天孙中山忽然来访，缉拿者毫无准备，那么经请示密商决定"可拿"之后，孙中山次日再来时完全可以待他一踏入使馆之门即行逮捕，为什么还要招待他吃过午饭，并请他登楼参观公使会客厅以及签押房之后仍不动手，而还要请他再登楼与人坐谈良久，然后更上一层楼之后再行逮捕呢？这么渲染虽然增强了笔记小说的可读性、传奇色彩，却失去了其可信性。比较起来还是当事人即被逮捕者

---

① 转引自罗家伦《中山先生伦敦被难史料考订》，第84—85页。

本人孙中山所写的《伦敦蒙难记》里的说法更为真实,说他是一被诱骗进使馆的大门之后就立刻遭到逮捕的。

一个基本的事实就是,孙中山的行踪,连日常起居都早已被清使馆严密监视,绝不可能任意由逃犯逍遥自在地出入使馆,贸贸然来,又翩然而去的。当年密探的报告也证明翻译官吴宗濂所著《随轺笔记》篡改历史。清使馆档案文件里存有司赖特侦探社密探于1896年10月12日写给马格里(即马卡尼)的报告说:10月10日(九月初四)"星期六这天我们还在葛兰旅店街八号侦察此人。我们跟他出来,到国会两院。在那地方,他停留了两个钟头以上。出来的时候,他步行到斯屈朗,看看店铺的窗子,回到葛兰旅店街八号,以后就不看见了。"①当年这些福尔摩斯式的私人侦探真是恪尽职守,从孙中山从住宿的旅店里出来后就一直尾随跟踪,直到一天事情办完后孙中山回旅店不再出来,简直形影不离,连被跟踪的人在街上看看店铺窗子的细小动作都没有逃过密探的眼睛。侦探的报告,与当事人获释后接受英国内政部调查所作的陈述是基本相符的,孙说:"星期六,即十日,我到过摄政公园、动物园和植物园。我去那里时是上午十一二点钟,一直逗留到下午三点钟。然后,我去到霍尔庞,四点钟左右返回寓所。从那以后,我除了只在附近进餐外,再没有外出。"②孙中山这里说的"摄政公园",正是侦探跟踪报告里所写的"国会两院"(上、下议院),即著名的Palace of Westminster(西敏宫殿,或译威斯敏斯特宫殿),这是当时英国最高政治机构议会所在地。摄政公园(国会两院)在泰晤士河畔,与远离泰晤士河的清使馆完全不在一个方位。《随轺笔记》说这一天"九月初四日(引者按:即公历10月10日),孙文行经使署之门……乃进署门,入厅事",可知纯系虚构故事。

不过学术上对此也有不同的见解,台湾一位孙中山研究者却从这本多有作伪的清吏笔记中挖掘出了不少"伦敦蒙难罗生门",收入所

---

① 转引自罗家伦《中山先生伦敦被难史料考订》,第39页,参见《孙中山年谱长编》上册,10月10日(九月初四日)条。

② 《向英国律师卡夫所作的陈述词》,《孙中山全集》第1卷,第38页。

著《孙中山研究》文集中的《孙中山向清吏下跪求饶——伦敦蒙难罗生门》一文中。此文最着力强调的是孙中山因自己大意，肆无忌惮，自进使馆送死，以力证清使馆逮捕孙中山并不违法；但该作者很明白仅凭"孙中山是自投罗网"一点，尚远远不够损其人格及政治品质，于是进一步演绎他掌握的罗生门故事，这就是该文的主题："孙中山向清吏下跪求饶"。

这个故事所依据的就是上面说到的那个急欲表功请赏的看管委员邓翻译所编撰的《邓翻译与孙文问答节略》。其实这个看管邓某如果想把谎言扯得比较符合情理一些，则不应写孙是向他这样一个听差（看管犯人的使馆学生）"跪下，叩头流泪"，表示"恩同再造，感德不忘"，而应说是向洋参赞马卡尼大人，或直接向钦差大臣龚照瑗写投降变节书；最为关键的是必须交出所有同党名单及联络地址，须知缴获逆党文件，破获乱党秘密组织才是清廷的当务之急；囚犯如果贪生怕死，向清廷献媚最有效的办法就是争取"立功"，帮助朝廷将逆党一网打尽，只有这样才有一线活命的机会，才有可能谈得上"恩同再造"，否则即使向这个职权卑微的清廷小吏"跪下"磕一百个响头也是白费。

研究历史，当然不能只停留在情理和逻辑分析上，关键仍是对史料进行辨识分析，不可尽信一面之孤证，尤其不能将一些凭空杜撰的虚假材料当成信史。至今我们在清使馆的存档中，在清廷总理衙门的密档中，在英国外交部的有关案卷里，甚至就是在清吏的《随轺笔记》及其附录的这个《邓翻译与孙文问答节略》里，都没有发现孙中山为了活命，为了感激"恩同再造"的清吏而出卖组织和同志的任何材料。事实所证明的是，从逮捕到释放，在关押孙中山的十余天里，清使馆连孙中山发动起义的革命党组织"兴中会"的名称都未曾嗅到；起义失败后，孙中山、陈少白、郑士良等领导人流亡海外，他们在日本分手时商量好了今后的潜伏任务、联络方式，尤其是郑士良因身份尚未暴露，又再潜回香港洞察内地形势、处理善后事宜，这些潜伏下来的革命党人的安全却并未因为孙中山被捕而受到威胁。不仅是在被关押的日子里，即使在获释后，孙中山在写的书中仍然极为谨慎，没有写出革命组织名称，只是虚拟了一个名目："中国少年会"（"Young China Party"，一译"中国少年党"，或"少年中国党"）。伦敦绑架案的一切资料表明，没有任何站得住的理由可以将清吏笔记故事视为信史；而且，即使完全坐实《邓翻译与孙文问答节略》里记录的内容，蒙难者虽经哈哈镜扭曲变形之后所显现的仍然是：沉着和睿智。

关于伦敦绑架案我们能看到的有几个方面的文件资料：一，孙中山本人的陈述（包括当时的信函、谈话和《伦敦蒙难记》等文献）；二，英国政府调查报告（包括外交部、内政部有关文件以及警察机关案卷等）；三，清公使与总理衙门往来密电密函（清使馆及总理衙门所保存的原始密档）；四，清使馆所雇伦敦司赖特侦探社密探的报告。这些均属于第一手档案资料，并且代表了对立双方的原始记录材料。而清吏笔记（《随轺笔记》）大多是转述、转录，并且该书已是事过三年之后（1899年）所追记（该书落款："时光绪二十五年八月，嘉定吴宗濂追识于汉皋铁路局于牟隐庐"）。这当然也很有参考价值，特别是其中录存的不见于清史档案的史料。但如果用清政府官吏蓄意歪曲事实的材料，去推翻能够互相印证的并且是来自两个对立方面的真正的原始档案资料，就与真正史家的眼光和治史方法相去甚远。至于将那些如"跪下，叩头流泪"、"恩同再造，感德不忘"等捏造的空洞不实之词当成史实传述，就更不足取，其论证方法与上世纪六七十年代大陆"文革"时期的"政审"、无限上纲的做法无异。

五

中国革命家遭绑架的消息传出之后，英国舆论哗然，清使馆大楼前一时聚众数百人，声援被囚禁的中国流亡者。绑架策划者哈里代·马卡尼则被媒体聚焦，成众矢之的。英政府对此事的态度比较客观，认为："该事为清使所作，责任亦由其承担。"也就是说此系政府行为，不应由执行者个人负责。事实也是如此，北京总理衙门布置捉拿钦犯的电令都是直接下达给公使龚照瑗的，然后再由公使布置下属具体执行。而且策划诱捕阴谋的并不止这个洋参赞一人，还有一个外界不知道的重要人物，他就是使馆中的一位重要官员龚心湛。《伦敦蒙难记》中没有提到龚心湛，因为他不在台前，新闻媒体也没有披露，孙中山和康德黎都根本不知晓其人。《随轺笔记·龚星宪计擒粤犯孙文复行释放缘由》倒有记录："星使之犹子仙舟司马（心湛）乃雇包探赴梨花埔守候。""孙既去，急密告仙舟，转禀星使。星使与马格里、王鹏九两参赞密商办法，皆曰：'可拿。'"文中写的仙舟司马即指龚心湛（1871—1943）。他是公使龚照瑗的侄子，但他比其伯父到使馆任职还要早，金陵同文馆毕业后即派驻外公使馆任职，是前任驻英公使薛福成的随员，其伯父龚照瑗到任后他仍然留任；民国之后回籍做官，曾任安徽省财政厅厅长、省长；由于皖系关系，在北洋军阀政府段祺瑞内阁中任过财政总长、内务总长兼交通总长，还曾一度代理国务总理。作为民国的高官，绑架孙中山自然是他最不光彩的事情，从《随轺笔记》里知道，雇密探跟踪孙中山有他，密谋捉拿绑架孙中山也有他。他最后一次与孙中山发生关联已是孙中山身后之事了。民国十四年（1925）孙中山在北京逝世时，时任北京临时执政府内务总长的龚心湛参加了悼念活动，他与次长王耒所献祭文云：

维中华民国十四年三月二十四日，龚心湛、王耒等，致祭于前临时大总统孙公之灵。曰：呜呼！惟公诞灵岭表，腾迹海隅。愤一姓之专制，为革命之先驱。既假手以底厥绩兮，而来轸不戒于前车。遂投袂以奋斗，历百折而不渝。夫岂袭尉佗之故事，亦庶几乎拿坡崙之所为。繄群帅之协谋，爰力疾而即路。维上药之无灵，遂一瞑以不顾。何彼苍之梦梦兮，乃一例视乎愚智？呜呼！公年未耄，公言甚大。欲贯澈民生主义，欲废除不平等条约。其言之售否当别论兮，要其理颠扑而不可破。嗟九州之方裂，特众木之相维。公固挟大名以去，而世恶能不悲？奠醊陈辞，谨为天下恸，而不系乎其私。呜呼哀哉！伏维尚飨。①

"奠醊陈辞，谨为天下恸"，不可不谓情真意切，这也许是当年的阴谋绑架者与时俱进了吧。祭文中写道"遂投袂以奋斗，历百折而不渝"，1896年的伦敦蒙难却是中山先生平生所历经的第一大挫折。

《随轺笔记》里还提到一个叫王鹏九的人："星使与马格里、王鹏九两参赞密商办法"，这个王鹏九其实只是一个供事，管理使馆后勤工作，将他说成参赞，应是误记。不过王的资历很老，光绪四年（1878）系以四品衔候选州同的资历随出使俄国全权大臣崇厚赴俄谈判；崇厚革职查办后曾纪泽任驻俄公使，继续留任王为使馆供事。之后十多年王鹏九在几任公使手下一直担任此职。他显然是一个办事可靠能干的人，参加捉拿朝廷要犯行动当然是一个合适人选，比如调配行动组人员、安排囚禁室以及布置偷运人犯，等等，都需要他负责。具体执行绑架行动的除了看管委员邓廷铿外，还派了两个使馆武弁，名叫车德文、谢邦清，他们就是《伦敦蒙难记》里所写的左右一边一个将孙中山夹着强行带进公使馆的两个人。所谓武弁者，并非公使馆外交武官，不过是使馆治安保卫人员而已，所以这种暴行正好发挥了他们的专长。此二人归看管委员邓廷铿指挥。

《随轺笔记》作者吴宗濂是清廷驻英法第三任公使刘瑞芬（芝田）的法文翻译官，到龚照瑗第五任公使时他已算是一位有一定资历的外交官了。李敖在他的《孙中山研究》里说："当时龚照瑗以候补三品京堂出使英、法、意、比四国，需要翻译人才，乃由安徽巡抚沈仲复推荐，由江苏嘉定的吴宗濂担任。"此说把吴宗濂的资历说浅了一点，龚照瑗任公使时，吴早已经在使馆做了七年的翻译官了。该研究者显然没有采用原始的可靠材料。

① 引自徐友春、吴志明编《孙中山奉安大典》，《江苏文史资料》第26辑，华文出版社1989年版。

当年吴宗濂虽不知名，绑架丑闻中也无人知晓他，但数年后他在自己的笔记里情不自禁地说出了自己，人们才知道他也是阴谋绑架的参加者。他在笔记中说："初八日，星使嘱宗濂代拟电稿，言唯有专雇一船，迳解粤省。"这不过是略表自己的功劳吧。像这种发给总理衙门的关于偷运囚犯的机密文电由他起草，无疑属于公使馆中的智囊人物。他笔记中所谓的"龚星宪计擒粤犯孙文"，也有他的谋划献计之功，虽然他并非主谋，但所撰多有歪曲事实之笔，包括所录存的经过蓄意编排的函电所产生的长期恶劣影响，却是当年阴谋策划者马卡尼望尘莫及的。曾纪泽出使英伦之际，曾翻阅前任驻英副使刘锡鸿所著《英轺私记》，以作出使之参考，但阅后他的评语是："看《英轺日记》，有意钓誉，立言皆无实际，不足取也。"[①]吴著《随轺笔记》虽不能说是"有意钓誉"、"不足取也"，但"有意歪曲，立言有悖实际"却是事实。民国之后此人也继续在北洋军阀政府中任职。冯自由于民国十七年（1928年）为编著《开国前革命史》，"曾托友人但植之（焘）向吴宗濂借读，借供史料，顾久久未得，无从选录。"[②]冯自由不知，对于这本所谓"计擒粤犯孙文"的书，吴氏此时即使十分迂腐，也应该知道已经很不合时宜了，他恐怕唯愿它绝迹都来不及，哪里还愿给人去"借供史料"呢。

　　已被载于中国近代史册的哈里代·马卡尼（Macartney Halliday 1833—1906）由于《伦敦蒙难记》而被钉在了历史的羞耻柱上，但是他倒是一个不能一笔抹黑的具有传奇性的人物。

　　哈里代·马卡尼取了一个中国名字叫马格里；他还有一个表字曰：清臣。曾纪泽一直很亲热地称他清臣。清使馆中人向孙中山说到他时则称马大人。

　　马格里于1833年生于苏格兰，爱丁堡大学（University of Edinburgh）医学专业毕业。第二次鸦片战争爆发，他作为军医于1858年随侵华军到中国。清政府屈服后，他随英军协同清政府助剿太平

----

① 曾纪泽：《出使英法俄国日记》，光绪四年八月十二日。
② 《革命逸史·孙总理被囚伦敦使馆之清吏笔记》。

军，继而被聘为淮军洋炮教习，深得李鸿章信任。以后他帮助李鸿章建立中国早期近代化兵工厂，起初于1863年在上海淞江建造了一个洋炮局，不久迁往苏州，建立苏州洋炮局。1865年夏李鸿章以江苏巡抚署理两江总督的名义，即命马格里在南京又建立起一个大规模的兵工厂"金陵制造局"，由马格里担任总监。从上海松江洋炮局、苏州洋炮局到金陵制造局，他为淮军效力十余年，成为中国近代军事工业中的一位有功之臣。但善始未必善终，他终因淮军内部的倾轧，在一次恶性事故中栽了跟头。1875年大沽口炮台试放金陵兵工厂出产的新炮，不料发生爆炸，当场炸死官兵7人。这并非偶发事故，毕竟对于军事工业他完全外行，后来又连续发生爆炸事件，直接原因是使用了劣质钢材。他因此丢官。但是第二年，仅赋闲一年的他很快就碰到了一个更适合他发挥才干的难得的机遇。当时英国驻华公使馆翻译官马嘉里在云南被杀事件刚刚解决，清政府应英国要求于1876年12月（光绪二年）派遣礼部左侍郎郭嵩焘（后复任兵部左侍郎）为钦差大臣赴英国"通好谢罪"，同时设立中国驻英国伦敦公使馆。英国驻华公使威妥玛和李鸿章力荐马格里充任翻译官随同郭嵩焘出使英国。他是以三品衔候选道充任三等英文翻译官的，到曾纪泽任公使之后晋升为二等参赞。这样，哈里代·马卡尼就由中国近代兵工厂的一位洋厂长，变成了大清帝国派驻国外的第一位洋人外交官了。他离开故乡时还只是一名英国青年军官，当他回到自己的国家时却已成为东方帝国的朝廷命官了。

然而在孙中山眼里这个清廷的洋爪牙不过是一个犹大式的人物。20年前中国公使郭嵩焘对他的这个洋人随员也有过相类似的感觉。郭嵩焘十分恼怒马格里业务上不称职，成事不足败事有余，多次在日记中述及，如光绪三年二月十二日日记云："夏弗斯白里①商禁鸦片烟一节，开示马格里应答之词，……讵是日马格里编造无数言语，而所开示之词，竟无一语及之。"②又，光绪三年二月十四日："议禁鸦

① 夏弗斯白里（Earl Shaftesbury），英国禁止鸦片烟会会长。
② 郭嵩焘：《伦敦与巴黎日记》，见钟叔河编《走向世界丛书》，岳麓书社2008年版。

片烟公会教士丹拿来，传夏弗斯伯里言，以初三日马格里传言竟无一合者，恐补刊新闻纸，益使人疑。其中惟荷兰国本拟禁烟，而误为种烟，情节过为违悖，无以对荷兰人，必得改正。丹拿能为此言，马格里乃至尽反吾所指授之言而自发议论，顽然不顾，使人茫然不解其心意之所属。"将"禁烟"译为"种烟"可见其翻译水平了。而且郭氏对其人格的评价也极低，郭氏本已憎其"愚谬专擅"，后发现他为副使刘锡鸿讲解西洋年鉴（*Almanach de Gotha*，《哥达年鉴》）颇为尽力，即在日记中写道："至是始知马格里之真为走卒才也。"[1]刘锡鸿得力于马格里的帮助确实不小，他的《英轺私记》即多来自马格里的见闻。由于马格里是朝廷所派，且系驻在国之洋人，郭嵩焘也只好忍受，感到百般无奈："马格里诸事生疏，而喜持意见专擅，亦予大运中之一劫星也，心实苦之。"[2]"马格里愚谬专擅，屡经训饬，略无悛改。"[3]

公允地说，作为走卒之才，他也并非一败涂地、一无所长，其外交上的才能得到充分施展是成为曾纪泽的僚属之后。此时驻英使馆已无刘锡鸿一般的奸佞之徒作祟（刘后调任驻德公使，后又与郭嵩焘同时被撤回国），用郭氏的话，就是再不会"熏蒸于刘锡鸿之积恶以与之化，无事不承其害"了。更重要的是，曾纪泽更懂得如何驾驭走卒之才，充分发挥其长处而避其短处，并且他本人又深通异国语言（英语），不会出现受蒙蔽欺瞒的情况，使馆随员只有诚实、尽心尽职才有可能被聘用、留任。马格里给曾氏的印象是"情形熟悉，办事实心"，因而也赢得了曾纪泽的信任重用。曾纪泽外交生涯中最光彩的一笔是为伊犁改约一案出使俄国谈判，争回了被俄国侵吞的新疆部分领土主权。这次谈判马格里作为曾纪泽的智囊团重要成员一同前往。此任的艰难，正如曾纪泽致丁日昌信中所说："夫全权大臣（按，指

---

① 见郭嵩焘《伦敦与巴黎日记》，光绪三年五月初七日。

② 同上书，光绪三年四月初三日。

③ 同上书，光绪三年十二月初二日。

崇厚）与一国帝王（按，指俄国沙皇）面订之件，忽欲翻异，施之至弱极小之邦，然且未肯帖然顺从，况以俄之强大，理所不能折，势所不能屈者乎？"这是说他此番赴俄是要去推翻沙皇与中国全权大臣所签订的中俄边界及通商条约，这岂不等于虎口拔牙吗？曾纪泽自己说得更贴切，这就如"探虎口而索已投之食"。

这样复杂艰巨的使命，应该说不是曾氏一人能够完成的，他率领了一个精干的外交人才队伍，马格里算是他的高参。出使俄国之前，马格里陪同曾纪泽与英外相密商，请英国支持中国的这次外交谈判，希望谈判"遇有争辩相持之际，望英使之驻俄都者从旁婉劝俄廷"[①]。这就是与英国商量联手牵制俄国。这个要求得到了英国政府的应允，因为英国在印度、中亚的利益正需要中国对俄国的牵制，同时英帝国也必须维护其在华势力。赴俄国谈判期间，中国官员与英、法驻俄公使一直保持着密切联络。正因为具有这样的国际政治形势，也正因为很好地掌控了这场外交斗争的有利形势，才有可能"探虎口而索已投之食"的。

在与俄国商改伊犁边界条约谈判中，这位洋参赞的表现在曾纪泽日记中留有不少痕迹，如光绪六年（1880）七月初二日曾氏在日记中写道："清臣来，久谈。与之展阅中、西地图，考核伊犁、塔尔巴哈台、喀什噶尔诸境。"十五日日记写道："与清臣谈极久，阅俄人所刻土耳吉斯坦暨伊犁等处地图。"虽然日记中仅寥寥两笔，其辛勤工作的情形可想而知。又，十六日日记："将译署奏定准驳约章，用三色笔批于随身条约之上。与清臣、日意格谈甚久。"日记里的另一个洋人顾问日意格（Prosper Marie Giquel， 1835-1886 ），是个法国军官，经历与马格里相似，也是第二次鸦片战争时随军来华，也参加了镇压太平军起义，后来协助左宗棠、沈葆桢创办福建船政局，被任命为正监督，是中国近代海军的一位重要创建人。他当时作为曾纪泽的随员赴俄参加谈判，显然是很需要他这样的在中法之间能够起斡旋协

---

① 曾纪泽：《出使英法俄国日记》，光绪六年四月廿五日。

出席"靖远"舰下水仪式的中外官员：中国驻英公使曾纪泽（右四），参赞马卡尼（左三）

调作用的洋参谋，正与马格里在中英之间所起作用一样。光绪六年八月十二日曾纪泽日记："摘录初五谕旨，因纪泽致俄外部文牍，未将应驳诸务全行商改，俄派使赴华，……至清臣、日意格处，将前此所拟商改全约之牍，修饰数处。"这是说俄国企图绕过中国钦差这个强硬谈判对手，直接去北京找总理衙门的大臣去谈，于是曾纪泽赶紧找马格里和日意格商量适当的妥协办法。八月廿九日日记："核改致布策函。阅昨日问答节略。至清臣、日意格处谈甚久。"布策是俄国驻中国公使，因中方的坚持，他终于被召回国与中国钦差大臣具体商改边界以及通商条约。九月初一日记："清臣、霭堂、日意格来，商订致布策函良久。"此时谈判已初见成效，九月初五的日记里说："至清臣室，与日意格查对地图极久，补编电寄译署，四十七字。"这是向北京总理衙门（译署）发电汇报谈判的进展以及初步结果。三个月后，曾纪泽在十二月十八日日记里写道："已初起，阅译署电报，知纪泽所商改俄国约章，已奉温旨俞允，深以为慰。"这是说已经接到圣旨，通过了他们商改的条款。廿九日日记："至清臣、日意格处久谈，偕二人至余室，商所改通商章程稿，……"此时已临近除夕了。到大年初二，光绪七年元月初二日记云："至清臣、日意格室商改条约章程。"十一日："清臣、日意格来，商议约章字句。核阅条约稿。"从这些极其简单的记载中，我们可以看到他们就是这样在紧张的工作中度过了1881年春节。①

曾纪泽没有埋没马格里的功劳，多次向总理衙门以及英国政府为他报功请赏。中俄伊犁条约签订后，马格里获得了英王奖赐的三等宝星。在郭嵩焘属下时他还只是一个英文翻译官，而此时他已是二品顶戴总领事衔二等参赞了。曾纪泽卸任之际，还致函英外相索尔兹伯里勋爵，请英王奖赏马格里二等宝星。

在以后的供职中他仍一如既往效忠于清政府，尤其可圈可点的是襄助薛福成（时任驻英法意比四国公使）与英国政府谈判，为签订中缅边界勘定条款起了重要作用。薛福成日记中录存了马格里为争中国属地的谏言：

二十四日记　马格里来信云：

> 昨遵总署来电，赴外部问滇缅界事曾发电戒饬管理缅甸大臣否。外部答云，英兵未曾实入中国边界，总署亦未指明英兵所在地名，是以印度部不能发电，等语。总署来电，仅言腾越西北地方。腾越西北，无论何处皆系穆雷江之北，本非缅甸所辖。英虽战胜缅甸，此地不归英属，昔曾侯已明告外部，今中国若不欲失管辖之权（此地即穆雷江之北，厄勒瓦谛江之东），现在必须竭力索问。此处即出翡翠之地，虽非尽中国人，却皆中国一类之人；风俗教化衣服，皆与中国同。中国可云："向归我辖，现仍欲管辖下去"，必能有效。从前中国四面皆有属地。今则俄在北边，既辖黑龙江大股之地，又欲觊觎喀什噶尔之西；朝鲜已为自主之国；日本灭琉球；英人踞缅甸；法人取越南；暹罗不肯再进贡中国。中国所有属地，仅馀西藏而已。非中国之不能管辖各地，实由中国于边界之事，太不加意。甚可诧也。②

---

① 以上均见曾纪泽《出使英法俄国日记》。

② 薛福成：《出使英法意比四国日记》，光绪十七年十二月二十四日，见钟叔河编《走向世界丛书》，岳麓书社2008年版。

所谓"非中国之不能管辖各地，实由中国于边界之事，太不加意。甚可诧也。"这话可说是对当时总理衙门诸大臣的批评。马格里的这一番言论与薛福成的想法甚为合拍，于是薛特记录了下来。

薛福成在马格里的得力辅佐下，与英政府经过艰难谈判，终于勘定滇缅边界。签约当日薛福成在日记中记道："自壬辰闰六月接总署电音，与英外部商办滇缅分界通商条约，发轫之初，势甚凿枘。又有印度部掣外部之肘，印度总督又掣外部、印度部之肘。凡关系紧要之件，往往既允复翻，无从得其要领。余督同参赞马格里，相机理论，刚柔互用，稍稍使就范围。"①

这就是一个英国籍的驻英中国外交官员的立场。从赴俄参加修改重订伊犁条约，到积极筹议续订中英滇缅边界及商务条款，这些在清政府外交史上非常少有的亮点，均包含有这位中国的洋外交官的劳绩。他效忠于所服务的国家，为自己所代表的国家的权益与西方列强包括自己的祖国进行针锋相对的论辩，如果用马克思主义的语言来评价，这是不折不扣的国际主义精神。因此他也获得了中英两国政府的褒奖。

伦敦绑架案结束后，清使馆随员曾广铨回国向总理衙门大臣翁同龢汇报了情况。翁同龢肯定地说："英人参赞马葛里忠于我，可用。"②正因为马格里对于清王朝的这种愚忠，他的这种职业道德使他缺失了"遍布英国的宽厚的公德精神"③，尤其是使他无视作为一个基督徒应有的博爱精神，竟然干出了违背国际公法、滥施外交特权、置人身保护权于不顾的阴谋勾当，其"奴才走卒"、"愚谬专擅"之本性暴露无遗。从这一面来说，郭嵩焘的眼力比曾纪泽锐利得多。

---

① 薛福成：《出使英法意比四国日记》，光绪二十年正月二十四日。

②《翁同龢日记》，光绪二十二年十一月廿七日，1896年12月31日。

③《伦敦蒙难记·致各报编辑》中语。

六

　　孙中山从囚禁室秘密传递出去的写给他的老师康德黎先生的求救信终于使得阴谋绑架计划化为泡影。当时无人了解这封求救信的历史意义——它不仅拯救了一个革命家的生命，更拯救了他的事业。孙中山在《伦敦蒙难记》里写道："最令我担心的是这种灾祸会降临在我为之斗争的大事业上，假若我被带回中国并被杀害，这一后果就会发生。""一旦我被囚运回国，他们一定会向海外公布我是被英政府通过合法手续移交的"，"如果我被带回中国并被杀害，人们会再一次相信这次革命斗争的失败又是由于英国的帮助所导致，这样我们的革命将没有希望了。"[①]阻止这个历史灾祸降临的就是这封密信，孙中山获释后将它记入了《伦敦蒙难记》（*Kidnapped in London*）书中。此信当时是偷偷写在两张小小的名片上的，写得很仓促，不过只有几句话：

　　I was kidnapped on Sunday last by two Chinamen， and forcibly taken into the Chinese Legation. I am imprisoned， and in a day or two I am to be shipped off to China， on board a specially-chartered vessel. I am certain to be beheaded. Oh！ Woe is me.[②]

中译文是：

　　上星期天我被两个中国人绑架，并被强行带进中国公使馆。我被关押起来，而且在一两天内将被遣送去中国，关在专门包租的一条船上。我肯定会被砍头。唉！我真是不幸。

---

　　① 《伦敦蒙难记》第四章，收入《国父全集》第五卷，台湾1973年版。
　　② 《伦敦蒙难记》第五章，收入《国父全集》第五卷，台湾1973年版。

许多年过去之后才知道《伦敦蒙难记》书中所记并非是按照原信抄录，是孙中山获救之后回忆补记的，因为送出的密函原件当时已不在康德黎先生手里了，当时康德黎为营救他的这位使他感到骄傲的学生，已经将这封求救信交给了律师，准备运用法律手段与中国公使馆交涉，或起诉中国公使馆，因为写有密信的这两张名片是公使馆非法逮捕旅英政治流亡者的有力证据。后来由于英国政府的及时干预，事件迅速得到解决，这就用不着再打官司了，这封求救密函对于孙中山和康德黎来说也就没有任何作用了，于是写在两张名片上的这封密信就一直留存在了律师那里。在写作《伦敦蒙难记》时，刚刚发生过的事情历历在目，写信人和收信者都清晰地记得写在名片上信的内容，无需特别去索回原件对照抄录。

15年之后，辛亥革命取得成功，当年孙中山在囚室里传出来的密信已是极其珍贵的革命历史文物了。幸运的是康德黎先生曾经委托的那位律师居然保留了这两张珍贵的名片，并遗留给了他的儿子。这位律师的儿子是位军人，可能文物意识比较淡薄，后来有人通过中国驻英使馆以很低廉的价钱从他那里买走；也许这位军人以为是卖给中国政府，就带有捐献的性质吧。这是民国十八年（1929年）的事，已经是孙中山去世之后的事情了。此信原物最终保存于何处，因没有见到有关资料，不得而知。好在这封密信的手迹已经流传于世了，现在我们可以从商务印书馆1930年出版的罗家伦先生所著《中山先生伦敦被难史料考订》一书中看到影印的手迹。罗氏是从当年原信收藏者处借到原件拍照影印的，所以比较清晰，原件名片上铅印的名字，密函上的铅笔字迹和墨水字迹，以及名片上的编码钉孔，罗著中均有详细介绍。

这封求救信是写在孙中山本人的两张名片上的，名片的两面都写了字。事后两张名片均标上了顺序，一张标记A，一张标记B，据罗著介绍。这是当年受康德黎先生委托的那位律师所编的文件号码。

两张名片正面均写有收信人的姓名及地址：

To Dr.   James Contlie

46 Dewonshire St

Dr. Y. S. Sun

中译:

德文榭街46号

杰姆斯·康德黎博士 收

Y. S. 孙医生

收信人地址姓名也可译为: "面交德文榭街46号杰姆斯·康德黎博士"。两张名片上均写明地址和姓名,这显然是为了使受托付传递密函的人能够很顺利地找到收信者。但毕竟对伦敦街道陌生,在牢中匆匆凭记忆拼写,难免不准确,街名Dewonshire,应该以《伦敦蒙难记》中所写Devonshire为准。写信人署名,则是利用名片上铅印的名字。这如果不看原件,只看复制图片是不好辨认的,多半会以为就是手写的,英文花体很漂亮,有点像汉字行书的味道。至于将Dr. Y. S. Sun译为孙医生还是孙博士,都是可以的,名片主人当时事实上已是一位获得了副博士学位的拥有开业执照的医生。考虑到他是给自己的老师写信,落款应该还是译他的职业名称较好。

名片A的正面,在姓名和地址之下写有一句铅笔字迹的附言:

Please take care of the man for me at present,   He is very poor
and will lost his work by doing for me.

中译:

现在请替我照顾这个人,他很穷,而且为了给我做事,他将
会失去他的工作。

名片A的背面是信的正文：

I was kidnapped into the Chinese Legation on Sunday and shall be smuggled out from England to China for death. Pray rescue me quick?

中译：

礼拜天我被绑架到中国公使馆，并将从英格兰偷运到中国去处死。恳求赶快救救我！

名片A正面手迹，名片上的圆"墨团"是文件钉孔

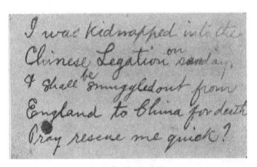

名片A背面手迹

名片B正面只写有地址和姓名，写信人落款同A片，也是恰到好处地用了名片上原有的铅印字，这样接到信的朋友一看到这个熟悉的名片，就会立刻想到名片主人发生意外了。背面文字接A片，为信文的第二段：

A ship is already charter by the C. L. for the service to take me to China and I shall be locked up all the way. Without communication to anybody. O! Woe to me!

中译：

　　为了遣送我到中国，中使馆早已包租了一条船，并且整个航程我将被关锁起来，与任何人不能联系。哎！我多么不幸！

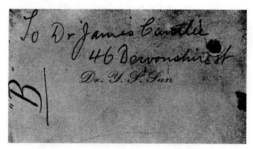

名片B正面手迹

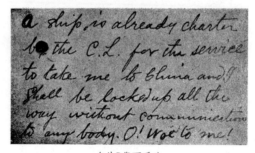

名片B背面手迹

　　将名片A和B的两段文字连起来并加上附言，中译全文是：

德文榭街46号

杰姆斯·康德黎博士收

Y. S. 孙医生

礼拜天我被绑架到中国公使馆，并将从英格兰偷运到中国去处死。恳求赶快救救我！

为了遣送我到中国，中使馆早已包租了一条船，并且整个航程我将被关锁起来，与任何人不能联系。哎！我多么不幸！

（现在请替我照顾这个人，他很穷，而且为了给我做事，他将会失去他的工作。）

如果将《伦敦蒙难记》书中所引的这封信与名片原件对照，就能看出，《伦敦蒙难记》是回忆重写的，毕竟不是在那种危险紧急的情形下所写，语言表达上确实更为准确，比如原件中第一句："I was kidnapped into the Chinese Legation on Sunday"（星期天我被绑架到中国公使馆）；而书中就将这一句改为两句表达：I was kidnapped on Sunday last by two Chinamen, and forcibly taken into the Chinese Legation.（上个星期天我被两个中国人绑架，并被强行带进中国公使馆。）重写之后就把当时被绑架的情形说得更具体一些了。原件说自己将被遣送到中国处死，仅说："for death"；而重新写的是："certain to be beheaded"（肯定会被砍头），就是说会抓回国去斩首示众。这就凶残得多了。

尽管重写后的文字优于原信，但毫无疑问名片上的原文更具有史学价值，更可以看到囚禁时所处的紧张危急的情形，比如"Pray rescue me quick！"（恳求赶快救救我！）这一句，像这样的渴望生还的呼救，重写时却删掉了。这句话如果保留下来就更好，更可以让读者感受到囚徒当时焦虑的心情。

密函附言："现在请替我照顾这个人，他很穷，而且为了给我做事，他将会失去他的工作。"孙中山后来写书时这句话没有写上，这也许是为了避免给人造成一种印象，认为送信者是为了饭碗才愿意伸出援助之手的吧；其实如果保留这句附言，从中也能看出在那样危急的情况下作为一个死囚还能想到替他送信的人是一个穷人，只是使馆里的一个仆人，显然当时他是非常镇定的。

至于最后发出的悲哀的叹息："Woe to me!"（原函文），改为主谓句："Woe is me."（《伦敦蒙难记》文）意思却是一样的，这是句成语，均源于《圣经·旧约全书》。《约伯记》第10章："If I am wicked, woe to me!"意思是："我若行恶，便有了祸！"《诗篇》第120篇："Woe is me, that I am an alien in Meshech, …"意思是："我多么悲哀呀，我这个在米设的外侨……"（旧译为："我寄居在米设……有祸了！"见南京中国基督教协会2000年版《圣经》）当然，后来人们说这句话时大多就是表示悲哀不幸，而没有懊悔和忏悔的意思，更没有原罪感了。

之后孙中山从牢房里又秘密传送出了第二封密信：

十月十一日，星期天，我在离中国公使馆门口不远的街上，被两个中国人拉入使馆。还没有进去之前，他们各在左右夹住我的一只手，竭力怂恿我入内和他们谈谈。当我进入后，他们把正门锁上，并强迫我上楼，推进一个房间，从那天起便将我关锁起来。如果他们做得到，就打算将我从英国偷偷运走；不然的话，也会在使馆里用别的方法杀害我。

我出生于香港，四五岁时才回到中国内地。把我当作一名合法的英国臣民，你能不能用这种方法来使我脱险？[①]

这封信比第一封信显然写得从容多了，此时他已得到了康德黎

———————

① 《致康德黎简（一八九六年十月十九日）》，《孙中山全集》第1卷第30页。

的回音，心里比较踏实了，于是再补写一封比较详细的信。此信重要的是后面一段，是和康德黎商量能否从国籍上考虑设法营救他。他认为如果能将他当做英殖民地香港的居民，清政府就无法引渡他，更不敢偷运出英国国境了。孙中山虽精于医术，但并非法学家或外交家，尤其此刻他身陷囹圄，被秘密关押，无法咨询了解自己可享之权利以及有关国际公法；他哪里知道，作为流亡旅居英国的侨民或政治避难者，他同样享有人身不受侵犯的权利，并非一定要成为香港居民，何况他万万不会想到他将是英国女王所称谓的"华人作桃源于英藩者"、"寄英宇下之华民"呢。

毫无疑问这封写在两张名片上的密函比清吏笔记更属于原始材料，更具有史料价值；《伦敦蒙难记》也更是值得学者们重视的历史文献。

1897年7月2日孙中山结束了英国的考察，乘轮东归，告别了英藩桃源，也离开了他平生第一次遭受劫难之地，须经历更大更多的劫难了。

多年之后，冯自由在《孙总理被囚伦敦使馆之清吏笔记》一文中记载了他所闻见的与伦敦绑架案有关的关于邓廷铿的一件小事：

> 辛亥革命后，邓（引者按，即看管委员邓廷铿）于民元二月尝诣南京临时大总统府投刺求谒孙总理。总统府副官某等知其曾陷害总理，欲治以汉奸之罪，特向总理请示。总理曰，桀犬吠尧，各为其主，已过之事，无庸深究，彼来求官，但不予之官足矣。即令副官护送邓出府，庶免发生危险，是可见总理之器量之广，殊非常人所及也。

冯自由是孙中山广州起义失败后逃亡日本时发展的兴中会会员，民国元年他担任南京临时政府总统府机要秘书，他的这个掌故，应是此案最末的花絮吧。

2011年4月写于《伦敦蒙难记》新译本出版之际

香山翠亨村故居二楼卧室，孙中山在此撰写了《上李鸿章书》

1915年孙中山在日本东京与梅屋庄吉夫妇合影

六

Kidnapped in London

KIDNAPPED IN LONDON

Being the Story of my

CAPTURE BY,

DETENTION AT,

AND

RELEASE FROM

The Chinese Legation, London

By

Sun Yat-Sen

BRISTOL

J. W. Arrowsmith,II Quay Street

LONDON

Simpkin, Marshall, Hamilton, Kent and Company Limited

1897

PREFACE

My recent detention in the Chinese Legation, 49 Portland Place, London, has excited so much interest, has brought me so many friends and has raised so many legal, technical and international points of law, that I feel I should be failing in my duty did I not place on public record, all the circumstances connected with the historical event.

I must beg the indulgence of all readers for my shortcomings in English composition, and confess that had it not been for the help rendered by a good friend, who transcribed my thoughts, I could never have ventured to appear as the Author of an English book.

SUN YAT SEN.

London, 1897.

1

Kidnapped in London

CHAPTER I.

THE IMBROGLIO.

When in 1892 I settled in Macao, a small island near the mouth of the Canton river, to practise medicine, I little dreamt that in four years time I should find myself a prisoner in the Chinese Legation in London, and the unwitting cause of a political sensation which culminated in the active interference of the British Government to procure my release. It was in that year however; and at Macao, that my first acquaintance was made with political life; and there began the part of my career which has been the means of bringing my name so prominently before the British people.

I had been studying medicine, during the year 1886, in Canton at the Anglo-American Mission, under the direction of the venerable Dr. Kerr, when in 1887 I heard of the opening of a College of Medicine at Hong Kong, and determined immediately to avail myself of the advantages it offered.

After five years' study (1887–1892) I obtained the diploma entitling me to style myself "Licentiate in Medicine and Surgery, Hong Kong."

Macao has belonged to Portugal for 360 years; but although the Government is Europeanised, the inhabitants are mostly Chinese, and the section of the population which styles itself Portuguese, consists really of Eurasians of several in-bred genera-

1

tions.

In my newly selected home, I found the Chinese authorities of the native hospital willing to help me forward in the matter of affording me opportunities to practise European medicine and surgery. They placed a ward at my disposal, supplied me with drugs and appliances from London, and granted me every privilege whereby to secure my introduction amongst them on a fair footing.

This event deserves special notice as marking a new and significant departure in China; for never before had the Board of Directors of any Chinese hospital throughout the length and breadth of the great empire given any direct official encouragement to Western medicine. Many patients, more especially surgical cases, came to my wards, and I had the opportunity of performing several of the major operations before the Directors. On the other hand, I had difficulty from the first with the Portuguese authorities. It was not the obstructive ignorance of the East, but the jealousy of the West, which stepped in to thwart my progress. The law of Portugal forbids the practice of medicine, within Portuguese territory, by any one who is not possessed of a Portuguese diploma, obtainable only in Europe. Under this rule the Portuguese doctors took refuge and fought my claims to practise. They first forbade me to practise amongst, or prescribe for, Portuguese; the dispensers in the pharmacies were not allowed to dispense prescriptions from the pen of a doctor of any alien nationality; consequently my progress was hampered from the first. After futile attempts to establish myself in Macao, and at considerable pecuniary loss, for I had settled down little dreaming of opposition, I was induced to go to Canton.

It was in Macao that I first learned of the existence of a political movement which I might best describe as the formation of a "Young China" party. Its objects were so wise, so modest, and so hopeful, that my sympathies were at once enlisted in its behalf, and I believed I was doing my best to further the interests of my country by joining it. The idea was to bring about a peaceful reformation, and we hoped, by forwarding modest schemes of reform to the Throne, to initiate a form of government more consistent with modern requirements. The prime essence of the movement was the establishment of a form of constitutional government to supplement the old-fashioned, corrupt, and worn-out system under which China is groaning.

It is unnecessary to enter into details as to what form of rule obtains in China at present. It may be summed up, however, in a few words. The people have no say whatever in the management of Imperial, National, or even Municipal affairs. The mandarins, or local magistrates, have full power of adjudication, from which there is no appeal. Their word is law, and they have full scope to practise their machinations with complete irresponsibility, and every officer may fatten himself with impunity. Extortion by officials is an institution; it is the condition on which they take office; and it is only when the bleeder is a bungler that the government steps in with pretended benevolence to ameliorate but more often to complete the depletion.

English readers are probably unaware of the smallness of the established salaries of provincial magnates. They will scarcely credit that the Viceroy of, say, Canton, ruling a country with a population larger than that of Great Britain, is allowed as his legal salary the paltry sum of £60 a year; so that, in order to live and maintain himself in office, accumulating fabulous riches the while, he resorts to extortion and the selling of justice. So-called education and the results of examinations are the one means of obtaining official notice. Granted that a young scholar gains distinction, he proceeds to seek public employment, and, by bribing the Peking authorities, an official post is hoped for. Once obtained, as he cannot live on his salary, perhaps he even pays so much annually for his post, licence to squeeze is the result, and the man must be stupid indeed who cannot, when backed up by government, make himself rich enough to buy a still higher post in a few years. With advancement comes increased licence and additional facility for self-enrichment, so that the cleverest "squeezer" ultimately can obtain money enough to purchase the highest positions.

This official thief, with his mind warped by his mode of life, is the ultimate authority in all matters of social, political, and criminal life. It is a feudal system, an *imperium in imperio,* an unjust autocracy, which thrives by its own rottenness. But this system of fattening on the public vitals—the selling of power—is the chief means by which the Manchu dynasty continues to exist. With this legalised corruption stamped as the highest ideal of government, who can wonder at the existence of a strong undercurrent of dissatisfaction among the people?

The masses of China, although kept officially in ignorance of what is going on in the world around them, are anything but

a stupid people. All European authorities on this matter state
that the latent intellectual ability of the Chinese is considerable;
and many place it even above that of the masses in any other
country, European or Asiatic. Books on politics are not allowed;
daily newspapers are prohibited in China; the world around, its
people and politics, are shut out; while no one below the grade
of a mandarin of the seventh rank is allowed to read Chinese
geography, far less foreign. The laws of the present dynasty are
not for public reading; they are known only to the highest
officials. The reading of books on military subjects is, in common
with that of other prohibited matter, not only forbidden, but is
even punishable by death. No one is allowed, on pain of death,
to invent anything new, or to make known any new discovery.
In this way are the people kept in darkness, while the government
doles out to them what scraps of information it finds will suit
its own ends.

The so-called "Literati" of China are allowed to study only
the Chinese classics and the commentaries thereon. These consist
of the writings of ancient philosophers, the works of Confucius
and others. But of even these, all parts relating to the criticism
of their superiors are carefully expunged, and only those parts
are published for public reading which teach obedience to
authorities as the essence of all instruction. In this way is China
ruled—or rather misruled—namely, by the enforcement of blind
obedience to all existing laws and formalities.

To keep the masses in ignorance is the constant endeavour
of Chinese rule. In this way it happened, that during
the last Japanese incursion, absolutely nothing was known of the

war by the masses of China, in parts other than those where the campaign was actually waged. Not only did the people a short way inland never hear of the war, but the masses had never even heard of a people called Japanese; and even where the whisper had been echoed, it was discussed as being a "rebellion" of the "foreign man."

With this incubus hanging over her, China has no chance of reform except it come from the Throne; and it was to induce the Throne to modifythis pernicious state of things that the "Young China" party was formed. Hoping that the Peking authorities, by their more extended contact during recent years with foreign diplomatists, might have learned something of constitutional rule, and might be willing to aid the people in throwing off their deplorable ignorance, I ventured, with others, to approach them, beseeching them, in all humility, to move in this direction for the welfare of China. These petitions only resulted in the infliction of many rigorous punishments. We had seized the moment when the Japanese were threatening Peking, and the Emperor, fearing that harsh dealings with the reformers might alienate many of his people, took no notice of them until peace was assured. Then an edict was issued denouncing the petitioners and commanding the immediate cessation of all suggestions of reform.

Finding the door closed to mild means, we grew more concrete in our notions and demands, and gradually came to see that some degree of coercion would be necessary. In all quarters we found supporters. The better classes were dissatisfied with the behaviour of our armies and fleets, and knew that corruption in its worst forms was the cause of their failure. This feeling was not confined to one locality, but was wide-spread and deep-rooted, and promised to take shape and find expression in decided action.

The headquarters of the "Young China" party was really in Shanghai, but the scene of action was to be laid in Canton. The party was aided in its course by one or two circumstances. First among these was the existence of discontented soldiery. Three-fourths of the Cantonese contingent were disbanded when the war in the North had ceased in 1895. This set loose a number of idle, lawless men; and the small section of their comrades who were retained in service were no better pleased than those dismissed. Either disband all or retain all, was their cry; but the authorities were deaf to the remonstrance. The reform party at once enlisted the sympathies of these men in their cause, and so gained numerical strength to their military resources.

Another chance coincidence hastened events. For some reason or other a body of police, discarding their uniform, set to work to loot and plunder a section of the city. After an hour or two, the inhabitants rose, and obtaining mastery of the quondam police, shut some half-dozen of the ringleaders up in their Guild-hall. The superintendent of the official police then sent out a force to release the marauders, and proceeded forthwith to plunder the Guildhall itself. A meeting of the inhabitants was immediately held, and a deputation of 1000 men sent to the Governor's residence to appeal against the action of the police. The authorities, however, told the deputation that such a proceeding was tantamount to a rebellion, and that they had no right to threaten their superiors. They thereupon arrested the ringleaders of the deputation, and sent the others about their business. The discontents soon became disaffected, and, the "Young China" party making advances, they readily joined the reformers.

Yet a third and a fourth incident helped to swell their ranks. The Viceroy, Li Han Chang (brother of the famous Viceroy Li), put a fixed tariff on all official posts throughout his two provinces, Kwang-Tung and Kwang-Si. This was an innovation which meant a further "squeeze" of the people, as the officials, of course, made the people pay to indemnify them for their extra payments. The fourth, and the most characteristically Chinese, method of extortion was afforded in the occasion of the Viceroy's birthday. The officials in his provinces combined to give their master a present, and collected money to the amount of a million taels (about £200,000). Of course the officials took the money from the richer merchants in the usual way, by threats, by promises, and by blackmailing. A follower of Li Han Chang, Che Fa Nung by name, further angered all the "Literati" by selling, to all who could afford to pay, diplomas of graduation for 3000 taels (about £500) each. The richer men and the "Literati" became thereby disaffected and threw in their lot with "Young China."

In this way the reform movement acquired great strength and coherence and wide-spread influence, and brought matters all too soon to a climax. The plan was to capture the city of Canton and depose the authorities, taking them by surprise and securing them in as quiet a way as possible, or, at any rate, without blood-shed. To ensure a complete *coup*, it was considered necessary to bring an overwhelming force to bear; consequently, two bodies of men were employed, one in Swatow and the other from the banks of the West river. These places were fixed upon as the Swatow men, for instance, were totally ignorant of the Cantonese language. Although only 180 miles north of Canton, the language of Swatow differs as much from that of Canton as English does from Italian. It was deemed wise to bring strangers in, as they were more likely to be staunch to the cause, since they could not communicate with, and therefore could not be tampered with by, Cantonese men. Nor would it be safe for them to disband or desert, as they would be known as strangers, and suspicion would at once fall on them were they found in Canton after the disturbance.

It was arranged that on a certain day in October, 1895, these men should march across country, one body from the south-west, the other from the north-east, towards Canton. All proceeded satisfactorily, and they commenced their advance. Frequent meetings of the Committee of Reformers were held, and arms, ammunition and dynamite were accumulated at the headquarters. The soldiers advancing across the country were to be still further strengthened by a contingent of four hundred men from Hong Kong. The day for the assemblage came and the southern men were halted within four hours march of the city. A guard of one hundred men, fully armed, was stationed around the Committee in their Guild; runners, some thirty in number, were despatched to the disaffected over the city to be ready for the following morning. Whilst the conspirators sat within their hall a telegram was received to the effect that the advancing soldiers had been stayed in their progress, and the reform movement forthwith became disconcerted. It was impossible to recall the messengers, and others could not be found who knew where the disaffected were resident. Further news came to hand rendering it impossible to proceed, and the cry arose *"Sauve qui peut."* A general stampede followed; papers were burnt, arms hidden, and telegrams despatched to Hong Kong to stop the contingent from that place. The telegram to the Hong Kong agent, however, only reached him after all his men had been got on board a steamer, which also carried many barrels of revolvers. Instead of dismissing the men as he should have done, he allowed them to proceed, and they landed on the wharf of Canton only to find themselves placed under arrest. The leaders in Canton fled, some one way, some another; I myself, after several hair-breadth escapes, getting on board a steam launch in which I sailed to Macao. Remaining there for twenty-four hours only, I proceeded to Hong Kong, where, after calling on some friends, I sought my old teacher and friend, Mr. James Cantlie. Having informed him that I was in trouble through having offended the Cantonese authorities, and fearing that I should be arrested and sent to Canton for execution, he advised me to consult a lawyer, which I immediately proceeded to do.

CHAPTER II.

MY CAPTURE.

I did not see Mr. Cantlie again, as Mr. Dennis, who directed my steps, constrained me to get away at once.

In two days time I went by Japanese steamer to Kobe, whence, after a few days' stay, I proceeded to Yokohama. There I changed my Chinese attire for a European costume *à la* Japanese. I removed my queue, allowed my hair to grow naturally and cultivated my moustache. In a few days I sailed from Yokohama for the Hawaiian Islands and there took up my quarters in the town of Honolulu, where I had many relations, friends and well-wishers. Wherever I went, whether in Japan, Honolulu, or America, I found all intelligent Chinese imbued with the spirit of reform and eager to obtain a form of representative government for their native land.

Whilst walking in the streets of Honolulu I met Mr. and Mrs. Cantlie and family, who were then on their way to England. They did not at first recognise me in my European dress, and their Japanese nurse at once addressed me in the Japanese language, taking me for a countryman. This happened frequently, Japanese everywhere at first taking me for one of themselves and only finding their mistake when they spoke to me.

I left Honolulu in June, 1896, for San Francisco, where I remained for a month before proceeding eastward. There I met many of my countrymen and was well received by them. I spent

11

three months in America, and came to Liverpool by the s.s. *Majestic*. In New York I was advised to beware the Chinese Minister to the United States, as he is a Manchurian, and has but little sympathy with Chinese generally and a reformer in particular.

On October 1st, 1896, I arrived in London and put up at Haxell's Hotel in the Strand. I went next day to Mr. Cantlie's, at 46 Devonshire Street, Portland Place, W., where I received a hearty welcome from my old friend and his wife. Lodgings were found for me at 8 Gray's Inn Place, Gray's Inn, Holborn. Henceforward I proceeded to settle down to enjoy my stay in London and to become acquainted with the many sights, the museums and the historical relics in this the very centre of the universe. What impressed me, a Chinaman, most was the enormous vehicular traffic, the endless and unceasing stream of omnibusses, cabs, carriages, wagons, and wheeled conveyances of humbler character which held the streets; the wonderful way in which the police controlled and directed the traffic, and the good humour of the people. The foot passengers are, of course, many, but they are not in such crowds as we find in Chinese streets. For one thing, our streets are much narrower, being, in fact, mere alleys; and, in the second place, all our goods are conveyed by human carriage, everything being slung from a bamboo pole carried across the shoulders. Yet even in the wide streets of Hong Kong our foot passenger traffic is in swarms.

I was just beginning to know Holborn from the Strand, and Oxford Circus from Piccadilly Circus, when I was deprived of my liberty in the fashion so fully described by the public press of the country.

I had been frequently at Mr. Cantlie's, almost daily in fact, and spent most of my time in his study. One day at luncheon he alluded to the Chinese Legation being in the neighbourhood, and jokingly suggested that I might go round and call there; whereat his wife remarked, "You had better not. Don't you go near it; they'll catch you and ship you off to China." We all enjoyed a good laugh over the remark, little knowing how true the womanly instinct was, and how soon we were to experience the reality. While dining one evening at Dr. Manson's, whom I had also known in Hong Kong, as my teacher in medicine, I was jokingly advised by him also to keep away from the Chinese Legation. I was well warned, therefore; but as I did not know where the Legation was, the warning was of little use. I knew that to get to Devonshire Street I had to get off the omnibus at Oxford Circus, and from thence go straight north up a wide street till I found the name Devonshire on the corner house. That was the extent of my knowledge of the locality at this time.

On Sunday morning, October 11th, at almost half-past ten, I was walking towards Devonshire Street, hoping to be in time to go to church with the doctor and his family, when a Chinaman approached in a surreptitious manner from behind and asked, in English, whether I was Japanese or Chinese. I replied, "I am Chinese." He then inquired from what province I came, and when I told him I was from Canton he said, "We are countrymen, and speak the same language; I am from Canton." It should be observed that English or "Pidgin," that is "business" English, is the common language between Chinamen from different localities.

A Swatow and a Cantonese merchant, although their towns are but 180 miles apart (less than the distance between London and Liverpool), may be entirely ignorant of each other's spoken language. The written language is the same all over China, but the written and spoken languages are totally different, and the spoken languages are many. A Swatow merchant, therefore, doing business in Hong Kong with a Cantonese man, speaks English, but writes in the common language of China. While upon this subject it may be well to state that the Japanese written language is the same in its characters as that used by the Chinese; so that a Chinaman and a Japanese when they meet, although having no spoken words in common, can figure to each other on the ground or on paper, and frequently make imaginary figures on one hand with the forefinger of the other to their mutual understanding.

My would-be Chinese friend, therefore, addressed me in English until he found my dialect. We then conversed in the Cantonese dialect. Whilst he was talking we were slowly advancing along the street, and presently a second Chinaman joined us, so that I had now one on each side. They pressed me to go in to their "lodgings" and enjoy a smoke and chat with them. I gently demurred, and we stopped on the pavement. A third Chinaman now appeared and my first acquaintance left us. The two who remained further pressed me to accompany them, and I was gradually, and in a seemingly friendly manner, led to the upper edge of the pavement, when the door of an adjacent house suddenly opened and I was half-jokingly and half-persistently compelled to enter by my companions, one on either side, who reinforced their entreaties by a quasi-friendly push. Suspecting nothing, for I knew not what house I was entering, I only hesitated because of my desire to get to Mr. Cantlie's in time for church, and I felt I should be too late did I delay. However, in good faith I entered, and was not a little surprised when the front door was somewhat hurriedly closed and barred behind me. All at once it flashed upon me that the house must be the Chinese Legation, thereby accounting for the number of Chinamen in mandarin attire, and for the large size of the house; while I also recollected that the Minister resided somewhere in the neighbourhood of Devonshire Street, near to which I must then be.

I was taken to a room on the ground floor whilst one or two men talked to me and to each other. I was then sent upstairs, two men, one on either side, conducting and partly forcing me to ascend. I was next shown into a room on the second floor and told I was to remain there. This room, however, did not seem to satisfy my captors, as I was shortly afterwards taken to another on the third floor with a barred window looking out to the back of the house. Here an old gentleman with white hair and beard came into the room in rather a bumptious fashion and said:

"Here is China for you; you are now in China."

Sitting down, he proceeded to interrogate me.

Asked what my name was, I replied "Sun."

"Your name," he replied, "is Sun Wen; and we have a telegram from the Chinese Minister in America informing us that you were a passenger to this country by the s.s. *Majestic*; and the Minister asks me to arrest you."

"What does that mean?" I enquired.

To which he replied:

"You have previously sent in a petition for reform to the Tsung-Li-Yamen in Peking asking that it be presented to the Emperor. That may be considered a very good petition; but now the Tsung-Li-Yamen want you, and therefore you are detained here until we learn what the Emperor wishes us to do with you."

"Can I let my friend know I am here?" I asked.

"No," he replied; "but you can write to your lodging for your luggage to be sent you."

On my expressing a wish to write to Dr. Manson, he provided me with pen, ink and paper. I wrote to Dr. Manson informing him that I was confined in the Chinese Legation, and asking him to tell Mr. Cantlie to get my baggage sent to me. The old gentleman, however,— whom I afterwards learned to be Sir Halliday Macartney,—objected to my using the word "confined," and asked me to substitute another. Accordingly I wrote: "I am in the Chinese Legation; please tell Mr. Cantlie to send my luggage here."

He then said he did not want me to write to my friend, and asked me to write to my hotel. I informed him that I was not at a hotel, and that only Mr. Cantlie knew where I was living. It was very evident my interrogator was playing a crafty game to get hold of my effects, and more especially my papers, in the hope of finding correspondence whereby to ascertain who my Chinese accomplices or correspondents were. I handed him the letter to Dr. Manson, which he read and returned, saying, "That is all right." I put it in an envelope and gave it to Sir Halliday Macartney in all good faith that it would be delivered.

CHAPTER III

MY IMPRISONMENT

Sir Halliday then left the room, shut the door and locked it, and I was a prisoner under lock and key. Shortly afterwards I was disturbed by the sound of carpentry at the door of my room, and found that an additional lock was being fixed thereto. Outside the door was stationed a guard of never less than two people, one of whom was a European; sometimes a third guard was added. During the first twenty-four hours the Chinese guards at the door frequently came in and spoke to me in their own dialect, which I understood fairly well. They did not give me any information as to my imprisonment—nor did I ask them any questions—further than that the old gentleman who had locked me up was Sir Halliday Macartney, the Ma-Ta-Yen, as they called him: *Ma* standing for "Macartney," *Ta-Yen* being the equivalent for "His Excellency." This is in the same category with the name under which the Chinese Minister passes here, Kung-Ta-Yen. *Kung* is his family name or surname; *Ta-Yen* indicates his title, meaning "His Excellency." He never gives his real name in public matters, thereby compelling every foreigner to unconsciously style him "His Excellency." I often wonder if he deals with the British Government under this cognomen solely; if he does, it is a disparagement and slight that is meant. Court and diplomatic etiquette in China is so nice, that the mere inflection of a syllable is quite enough to change the meaning of any communication to the foreigner from a compliment to a slight. This is constantly striven after in all dealings with foreigners, and it requires a very good knowledge of Chinese literature and culture indeed, to know that any message delivered to a

18

foreigner does not leave the Chinese diplomatist hugging himself
with delight at having insulted a foreigner of high rank, without
his knowing it. To the people around him he thereby shows his
own preëminence, and how the "foreign devils"—the Yang Quei
Tze—are his inferiors.

Several hours after my imprisonment, one of the guard came
into my room and told me that Sir Halliday Macartney had
ordered him to search me. He proceeded to take my keys, pencil
and knife. He did not find my pocket in which I had a few
bank notes; but he took the few unimportant papers I had. They
asked me what food I wanted, and at my request brought me
some milk which I drank.

During the day two English servants came to light the fire,
bring coals and sweep the room. I asked the first who came to
take a letter out for me, and being promised that this would be
done, I wrote a note addressed to Mr. Cantlie, 46 Devonshire
Street, W. When the second servant came I did the same thing.
I did not, of course, know till later what had happened to my
letters, but both men said they had sent them. That (Sunday)
evening an English woman came in to make up my bed. I did
not address her at all. All that night I had no sleep, and lay
with my clothes on.

On the following day—Monday, 12th October—the two
English servants came again to attend to the room, and brought
coals, water and food. One said he had sent the note with which
I had entrusted him, while the other, Cole, said he could not get
out to do so. I suspected, however, that my notes had never

reached their destination.

On Tuesday, the 13th, I again asked the younger manservant —not Cole—if he had delivered my letter and had seen Mr. Cantlie. He said he had; but as I still doubted him, he swore he had seen Mr. Cantlie, who on receiving the note said, "All right!" Having no more paper, I wrote with pencil on the corner of my handkerchief, and asked him to take it to my friend. At the same time I put a half-sovereign in his hand, and hoped for the best I was dubious about his good faith, and I found that my suspicions were but too well-founded; for I ascertained subsequently he went immediately to his employers and disclosed all.

On the fourth day of my imprisonment Mr. Tang, as he is called, came to see me, and I recognised in him the man who had kidnapped me. He sat down and proceeded to converse with me.

"When I last saw you," he began, "and took you in here, I did so as part of my official duty: I now come to talk with you as a friend. You had better confess that you are Sun Wen; it is no use denying it: everything is settled." In a vein of sarcastic-pseudo flattery he continued: "You are well known in China: the Emperor and the Tsung-Li-Yamen are well acquainted with your history; it is surely worth your while dying with so distinguished a name as you have made for yourself upon you." (This is a species of Oriental flattery scarcely perhaps to be appreciated by Western minds; but it is considered everything in China, how and under what name and reputation you *die*.)"Your being here," he proceeded, "means life or death. Do you know that?"

"How?" I asked. "This is England, not China. What do you propose to do with me? If you wish extradition, you must let my imprisonment be known to the British Government; and I do not think the Government of this country will give me up."

"We are not going to ask legal extradition for you," he replied. "Everything is ready; the steamer is engaged; you are to be bound and gagged and taken from here, so that there will be no disturbance; and you will be placed on board in safe keeping. Outside Hong Kong harbour there will be a Chinese gunboat to meet you, and you will be transferred to that and taken to Canton for trial and execution."

I pointed out that this would be a risky proceeding, as I might have the chance of communicating with the English on board on the way. This, however, Tang declared would be impossible, as, said he, "You will be as carefully guarded as you are here, so that all possibility of escape will be cut off." I then suggested that the officers on board might not be of the same mind as my captors, and that some of them might sympathise with me and help me.

"The steamboat company," replied Tang, "are friends of Sir Halliday Macartney's and will do what they are told."

In reply to my questions he told me that I should be taken by one of the "Glen" Line of Steamers, but that my departure would not take place that week (this was October 14th), as the Minister was unwilling to go to the expense of exclusively chartering the steamer, and he wished to have the cargo shipped first, so that only the passenger tickets would have to be paid for.

"Some time next week," he added, "the cargo will be embarked and you will go then."

On my remarking that this was a very difficult plan to put into execution, he merely said:

"Were we afraid of that, we could kill you here, because this is China, and no one can interfere with us in the Legation."

For my edification and consolation he then quoted the case of a Korean patriot, who, escaping from Korea to Japan, was induced by a countryman of his to go to Shanghai, where he was put to death in the British concession. His dead body was sent back by the Chinese to Korea for punishment, and on arrival there it was decapitated, while the murderer was rewarded and given a high political post. Tang was evidently fondly cherishing the belief that he would be similarly promoted by his government for arresting me and securing my death.

I asked him why he should be so cruel, to which he replied:

"This is by order of the Emperor, who wants you captured at any price, alive or dead."

I urged that the Korean case was one of the causes of the Japanese war, and that my capture and execution might lead to further trouble and great complications.

"The British Government," I said, "may ask for the punishment of all the members of this Legation; and, as you are a countryman of mine, my people in the province of Kwang-Tung may revenge themselves on you and your family for your treatment of me."

He then changed his tone, desisted from his arrogant utterances, and remarked that all he was doing was by the direction of the Legation, and that he was merely warning me in a friendly way of my plight.

CHAPTER IV.

PLEADING WITH MY GAOLERS FOR LIFE.

At twelve o'clock the same night Tang returned to my room and re-opened the subject. I asked him, if he was really a friend of mine, what he could do to help me.

"That is what I came back for," he replied, "and I want to do all I can, and will let you out by-and-by. Meantime," he continued, "I am getting the locksmith to make two duplicate keys, one for your room and one for the front door."

Tang had to take this step, he said, as the keys were kept by the confidential servant of the Minister, who would not part with them.

To my inquiry as to when he could let me out, he stated that it would be impossible till the following day, and that he could probably manage it at two a.m. Friday morning.

As he left the room he counselled me to be ready to get out on the Friday.

After his departure I wrote down a few words on a paper to give to the servants to take to Mr. Cantlie.

Next morning, Thursday, October 15th, I gave the note to the servant; but, as Tang told me on the afternoon of that day, it was handed by the servant to the Legation authorities.

24

Tang declared that by my action I had spoiled all his plans for rescuing me, and that Sir Halliday Macartney had scolded him very much for telling me how they intended to dispose of me.

I thereupon asked him if there was any hope for my life, to which he replied:

"Yes, there is still great hope; but you must do what I tell you."

He advised me to write to the Minister asking for mercy. This I agreed to do, and asked for pen, ink and paper. These Tang told Cole to bring me.

I asked, however, that Chinese ink and paper should be supplied me, as I could not write to the Chinese Minister in English.

To this Tang replied:

"Oh, English is best, for the Minister is but a figure-head; everything is in Macartney's hands, and you had better write to him."

When I asked what I should write, he said:

"You must deny that you had anything to do with the Canton plot, declare that you were wrongly accused by the mandarins, and that you came to the Legation to ask for redress."

I wrote to his dictation a long letter to this effect in Tang's presence.

Having addressed the folded paper to Sir Halliday Macartney (whose name Tang spelt for me, as I did not know how) I handed it to Tang, who went off with it in his possession, and I never saw the intriguer again.

This was no doubt a very stupid thing to have done, as I thereby furnished my enemies with documentary evidence that I had come voluntarily to the Legation. But as a dying man will clutch at anything, so I, in my strait, was easily imposed upon.

Tang had informed me that all my notes had been given up by the servants, so that none of them had reached my friends outside. I then lost all hope, and was persuaded that I was face to face with death.

During the week I had written statements of my plight on any scraps of paper I could get and thrown them out of the window. I had at first given them to the servants to throw out, as my window did not look out on the street; but it was evident all of them had been retained. I therefore attempted to throw them out at my own window myself, and by a lucky shot one fell on the leads of the back premises of the next house.

In order to make these missives travel further I weighted them with coppers, and, when these were exhausted, two-shilling pieces, which, in spite of the search, I had managed to retain on my person. When the note fell on the next house I was in hopes that the occupants might get it. One of the other notes, striking a rope, fell down immediately outside my window. I requested a servant—not Cole—to pick it up and give it me; but instead of doing so he told the Chinese guards about it, and they picked it up.

Whilst searching about, the letter on the leads of the next house caught their attention, and, climbing over, they got possession of that also, so that I was bereft of that hope too. These notes they took to their masters.

I was now in a worse plight than ever, for they screwed up my window, and my sole means of communication with the outside world seemed gone.

My despair was complete, and only by prayer to God could I gain any comfort. Still the dreary days and still more dreary nights wore on, and but for the comfort afforded me by prayer I believe I should have gone mad. After my release I related to Mr. Cantlie how prayer was my one hope, and told him how I should never forget the feeling that seemed to take possession of me as I rose from my knees on the morning of Friday, October 16th—a feeling of calmness, hopefulness and confidence, that assured me my prayer was heard, and filled me with hope that all would yet be well. I therefore resolved to redouble my efforts, and made a determined advance to Cole, beseeching him to help me.

When he came in I asked him: "Can you do anything for me?"

His reply was the question: "What are you?"

"A political refugee from China," I told him.

As he did not seem to quite grasp my meaning, I asked him if he had heard much about the Armenians. He said he had, so I followed up this line by telling him that just as the Sultan of Turkey wished to kill all the Christians of Armenia, so the Emperor of China wished to kill me because I was a Christian, and one of a party that was striving to secure good government for China.

"All English people," I said, "sympathise with the Armenians, and I do not doubt they would have the same feeling towards me if they knew my condition."

He remarked that he did not know whether the English Government would help me, but I replied that they would certainly do so, otherwise the Chinese Legation would not confine me so strictly, but would openly ask the British Government for my legal extradition.

"My life," I said to him, "is in your hands. If you let the matter be known outside, I shall be saved; if not, I shall certainly be executed. Is it good to save a life or to take it? Whether is it more important to regard your duty to God or to your master?—to honour the just British, or the corrupt Chinese, Government?"

I pleaded with him to think over what I had said, and to

give me an answer next time he came, and tell me truly whether he would help me or not.

He went away, and I did not see him till next morning. It may well be imagined how eager I was to learn his decision. While engaged putting coals on the fire he pointed to a paper he had placed in the coal scuttle. On the contents of that paper my life seemed to depend. Would it prove a messenger of hope, or would the door of hope again be shut in my face? Immediately he left the room I picked it up and read:

"I will try to take a letter to your friend. You must not write it at the table, as you can be seen through the keyhole, and the guards outside watch you constantly. You must write it on your bed."

I then lay down on my bed, with my face to the wall, and wrote on a visiting card to Mr. Cantlie. At noon Cole came in again, and I pointed to where my note was. He went and picked it up, and I gave him all the money I had about me—£20. Mr. Cantlie's note in reply was placed by Cole behind the coal scuttle, and by a significant glance he indicated there was something there for me. When he had gone I anxiously picked it up, and was overjoyed to read the words: "Cheer up! The Government is working on your behalf, and you will be free in a few days." Then I knew God had answered my prayer.

During all this time I had never taken off my clothes. Sleep came but seldom, only in snatches, and these very troubled. Not until I received my friend's cheering news did I get a semblance of real rest.

My greatest dread was the evil that would befall the cause for which I had been fighting, and the consequences that would ensue were I taken to China and killed. Once the Chinese got me there, they would publish it abroad that I had been given up by the British Government in due legal fashion, and that there was no refuge in British territory for any of the other offenders. The members of "the Party" will remember the part played by England in the Taiping rebellion, and how by English interference that great national and Christian revolution was put down. Had I been taken to China to be executed, the people would have once more believed that the revolution was again being fought with the aid of Britain, and all hopes of success would be gone.

Had the Chinese Legation got my papers from my lodgings, further complications might have resulted to the detriment of many friends. This danger, it turned out, had been carefully guarded against by a thoughtful lady. Mrs. Cantlie, on her own responsibility, had gone to my lodgings, carefully collected my papers and correspondence, and within a few hours of her becoming acquainted with my imprisonment, there and then destroyed them. If some of my friends in various parts of the world have had no reply to their letters, they must blame this considerate lady for her wise and prompt action, and forgive my not having answered them, as I am minus their addresses, and in many cases do not even know their names. Should the Chinese authorities again entrap me, they will find no papers whereby my associates can be made known to them.

I luckily did not think of poison in my food, but my state of mind was such that food was repulsive to me. I could only get down liquid nourishment, such as milk and tea, and occasionally an egg. Only when my friend's note reached me could I either eat or sleep.

CHAPTER V.

THE PART MY FRIENDS PLAYED.

Outside the Legation, I of course knew nothing of what was going on. All my appeals, all my winged scraps I had thrown out at the window, all my letters I had handed officially to Sir Halliday Macartney and Tang, I knew were useless, and worse than useless, for they but increased the closeness of my guard and rendered communication with my friends more and more an impossibility.

However, my final appeal on Friday morning, October 16th, had made an impression, for it was after that date that Cole began to interest himself in my behalf. Cole's wife had a good deal to do with the initiative, and it was Mrs. Cole who wrote a letter to Mr. Cantlie on Saturday, October 17th, 1896, and so set the machinery going. The note reached Devonshire Street at 11 p.m. Imagine the Doctor's feelings when he read the following:

"There is a friend of yours imprisoned in the Chinese Legation here since last Sunday. They intend sending him out to China, where it is certain they will hang him. It is very sad for the poor man, and unless something is done at once, he will be taken away and no one will know it. I dare not sign my name; but this is the truth, so believe what I say. Whatever you do must be done at once, or it will be too late. His name is, I believe, Lin Yin Sen."

No time was evidently to be lost. Late as it was, after ascertaining Sir Halliday Macartney's address, Mr. Cantlie set out

32

to find him. He little knew that he was going straight to the head centre of all this disgraceful proceeding. Luckily or unluckily for me, one will never know which, he found the house, 3 Harley Place, shut up. It was 11.15 p.m. on Saturday night, and the policeman on duty in the Marylebone Road eyed him rather suspiciously as he emerged from the compound in which the house stands. The policeman said that the house was shut up for six months, the family having gone to the country. Mr. Cantlie asked how he knew all this, and the policeman retorted that there had been a burglary attempted three nights previously, which led to close enquiries who the tenants were; therefore, the information he had, namely a six months' "anticipated" absence, was evidently definite and precise. Mr. Cantlie next drove to Marylebone Lane Police Office, and laid the matter before the Inspector on duty. He next went to Scotland Yard and asked to see the officer in charge. A Detective Inspector received him in a private room, and consented to take down his evidence. The difficulty was to get anyone to believe so improbable a story. The Police authority politely listened to the extraordinary narrative, but declared that it was impossible for Scotland Yard to take the initiative, and Mr. Cantlie found himself in the street about 1 a.m., in no better plight than when he set out.

Next morning Mr. Cantlie went to Kensington to consult with a friend as to whether or not there was any good in asking the head of the Chinese Customs in London to approach the Legation privately, and induce them to reconsider their imprudent action and ill-advised step.

Not receiving encouragement in that direction, he went again to 3 Harley Place, in hopes that at least a caretaker would be in possession, and in a position to at least tell where Sir Halliday Macartney could be found or reached by telegram. Beyond the confirmation of the policeman's story that burglary had been attempted, by seeing the evidence of "jemmies" used to break open the door, no clue could be found as to where this astute orientalised diplomatist was to be unearthed.

Mr. Cantlie then proceeded to Dr. Manson's house, and there, at his front door, he saw a man who proved to be Cole, my attendant at the Legation. The poor man had at last summoned up courage to disclose the secret of my imprisonment, and in fear and trembling sought out Mr. Cantlie at his house; but being told he had gone to Dr. Manson's, he went on there and met both the doctors together. Cole then presented two cards I had addressed to Mr. Cantlie, stating:

"I was kidnapped on Sunday last by two Chinamen, and forcibly taken into the Chinese Legation. I am imprisoned, and in a day or two I am to be shipped off to China, on board a specially-chartered vessel. I am certain to be beheaded. Oh! woe is me."

Dr. Manson heartily joined with his friend in his attempt to rescue me, and proceeded to interrogate Cole. Mr. Cantlie remarked:

"Oh, if Sir Halliday Macartney were only in town, it would be all right. It is a pity he is away; where *can* we find him?"

Cole immediately retorted:

"Sir Halliday is in town, he comes to the Legation every day; it was Sir Halliday who locked Sun in his room, and placed me in charge, with directions to keep a strict guard over the door, that he should have no means of escape."

This information was startling, and placed the difficulty of release on a still more precarious footing. The proceedings would have to be still more carefully undertaken, and the highest authorities would have to be called in, were these crafty and masterful men to be outwitted.

Cole, in answer to further interrogations, said that it was given out in the Legation that I was a lunatic; that I was to be removed to China on the following Tuesday (that was in two days more); that he did not know by what line of ships I was going, but a man of the name of McGregor, in the City, had something to do with it. It also came out that two or three men dressed as Chinese sailors had been to the Legation during the week, and Cole had no doubt their visit had something to do with my removal, as he had never seen men of that description in the house before.

Cole left, taking a card with the names of my two friends upon it to deliver to me, in the hopes that its advent would allay my fears, and serve as a guarantee that Cole was actually working on my behalf at last. The two doctors then set out to Scotland Yard to try the effects of a further appeal in that direction. The Inspector on duty remarked: "You were here at

12.30 a.m. this morning. I am afraid it is no use your coming here again so soon." The paramount difficulty was to know where to go to represent the fact that a man's life was in danger; that the laws of the country were being outraged; that a man was to be practically given over, in the Metropolis of the British Empire, to be murdered.

On quitting the premises they took counsel together, and decided to invade the precincts of the Foreign Office. They were told the resident clerk would see them at five p.m. At that hour they were received, and delivered their romantic tale to the willing ears of the courteous official. Being *Sunday, of course* nothing further could be done, but they were told that the statement would be laid before a higher authority on the following day. But time was pressing, and what was to be done? That night might see the tragedy completed and the prisoner removed on board a vessel bound for China. What was most dreaded was that a foreign ship would be selected; and under a foreign flag the British authorities were powerless. The last hope was that, if I were removed before they succeeded in rousing the authorities and the vessel actually got away, that it might be stopped and searched in the Suez Canal; but, were I shipped on board a vessel under a flag other than British, this hope would prove a delusion. With this dread upon them, they decided to take the decisive step of going to the Legation, and telling the Chinese that they were acquainted with the fact that Sun was a prisoner in their hands, and that the British Government and the police knew of their intention to remove him to China for execution. Dr. Manson decided he should go alone, as Mr. Cantlie's name in connection with Sun's was well known at the Legation.

Accordingly Dr. Manson called alone at 49 Portland Place. The powdered footman at the door was asked to call one of the English-speaking Chinamen. Presently the Chinese interpreter, my captor and tormentor, Tang himself, appeared. Dr. Manson said he wanted to see Sun Yat Sen. A puzzled expression fell o'er Tang's face, as though seeking to recall such a name. "Sun! — Sun! there is no such person here." Dr. Manson then proceeded to inform him that he was quite well aware that Sun was here; that he wished to inform the Legation that the Foreign Office had been made cognisant of the fact; and that Scotland Yard was posted in the matter of Sun's detention. But a Chinese diplomatist is nothing if not a capable liar, and Tang's opportunity of lying must have satisfied even his Oriental liking for the *rôle*. With the semblance of truth in his every word and action, Tang assured his interrogator that the whole thing was nonsense, and that no such person was there. His openness and frankness partly shook Dr. Manson's belief in my condition, and when he got back to Mr. Cantlie's he was so impressed with the apparent truthfulness of Tang's statement, that he even suggested that the tale of my imprisonment might be a trick by myself to some end—he knew not what. Thus can my countrymen lie; Tang even shook the belief of a man like Dr. Manson, who had lived in China twenty-two years; who spoke the Amoy dialect fluently; and was thereby more intimately acquainted with the Chinese and their ways than nine-tenths of the people who visit the Far East. However, he had to dismiss the thought, as no ulterior object could be seen in a trick of the kind. Tang is sure to rise high in the service of his country; a liar like that is sure to get his reward amongst a governing class who exist and thrive upon it.

It was seven o'clock on Sunday evening when the two doctors desisted from their labours, parted company, and considered they had done their duty. But they were still not satisfied that I was safe. The danger was that I might be removed that very night, especially since the Legation knew the British Government were now aware of the fact, and that if immediate embarkation were not possible, a change of residence of their victim might be contemplated. This was a very probable step indeed, and, if it had been possible, there is no doubt it would have been accomplished. Luckily for me, the Marquis Tseng, as he is called, had shortly before left London for China, and given up his residence. Had it not been so, it is quite possible the plan of removal to his house would have recommended itself to my clever countryman; and when it was accomplished, they would have thrown themselves upon the confidence and good friendship of the British, and asked them to search the house. That ruse could not be carried out; but the removal to the docks was quite feasible. It was expected I was to sail on Tuesday, and, as the ship must be now in dock, there was nothing more likely than that the "lunatic" passenger should be taken on board at night, to escape the excitement and noise of the daily traffic in the streets.

CHAPTER VI.

THE SEARCH FOR A DETECTIVE.

With all this in his mind Mr. Cantlie set forth again, this time to search out some means of having the Legation watched. He called at a friend's house and obtained the address of Slater's firm of private detectives in the City. Hither he went; but Slater's office was closed.

On Sunday it would seem no detectives are required. Can no trouble arise on Sunday in England? It must be remembered that the division of the month is but an artificial and mundane convenience, and crime does not always accommodate itself to such vagaries of the calendar as the portioning the month into weeks. However, there was the hard fact, Slater's office was shut, and neither shouting, bellringing, nor hard knocks could elicit any response from the granite buildings in Basinghall Street.

A consultation in the street with a policeman and the friendly cabman, who was taken into the secret of my detention, ended in a call at the nearest police station. Here the tale had to be unfolded again, and all the doubts as to the doctor's soberness and sanity set at rest before anything further could be attempted.

"Where was the place?"

"Portland Place, West."

"Oh! it is no good coming here, you must go back to the

39

West End; we belong to the City police."

To the doctor's mind neither eastern nor western police were of any avail.

"However," he persisted, "could a detective not be obtained to watch the house?"

"No. It was out of the power of the City police to interfere in the West End work."

"Have you not some old police constable, a reserve man, who would be willing to earn a little money at a job of the kind?" Mr. Cantlie asked.

"Well, there might be—let us see."

And here a number of men fell goodnaturedly to discussing whom they could recall to memory. Well, yes; they thought So-and-so would do.

"Where does he live?"

"Oh! he lives in Leytonstone. You could not get him to-night: this is Sunday, you know."

Sunday I should think it was, and my head in the balance. After a long discussion a man's name was suggested, and they got rid of the persistent doctor. The man's address was Gibston Square, Islington.

But before starting thence, Mr. Cantlie thought he would give the newspapers the whole tale, so he drove to the *Times* Office and asked for the sub-editor. A card to fill in was handed him as to the nature of his business; and he wrote:

"Case of Kidnapping at the Chinese Legation!"

This was 9 p.m., and he was told no one would be in until 10 p.m.

Away then he went to Islington in search of his "man." After a time the darkly-lit square was found, and the number proving correct, the abode was entered. But again disappointment followed; for "he could not go, but he thought he knew a man that would." Well, there was no help for it; but where did this man live? He was a wonderful chap; but the card bearing his address could not be found. High and low was it looked for: drawers and boxes, old packets of letters and unused waist-coats were searched and turned out. At last, however, it was unearthed, and then it was known that the man was not at home, but was watching a public-house in the City.

Well, even this was overcome, for the Doctor suggested that one of the numerous children that crowded the parlour should be sent with a note to the home address of the detective, whilst the father of the flock should accompany the Doctor to the City in search of the watcher. At last the hansom cab drew up at a little distance from a public-house, somewhere in the neighbourhood of the Barbican, and the place was reconnoitred. But no watcher could be seen around, and a futile search was settled in this way: that the public-house should be watched until eleven o'clock, when the house closed, at which time in all probability the "man" would be forthcoming. Mr. Cantlie left his erstwhile friend outside the house and set off again for the *Times* Office. There he was received in "audience" and his statement was taken down, and the publication of the tale was left to the *Times*' discretion. By this time it was 11.30 p.m. on Sunday, and at last the restless Doctor sought his home. He was somewhat chagrined to find that at 12 midnight his expected detective had not yet appeared, but, nothing daunted, he prepared to keep watch himself. He said good-night to his wife, and set out to observe the Legation, ready to interfere actively if need be.

However, as he strode forth with valiant intent, the Doctor encountered his expected "man" in the street, and immediately posted him. His Gibston Square friend had proved himself reliable and sent his deputy. The windows of the Legation, late as it was,—past twelve at night,—were still lit up, indicating a commotion within, the result, no doubt, of Dr. Manson's intimation that their evil ways were no longer unknown. The "man" was placed in a hansom cab in Weymouth Street, under the shadow of a house on the south side of the street, between Portland Place and Portland Road. It was a beautiful moonlight night, and both the Legation entrances could be clearly seen. The hansom cab was a necessary part of the sentinel on duty, as, supposing I had been hurried from the house across the pavement and into a carriage, I should have been carried beyond the reach of a person on foot in a few minutes. Cabs cannot be had at any moment in the early morning hours; hence the necessary precaution of having the watchman in a position by which he could follow in pursuit, if he were required so to do. The newspapers had it, that the cab was intended to carry me off when the rescue party had freed me, but this is another part of the story which I will relate later on.

At 2 a.m. the Doctor got to bed, and having informed the Government, told the police, given the tale to the newspapers, posted private detectives for the night, his day's work was finished and practically my life was saved, although I did not know it.

CHAPTER VII.

THE GOVERNMENT INTERVENE.

On Monday, October 19th, Slater's office was again asked for detectives, and, when they came, they were posted with instructions to watch the Legation night and day.

At 12 noon, by appointment at the Foreign Office, Mr. Cantlie submitted his statement in writing. The Foreign Office were evidently anxious that some less official plan of release should be effected than by their active interference, in the hopes that international complications might be averted.

Moreover, the proofs of my detention were mere hearsay, and it was unwise to raise a question which seemed to be founded on an improbable statement. As a step in the evidence, enquiry was made at the "Glen" Line Office, and when it was found that a passage had been asked for, the Government then knew by direct evidence that the tale was not only true, but that actual steps for its execution had been carefully laid. From this moment the affair passed into Government hands, and my friends were relieved of their responsibility.

Six detectives were told off by Government for duty outside the Legation, and the police in the neighbourhood were made cognisant of the facts and apprised to be vigilant.

The police had, moreover, my photograph, which I had had taken in America in my European dress. To the eye of the foreigner, who has not travelled in China, all Chinese are alike,

44

so that an ordinary photograph was not likely to be of much assistance; but in this photograph I wore a moustache and had my hair "European fashion."

No Chinaman wears a moustache until he has attained the "rank" of grandfather; but even in the country of early marriages, I, who have not yet attained the age of thirty, can scarcely aspire to the "distinction."

On Thursday, October 22nd, a writ of *Habeas Corpus* was made out against either the Legation or Sir Halliday Macartney, I know not which, but the Judge at the Old Bailey would not agree to the action, and it fell through.

On the afternoon of the same day a special correspondent of the *Globe* called at Mr. Cantlie's house and asked him if he knew anything about a Chinaman that had been kidnapped by the Chinese Legation. Well, he thought he did; what did the *Globe* know about it? The Doctor said he had given the information to the *Times* on Sunday, October 18th, five days before, and further supplemented it by additional information on Monday, October 19th, and that he felt bound to let the *Times* make it public first. However, Mr. Cantlie said, "Read over what you have written about the circumstance, and I will tell you if it is correct." The information the *Globe* had received proving correct, the Doctor endorsed it, but requested his name not to be mentioned.

Of course many persons were acquainted with the circumstances long before they appeared in print. Some two or three hundred people knew of my imprisonment by Tuesday morning, and it was a wonder that the ever eager correspondents did not know of it before Thursday afternoon. However, once it got wind there was no hushing the matter up, for from the moment the *Globe* published the startling news, there was no more peace at 46 Devonshire Street, W.

Within two hours after the issue of the fifth edition of the *Globe*, Mr. Cantlie was interviewed by a Central News and a *Daily Mail* reporter. He was too reticent to please them, but the main outlines were extracted from him.

The two searchers after truth next called at the Chinese Legation and asked to see Sun. They were met by the ever-ready and omnipresent Tang, who denied all knowledge of such a man. Tang was shown the report in the *Globe*, at which he laughed merrily and said the whole thing was a huge imposition. The Central News reporter, however, said it was no good denying it, and that if Sun was not given up, he might expect 10,000 men here to—morrow to pull the place about his ears. Nothing, however, moved Tang, and he lied harder than ever.

Sir Halliday Macartney was next unearthed at the Midland Hotel and interviewed. His statements are best gathered from the Press reports.

INTERVIEWS WITH SIR HALLIDAY MACARTNEY.

Sir Halliday Macartney, Counsellor of the Chinese Legation, visited the Foreign Office at 3.30 yesterday afternoon. In conversation with a press representative, Sir Halliday said: I am unable to give you any information about the man detained at the

Legation, beyond what has already appeared in print. On being informed that the Foreign Office had just issued an announcement to the effect that Lord Salisbury had requested the Chinese Minister to release the prisoner, Sir Halliday admitted that this was so, and in answer to a further question as to what would be the result of the request, replied: "The man will be released, but this will be done strictly without prejudice to the rights of the Legation involved."

In course of a later conversation with a representative of the press, Sir Halliday Macartney said: Sun Yat Sen is not the name of the man whom we have in detention upstairs. We have no doubt of his real identity, and have been from time to time fully informed of all his movements since he set foot in England. He came of his own free will to the Legation, and was certainly not kidnapped or forced or inveigled into the premises. It is quite a usual thing for solitary Chinamen in London to call here to make casual inquiries, or to have a chat with a countryman. There appears, moreover, to be some ground for suspecting that this peculiar visitor, believing himself unknown, came with some idea of spying on us and getting some information. Nobody knew him by sight. When he called he got into conversation with one of our staff, and was afterwards introduced to me. We chatted for awhile, and some remarks he made led me after he had gone to suspect he might be the person we were having watched. These suspicions being confirmed, he was, on returning the following day, detained, and he is still under detention pending instructions from the Chinese Government.

Speaking on the international side of the matter, Sir Halliday said: The man is not a British, but a Chinese, subject. We contend that for certain purposes the Legation is Chinese territory, where the Chinese Minister alone has jurisdiction. If a Chinaman comes here voluntarily, and if there are charges or suspicions against him, we contend that no one outside has any right to interfere with his detention. It would be quite different if he were outside this building, for then he would be on British territory, and we could not arrest him without a warrant.

Answering further questions, Sir Halliday mentioned that the man was not treated like a prisoner, and every consideration had been paid to his comfort. Sir Halliday ridiculed the statement which has appeared that the captive might be subjected to torture or undue pressure. He added a statement that a letter of inquiry had been received from the Foreign Office on the subject, which would receive immediate attention.

The Central News says: Sir Halliday Macartney, on his return to the Chinese Legation from the Foreign Office, proceeded to the bedside of the Minister Kung Ta Jen, and explained to him that Lord Salisbury had insisted upon the release of Sun Yat Sen.

It is not for me to discuss the behaviour of Sir Halliday Macartney; I leave that to public opinion and to his own conscience. In his own mind, I have no doubt, he has reasons for his action; but they seem scarcely consistent with those of a sane man, let alone the importance of the position he occupies. I expect Tang expressed the position pretty exactly when he told me that "the Minister is but a figure—head here, Macartney is the ruler."

Various reports of an intended rescue crept into the newspapers. The following is an example:

AN INTENDED RESCUE.

In reference to the arrest of Sun Yat Sen, it has been ascertained that his friends had arranged a bold scheme to bring about his rescue. Had they not been definitely assured by the Foreign Office and Scotland Yard that no harm whatever should come to him, his rescue was to be effected by means of breaking the window of his room, and descending from the roof of No. 51 Portland Place, the residence of Viscount Powerscourt. His friends had succeeded in informing him of the plan they intended to pursue, and although information which was subsequently obtained pointed to the fact that Sun Yat Sen was being kept handcuffed, a promise of inside assistance in opening the window satisfied his friends of the feasibility of the plan. Indeed, so far matured was the scheme, that a cab was held in waiting to convey Sun Yat Sen to the home of a friend. By the prisoner's friends it is declared that Long, the interpreter at the Legation, was one of the Chinamen who actually decoyed Sun into the Legation, though he was invariably the most positive subsequently in denying that such a man had ever been inside the Legation walls. His friends declare that Sun was dressed in English clothes, and so far from his being a typical Oriental, when dressed according to Western fashion was invariably taken for an Englishman. He is declared to be a man of unbounded good nature and of the gentlest disposition in Hongkong, and the various places where he practised medicine he obtained a reputation for skill and benevolence towards the poor. He is believed to have been in a great extent the tool of the Canton conspirators, though he never hesitated to condemn the cruel and oppressive Government of the Viceroy of Canton. He is said to have journeyed throughout Canton in the interests of his society, and the plot itself is declared to be the most widespread and formidable since the present Emperor commenced to reign.

The real facts are these. Cole sent the following communication to Mr. Cantlie on October 19th, 1896: "I shall have a good opportunity to let Mr. Sun out on to the roof of the next house in Portland Place to—night. If yon think it advisable, get permission from the occupants of the house to have someone waiting there to receive him. If I am to do it, find means to let me know." Mr.Cantlie went with this letter to Scotland Yard and requested that a constable be posted with himself on the roof of the house in question; but the Scotland Yard authorities, thinking it was an undignified proceeding, dissuaded him from his purpose, and gave it as their firm conviction that I should walk out by the front door in a day or two.

CHAPTER VIII.

RELEASED.

On October 22nd Cole directed my attention to the coal scuttle, and when he left the room I picked up a clipping from a newspaper, which proved to be the *Globe*. There I read the account of my detention, under the heading: *"Startling Story! Conspirator Kidnapped in London! Imprisonment at the Chinese Embassy!"* And then followed a long and detailed account of my position. At last the Press had interfered, and I felt that I was really safe. It came as a reprieve to a condemned man, and my heart was full of thankfulness.

Friday, October 23rd, dawned, and the day wore on, and still I was in durance. At 4.30 p.m., however, on that day, my English and Chinese guards came into the room and said "Macartney wants to see you downstairs." I was told to put on my boots and hat and overcoat. I accordingly did so, not knowing whither I was going. I descended the stairs, and as it was to the basement I was being conducted, I believed I was to be hidden in a cellar whilst the house was being searched by the command of the British Government. I was not told I was to be released, and I thought I was to enter another place of imprisonment or punishment. It seemed too good to be true that I was actually to be released. However, Mr. Cantlie presently appeared on the scene in company with two other men, who turned out to be Inspector Jarvis from Scotland Yard, and an old man, the messenger from the Foreign Office.

Sir Halliday Macartney then, in the presence of these gentlemen,

51

handed me over the various effects that had been taken from me, and addressed the Government officials to the following effect:—

"I hand this man over to you, and I do so on condition that neither the prerogative nor the diplomatic rights of the Legation are interfered with," or words to that effect. I was too excited to commit them to memory, but they seemed to me then, as they do now, senseless and childish.

The meeting related above took place in a passage in the basement of the house, and I was told I was a free man. Sir Halliday then shook hands with us all, a post–Judas salutation, and we were shown out by a side–door leading to the area. From thence we ascended the area steps, and issued into Weymouth Street from the back door of the Legation.

It will perhaps escape observation and pass out of mind as but a minor circumstance that we were sent out by the *back* door of the Legation.

The fact of the rescue was the all important measure in the minds of the little group of Englishmen present; not so, however, with my astute countryman; not so especially with Sir Halliday Macartney, that embodiment of retrograde orientalism.

The fact that the representatives of the British Government were shown out by the back door, as common carrion, will redound to the credit of the Minister and his *clientelle* in the high courts of their country. It was intended as a slight and insult, and it was carried out as only one versed in the Chinese methods of dealing with foreigners can appreciate. The excuse, no doubt, was that the hall was crowded with reporters; that a considerable throng of people had assembled in the street outside the building; that the Foreign Office was anxious that the affair should be conducted quietly without demonstration. These, no doubt, were the reasons present in the ever-ready minds of these Manchurian rapscallions and their caretaker Macartney.

To English ways of looking at things, the fact of my release was all that was cared for; but to the Chinese the manner of the release wiped out all the triumph of British diplomacy in obtaining it. Both had their triumph, and no doubt it brought them equal gratification.

It was not an imposing party that proceeded to the Chinese Legation that Friday afternoon in October; but one member of it, the venerable old messenger from the Foreign Office, had a small note concealed in the depths of his great-coat pocket that seemed to bear great weight. It must have been short and to the point, for it took Macartney but two or three seconds to master its contents. Short it may have been, but it bore the sweet message of freedom for me, and an escape from death, and what I dreaded more, the customary exquisite torture to which political prisoners in China are submitted to procure confession of the names of accomplices.

In Weymouth Street a considerable crowd had assembled, and the everpresent newspaper reporter tried to inveigle me there and then into a confession. I was, however, speedily put into a fourwheeled cab, and, in company with Mr. Cantlie, Inspector

Jarvis, and the messenger, driven off towards Scotland Yard. On the way thither Inspector Jarvis gravely lectured me on my delinquencies, and scolded me as a bad boy, and advised me to have nothing to do any more with revolutions. Instead of stopping at Scotland Yard, however, the cab drew up at the door of a restaurant in Whitehall, and we got out on the pavement. Immediately the newspaper men surrounded me; where they came from I could not tell. We had left them a mile away in Portland Place, and here they were again the moment my cab stopped. There is no repressing them; one man had actually, unknown to us, climbed up on the seat beside the driver. He it was that stayed the cab at the restaurant, knowing well that if once I was within the precincts of Scotland Yard they could not get at me for some time. Unless the others—some dozen in number—were on the roof of my cab, I cannot understand where they sprang from. I was hustled from the pavement into the back premises of the hostelry with much more violence than ever was expended upon me when originally taken within the Chinese Legation, and surrounded by a crowd thirsting for knowledge as eagerly as my countrymen thirsted for my head. Pencils executed wonderful hieroglyphics which I had never seen before, and I did not know until that moment that English could be written in what seemed to me cuneiform characters. I found out afterwards it was in shorthand they were writing.

I spoke until I could speak no more, and it was only when Mr. Cantlie called out "Time, gentlemen!" that I was forcibly rescued from their midst and carried off to Scotland Yard. At the Yard I was evidently regarded as a child of their own delivery, and Jarvis's honest face was a picture to behold. However, the

difficult labour was over, and here I was free to make my own
confession. I was detained there for an hour, during which time
I made a full statement of the circumstances of my capture and
detention. This was all taken down and read over to me, and
I appended my signature and bade a cordial adieu to my friends in
the police force. Mr. Cantlie and myself then hied ourselves
homewards, where a hospitable welcome was accorded me, and
over an appetising dinner, a toast to my "head" was drunk with
enthusiasm.

During the evening I was frequently interviewed, and it was
not until a late hour that I was allowed to rest. Oh! that first
night's sleep! Shall I ever forget it? For nine hours did it last,
and when I awoke it was to the noise of children romping on
the floor above me. It was evident by their loud, penetrating
voices some excitement was on hand, and as I listened I could
hear the cause of it. "Now, Colin, you be Sun Yat Sen, and
Neil will be Sir Halliday Macartney, and I will rescue Sun."
Then followed a turmoil; Sir Halliday was knocked endways,
and a crash on the floor made me believe that my little friend
Neil was no more. Sun was brought out in triumph by Keith,
the eldest boy, and a general amnesty was declared by the
beating of drums, the piercing notes of a tin whistle, and the
singing of "The British Grenadiers." This was home and safety,
indeed; for it was evident my youthful friends were prepared to
shed the last drop of their blood on my behalf.

During Saturday, October 24th, I was interviewing all day.
The one question put was, "How did you let the doctors know?"
and the same question was addressed to Mr. Cantlie many scores

of times. We felt, however, that our tongues were tied; as, by answering the query, we should be incriminating those who, within the Legation walls, had acted as my friends, and they would lose their positions. However, when Cole resolved to resign his appointment, so that none of the others should be wrongly suspected, there was no object in hiding who had been the informant. It is all very well to say that I bribed him; that is not the case. He did not understand that I gave him the money by way of fee at all; he believed I gave it him to keep for me; he told Mr. Cantlie he had the £20 the day he got it, and offered to give it to him for safe keeping. When I came out Cole handed the money back to me, but it was the least I could do to urge him to keep it. I wish it had been more, but it was all the ready money I had. Cole had many frights during this time, but perhaps the worst scare he got was at the very first start. On the Sunday afternoon, October 18th, when he had made up his mind to help me practically, he took my notes to Mr. Cantlie, in his pocket, at 46 Devonshire Street. The door was opened and he was admitted within the hall. The doctor was not at home, so he asked to see his wife. Whilst the servant was gone to fetch her mistress, Cole became conscious of the presence of a Chinaman watching him from the far end of the hall. He immediately suspected that he had been followed or rather anticipated, for here was a Chinaman, pigtail and all, earnestly scrutinising him from a recess. When Mrs. Cantlie came down she beheld a man, trembling with fear and pale from terror, who could hardly speak. The cause of this alarm was a model of a Chinaman, of most life—like appearance, which Mr. Cantlie had brought home with him amongst his curios from Hong Kong. It has frightened many other visitors with less tender consciences than Cole's, whose overwrought nerves actually endowed the figure with a halo of terrible reality. Mrs. Cantlie relieved Cole's mind from his fear and sent him in to find her husband at Dr. Manson's. My part of the tale is nearly ended; what further complications in connection with this affair may arise I cannot say. There is not time, as yet, to hear how the papers in other English-speaking countries will deal with the subject, and as Parliament has not yet assembled I cannot say what questions appertaining to the event may be forthcoming. I have, however, found many friends since my release. I have paid several pleasant visits to the country. I have been dined and feasted, and run a good chance of being permanently spoiled by my well-wishers in and around London.

APPENDIX.

I append a few of the numerous articles called forth by my arrest. The first is a letter from Professor Holland to *The Times*, and is headed:

THE CASE OF SUN YAT SEN.

To the Editor of THE TIMES.

Sir,—The questions raised by the imprisonment of Sun Yat Sen are two in number. First, was the act of the Chinese Minister in detaining him an unlawful act? And secondly, if so, what steps could properly have been taken to obtain his release had it been refused?

The reply to the former question is not far to seek. The claim of an Ambassador to exercise any sort of domestic jurisdiction, even over members of his suite, is now little heard of, although, in 1603, Sully, when French Ambassador, went so far as to sentence one of his *attachés* to death, handing him over to the Lord Mayor for execution. I can recall but one instance of an attempt on the part of a Minister to exercise constraint against a person unconnected with his mission. In 1642, Leitao, Portuguese Minister at the Hague, detained in his house a horse-dealer who had cheated him. The result was a riot, in which the hotel was plundered, and Wicquefort remarks upon the transaction that Leitao, who had given public lectures on the Law of Nations, ought to have know *qu'il ne lui estoit pas permis de faire une prison de sa maison*. Sun Yat Sen, while on British soil as a *subditus temporarius*, was under the protection of our Laws, and

58

his confinement in the Chinese Legation was a high offence against the rights of the British Crown.

The second question, though not so simple, presents no serious difficulty. A refusal on the part of the Chinese Minister to release his prisoner would have been a sufficient ground for requesting him to leave the country. If this mode of proceeding would have been too dilatory for the exigencies of the case, it can hardly be doubted that the circumstances would have justified an entry upon the Legation premises by the London police. An Ambassador's hotel is said to be "extra-territorial," but this too compendious phrase means no more than that the hotel is for certain purposes inaccessible to the ordinary jurisdiction of the country in which it stands. The exemptions thus enjoyed are, however, strictly defined by usage, and new exemptions cannot be deduced from a metaphor. The case of Gyllenburg, in 1717, showed that if a Minister is suspected of conspiring against the Government to which he is accredited he may be arrested and his cabinets may be ransacked. The case of the coachman of Mr. Gallatin, in 1827, establishes that, after courteous notice, the police may enter a Legation in order to take into custody one of its servants who has been guilty of an offence elsewhere. There is also a general agreement that, except possibly in Spain and in the South American Republics, the hotel is no longer an asylum for even political offenders. Still less can it be supposed that an illegal imprisonment in a Minister's residence will not be put an end to by such action of the local police as may be necessary.

It seems needless to inquire into the responsibility which would rest upon the Chinese authorities if Sun Yat Sen was, as he alleges, kidnapped in the open street, or would have rested upon them had they removed him through the streets, with a view to shipping him off to China. Acts of this kind find no defenders. What is admitted to have occurred is sufficiently serious, and was doubtless due to excess of zeal on the part of the subordinates of the Chinese Legation. International law has long been ably taught by Dr. Martin at the Tung-wen College of Peking, and the Imperial Government cannot be supposed to be indifferent to a strict conformity to the precepts of the science on the part of its representatives at foreign Courts.

I am, Sir, your obedient servant,

T. E. HOLLAND.

Oxford, October 24th.

Another legal opinion is referred to below:

LEGAL OPINION.

Mr. Cavendish, one of the best authorities on the law of extradition, informed an interviewer at Bow Street yesterday that, speaking from memory, he could cite no case at all parallel with the case of Sun Yat Sen. The case of the Zanzibar Pretender was, of course, in no way parallel, for he took refuge in the German Consulate. He threw himself on the hospitality of the German Government, which, following the procedure sanctioned by International Law, refuses to give him up, and conveyed him to German territory on the mainland. Sun Yat Sen's case was that of an alleged Chinese subject, having come within the walls of the Legation of his own country, was arrested by representatives of his own Government for an offence against that Government. Mr. Cavendish assumed that if the facts were as stated, the case could only be dealt with by diplomatic representation on the part of our Foreign Office, and not by any known legal rule.

The next is a letter from Mr. James G. Wood to the same paper discussing some of the points of law raised in Professor Holland's letter:

To the Editor of THE TIMES.

Sir,—The second question proposed by Professor Holland, though fortunately, under the circumstances, not of present importance, is deserving of careful consideration. I venture to think his answer to it unsatisfactory.

It is suggested that on a refusal by the Chinese Minister to release his prisoner, "it can hardly be doubted that the circumstances would have justified an entry on the Legation premises by the London police." But why there should not be such a doubt is not explained. This is not solving the question but guessing at its solution. The London police have no roving commission to release persons unlawfully detained in London houses; and anyone attempting to enter for such a purpose could be lawfully resisted by force.

The only process known to the law as applicable to a case of unlawful detention is a writ of *habeas corpus*, and this is where the real difficulty lies. Could such a writ be addressed to an

Ambassador or any member of the Legation? Or if it were, and it were disregarded, could process of contempt follow? I venture to think not; and I know of no precedent for such proceeding.

I agree that the phrase that an Ambassador's hotel is extraterritorial is so metaphysical as to be misleading. It is, in fact, inaccurate. The more careful writers do not use it. The true proposition is not that the residence is extraterritorial in the sense in which a ship is often said to be so, but the Minister himself is deemed to be so; and as a consequence he and the members of his family and suite are said to enjoy a complete immunity from all civil process. It is not a question of what may or may not be done in the residence, but what may or may not be done to individuals. That being so, the process I have mentioned appears to involve a breach of the comity of nations.

To adduce cases where the police have under a warrant entered an Embassy to arrest persons who have committed an offence elsewhere to found the proposition that "the local police may take action to put an end to an illegal imprisonment," begun and continued within the Embassy, does not land us on safe ground. There is no common feature in the two cases.

I am, Sir, your obedient servant,

JAMES G. WOOD.

October 27th.

THE SUPPOSED CHINESE REVOLUTIONIST.

[From the China Mail, Hong Kong, Dec. 3rd, 1896.]

Sun Yat Sen, who has recently been in trouble in London through the Chinese Minister attempting to kidnap him for execution as a rebel, is not unlikely to become a prominent character in history. Of course, it would not be right to state, until a duly constituted court of law has found, that a man is definitely connected with any illegal movement, or that any movement with which he is connected is definitely anti-dynastic. The only suggestion of Dr. Sun Yat Sen being a rebel in any sense comes from the Chinese Legation in London and the officials of Canton. But without any injury to him it may be safely said that he is a remarkable man, with most enlightened views on the undoubtedly miserable state of China's millions, and that there are many Chinese who feel very strongly on the subject and try now and then to act very strongly. The allegation of the officials is that these people tried to accomplish a revolution in October, 1895, and that Sun Yat Sen was a leader in the conspiracy. Foreigners, even those resident in the Far East, had little knowledge how near the long-expected break-up of China then was. As it happened, the outbreak missed fire, and what little attention it did attract was of the contemptuous sort. The situation was, however, one of as great danger as any since the Tai Pings were suppressed, and the organisation was much more up-to-date and on a more enlightened basis than even that great rebellion. In fact, it was the intelligence of the principal movers that caused the movement to be discountenanced at an early stage as premature, instead of struggling on with a more disastrous failure in view, for the revolution is only postponed, not abandoned for ever. The origin of the movement cannot be specifically traced; it arose from the general dissatisfaction of Chinese with Manchu rule, and it came to a head on the outbreak of war between China and Japan. The malcontents saw that the war afforded an opportunity to put their aspirations into shape, and they promptly set to work. At first, that is to say before China had been so soundly thrashed all along the line, they had in view purely lawful and constitutional measures, and hoped to effect radical changes without resort to violence. Dr. Sun worked hard and loyally to fuse the inchoate elements of disaffection brought into existence by Manchu misgovernment, and to give the whole reform movement a purely constitutional form, in the earnest hope of raising his wretched country out of the Slough of Despond in which it was and is sinking deeper daily. His was the master-mind that strove to subdue the wild uncontrollable spirits always prominent in Chinese reactionary schemes, to harmonise conflicting interests, not only as between various parties in his own country but also as between Chinese and foreigners, and as between various foreign Powers. The most difficult problem was to work out the sequel of any upheaval—to anticipate and be ready in advance to deal with all the complications bound to ensue as soon as the change took place. Moreover he had to bear in mind that any great reform movement must necessarily depend very largely on the aid of foreigners, of nations and individuals as well, while there is throughout China an immense mass of anti-foreign prejudice which would have to be overcome somehow. The task was stupendous, hopeless in fact, but he recognised that the salvation of China depended and still depends on something of the sort being some day rendered possible, and that the only way to accomplish it was to try, try, try again. That is to say, last year's attempt was not likely to succeed, but was likely to bring success a stage nearer, and in that sense it was well worth the effort to an ardent patriot. Dr. Sun was the only man who combined a complete grasp of the situation with a reckless bravery of the kind which alone can make a national regeneration. He was born in Honolulu, and had a good English education. He has travelled extensively in Europe and America, and is a young man of remarkable attainments. He was for some time a medical student in Dr. Kerr's School in Tientsin, and afterwards was on the staff of the Alice Memorial Hospital in Hong Kong. He is of average height, thin and wiry, with a keenness of expression and frankness of feature seldom seen in Chinese. An unassuming manner and an earnestness of speech, combined with a quick perception and resolute judgment, go to impress one with the conviction that he is in every way an exceptional type of his race. Beneath his calm exterior is hidden a personality that cannot but be a great influence for good in China sooner or later, if the Fates are fair. In China, any advocate of reform or any foe of corruption and oppression is liable to be regarded as a violent revolutionist, and summarily executed. It has been the same in the history of every country when freedom and enlightenment were in their infancy, or not yet born. The propaganda had therefore to be disseminated with the greatest care, and at imminent peril. First, an able and exhaustive treatise on political matters was published in Hong Kong, and circulated all over China, especially in the south, where it created a sensation, early in 1895. It was most cautiously worded, and the most censorious official could not lay his finger on a word of it and complain; but it depicted in vivid colours the beauties of enlightened and honest government, contrasted with the horrors of corrupt and tyrannical misgovernment. This feeler served to show how much voluntary reform could be expected of Chinese officialdom, for it had as much effect as a volume of sermons thrown among a shoal of sharks. Then it became no longer possible to control the spirits of insurrection. Steps were at once taken to organise a rebellion, with which it is alleged, but not yet proved, that Dr. Sun Yat Sen was associated. Before the war there had been insurrectionary conspiracies—in fact, such things are chronic in China. The navy was disaffected, because of certain gross injustices and extortions practised on the officers and men by the all-powerful mandarins. The commanders of land forces and forts were not much different, and many civilian officials were willing to join in a rising. No doubt much of the support accorded to the scheme was prompted by ulterior motives, for there are more of that sort than of any other in China. The rebellion was almost precipitated in March, when funds were supplied from Honolulu, Singapore, Australia, and elsewhere; but men of the right sort were still wanting, and arms had not been obtained in great quantity, and wiser counsels prevailed. It would have been better perhaps if wiser counsels had prevailed in October, but wisdom cannot come without experience, and for the sake of the experience the leaders of the abortive revolution do not greatly regret their action. Some indeed drew out as soon as it became certain that violent measures were to be adopted; but the penalty of death would not be obviated by that, and it was at imminent risk of his life that Dr. Sun had been travelling throughout the length and breadth of China, preaching the gospel of good government and gathering recruits for constitutional reform. His allies, never very confident in pacific methods, planned a bold *coup d'état*, which might have gained a momentary success, but made no provision for what would happen in the next few moments. Men were drafted to Hong Kong to be prepared for an attack on Canton; arms and ammunition were smuggled in cement-casks;

money was subscribed lavishly, foreign advisers and commanders were obtained, and attempts were made, without tangible result, to secure the co-operation of the Japanese Government. What would have been the result if the verbal sympathy of Japanese under-officials had been followed by active sympathy in higher quarters, none can tell; the indemnity, the Liao-tung settlement, the commercial treaty, the whole history of the relations between Japan and China and Europe since the war might have been totally different. Every detail of the plot was arranged, but before the time for striking the blow, treachery stepped in. A prominent Chinese merchant of Hong Kong had professed adherence to the reform movement, for he had much to gain by it; then he concluded that he could gain more by playing into the hands of the official vampires, for he was connected with one of the many syndicates formed to compete for railway and mining concessions in China after the war. So he gave information, and the cement was examined, with the result that the whole *coup d'état* was nothing more than a flash in the pan. Dr. Sun happened to be in Canton at the time, and was accused of active participation in the violent section of the reform movement. In China, to be innocent is not to be safe; an accusation is none the less dangerous for being utterly unfounded. Sun had to fly for his life, without a moment's deliberation as to friends or property or anything else; and for two or three weeks he was a fugitive hiding in the labyrinthine canals and impenetrable pirate-haunts of the great Kwang-tung Delta. A report has been published that forty or fifty of his supposed accomplices were executed, and a reward was offered for his arrest, but he got away to Honolulu and thence to America. The story goes that this indomitable patriot immediately set to work converting the Chinese at the Washington

Embassy to the cause of reform, and that after-wards he tried to
do the same in London; that one of the Chinese in the Legation
at Washington had professed sympathy with the apostle of
enlightenment, and then thought more money could be made on
the other side, and so telegraphed to the London Embassy to
arrest Sun and kidnap him back to China by hook or by
crook. However that may be, he was captured and confined
in a most outrageous manner in the London Legation, whatever
plausible piffle may be put forward by Sir Halliday Macartney,
or any servile prevaricator; and it is due to Dr. Cantlie, Sun's
friend and teacher in Hong Kong, that one of the best men
China has ever produced was rescued by British justice from
the toils of treacherous mandarindom. All who know Dr.
Cantlie—and he is well known in many parts of the world—
agree that a more upright, honourable and devoted benefactor of
humanity has never breathed. Dr. Sun is in good hands, and
under the protection of such a man as Dr. Cantlie there can be
little doubt that he will pursue his chosen career with single-hearted
enthusiasm and most scrupulous straight–forwardness of methods,
until at last the good work of humanising the miserable condition
of the Chinese Empire is brought to a satisfactory state of
perfection.

A leading article in The Times of Saturday, October
24th, 1896, discusses the question very fully:

While the "Concert of Europe" is supposed to be making
steady progress towards the establishment of harmony amongst
the constituent Powers, the ordinarily smooth course of diplomatic
intercourse has been ruffled by a curious violation of law and
custom at the Chinese Legation—a violation which might have

led to tragic consequences, but which has so turned out as to present chiefly a ludicrous side for our consideration. Through a communication made on Thursday to our contemporary the *Globe*, it became known that a Chinese visitor to England, a doctor named Sun Yat Sen, was imprisoned at the house of the Chinese Minister, and that it was supposed to be the intention of his captors to send him under restraint to his own country, there to receive such measure of justice as a Chinese tribunal might be expected to extend to an alleged conspirator. Fortunately for the prisoner, he had studied medicine at Hong Kong, where he had made the acquaintance and had won the friendly regard of Mr. Cantlie, the Dean of the Hong Kong Medical College, and of Dr. Manson, both of whom are now residing in London. Sun Yat Sen was sufficiently supplied with money, and he succeeded in finding means of communication with these English friends, who at once took steps to inform the police authorities and the Foreign Office of what was being done, while, at the same time, they employed detectives to watch the Legation, in order to prevent the possibility of the prisoner being secretly conveyed away. Lord Salisbury, as soon as he was informed of what had occurred, made a demand for the immediate release of the prisoner, who was forthwith set at liberty, and was taken away by Mr. Cantlie and Dr. Manson, who attended in order to identify him as the person they had known. He has since furnished representatives of the Press with an account of the circumstances of his capture and detention, an account which differs in important respects from that of the Chinese authorities. If the Chinese had accomplished their supposed object, and had smuggled Sun Yat Sen on shipboard, to be tried and probably executed in China, our Foreign Office would have had to deal with an offence against the comity of nations for which it would have been necessary to demand and obtain the punishment of all concerned. The failure of the attempt may perhaps be held to bring it too near the confines of comic opera to furnish a subject for anything more than serious remonstrance.

The offence alleged against Sun Yat Sen is that his medical character is a mere cloak for other designs, and that he is really Sun Wên, the prime mover in a conspiracy which was discovered in 1894, and which had for its object the dethronement of the present reigning dynasty, The first step of the conspirators was to be the capture of the Viceroy of Canton, who was to be kidnapped when inspecting the arsenal; but the plot, like most plots, leaked out or was betrayed, and fifteen of the ringleaders were arrested and decapitated. Sun Wên saved himself by timely flight, and made his way through Honolulu and America to this country, being all the time carefully watched by detectives. On reaching England, at the beginning of the present month, he called upon his old friends, Mr. Cantlie and Dr. Manson, and prepared to commence a course of medical study in London A few days later he disappeared, and on the evening of last Saturday Mr. Cantlie was informed of his position. Sun Wên, or Sun Yat Sen, whichever he may be alleges that he was walking in or near Portland Place on the 11th inst., when he was accosted in the street by a fellow-countryman, who asked whether he was Chinese or Japanese; and, being told in reply that he was Chinese and a native of Canton, hailed him as a fellow provincial, and kept him in conversation until a second and then a third Chinaman joined them. One of the three left, while the other two walked slowly on until they reached the Legation, when the others invited Sun to enter, and supported the invitation by the exercise of a certain amount of force. As soon as he was inside, the door was shut and he was conveyed upstairs to a room where, as he alleges, he was seen by Sir Halliday Macartney, and in which he was afterwards kept close prisoner until released by the intervention of Lord Salisbury. The officials of the Chinese Legation, on the other hand, assert that the man came to the Legation of his own accord on Saturday, the 10th, and entered into conversation, talking about Chinese affairs, and appearing to want only a chat with some of his fellow-countrymen, after having which he went away; and that it was not until after he had gone that suspicion was excited that he might be the notorious Sun Wên, who had fled from justice at home, whose passage through America and departure for England had already been telegraphed to the Legation, and who was actually then being watched by a private detective in the employment of the Chinese Government. Sun came to the Legation a second time, on Sunday, the 11th, and then, evidence of his identity having been obtained, he was made prisoner. It had been supposed that he was about to return to Hong Kong as to a convenient base for further operations; and it was the intention of the Chinese Government to ask for his extradition as soon as he arrived there. In the meanwhile the actual presence of the supposed conspirator in the Legation furnished a temptation which it was found impossible to resist, and he was locked up until instructions with regard to him could arrive from Pekin. There can be little doubt that these instructions, if they had been received and could have been acted upon, would have effectually destroyed his power to engage in any further conspiracies; and it may be assumed that the intervention of Lord

Salisbury was not too early. Even as it was Sun appears to have suffered considerable anxiety lest the food supplied to him at the Legation should be unwholesome in its character.

The simple process of cutting a knot is often preferable to the labour of untying it, and we are not very much surprised that the Chinese Minister or his representative should have authorized the adoption of the course which has happily failed of success. But we cannot conceal our surprise that Sir Halliday Macartney, himself an Englishman, should have taken any part in a transaction manifestly doomed to failure, and the success of which would have been ruinous to all engaged in it. The Chinese Minister is said to have surrendered his prisoner "without prejudice," as lawyers say, to his assumed rights; but he appears to have claimed a right which is not acknowledged by any civilized country, and which would be intolerable if it were exercised. It would be a somewhat similar proceeding if the Turkish Ambassador were to inveigle some of the leading members of the Armenian colony in London into the Embassy, in order to despatch them, gagged and bound, as an offering to his Imperial Majesty the Sultan, or if Lord Dufferin had in the same way made a private prisoner of Tynan, and had sent him to stand his trial at the Old Bailey. It is well recognised that the house of a foreign mission is regarded as a portion of the country from which the mission is sent, and that not only the Minister himself, but also the recognised members of his suite, enjoy an immunity from liability to the laws of the country to which the Ambassador is accredited; but this hardly entitles the Ambassador to exercise powers of imprisonment or of criminal jurisdiction, and the privileges of the Embassy as a place of refuge for persons unconnected with it are strictly limited to the ground on which it stands, Even if the Chinese Minister could not have been prevented from keeping Sun in custody, he would have been liberated by the police as soon as he was brought over the threshold to be conveyed elsewhere. It is fortunate that he did not suffer from any form of illness; for if he had died during his imprisonment, it is very difficult to say what could have been done in consequence. Evidence would have been very hard to procure; and, even if it had been procured, the persons of the Minister and of his servants would have been sacred. Probably the only course would have been to demand that the Minister should be recalled, and that he should be put upon his trial in his own country; a demand which might perhaps have been readily complied with, but which might not improbably have led to what Englishmen would describe as a miscarriage of justice. We think that this country, almost as much as the prisoner, may be congratulated upon the turn of events; and we have no doubt that the Foreign Office will find ways and means of making the rulers of the Celestial Empire understand that they have gone a little too far, and that they must not commit any similar offence in the future.

This Article called forth a remonstrance from Sir Halliday Macartney, in which he stated his views:

To the Editor of The Times.

Sir,—In your leading article of to-day, commenting on the alleged kidnapping of an individual, a Chinese subject, calling himself, amongst numerous other aliases, by the name of Sun Yat Sen, you make some remarks with regard to me which I cannot but consider as an exception to the fairness which in general characterises the comments of *The Times*.

After stating the case as given by the two opposite parties, in the surprise which you express at my conduct, you take it for granted that the statement of Sun Yat Sen is the correct one and that of the Chinese Legation the wrong one.

I do not know why you make this assumption, for you undoubtedly do so when you say the case is as if the Turkish Ambassador had inveigled some of the members of the Armenian colony of London into the Embassy with a view to making them a present to his Majesty the Sultan.

Now, I repeat what I have said before—that in this case there was no inveiglement. The statement of Sun Yat Sen—or, to call him by his real name, Sun Wên—that he was caught in the street and hustled into the Legation by two sturdy Chinamen is utterly false.

He came to the Legation unexpectedly and of his own accord, the first time on Saturday, the 10th, the second on Sunday, the 11th.

Whatever the pundits of international law may think of his detention, they may take it as being absolutely certain that there was no kidnapping and that he entered the Legation without the employment of force or guile.

I am, Sir, your obedient servant,

Halliday Macartney.

Richmond House.
49 Portland Place, W.,
Oct. 24th.

Sir Halliday Macartney's remarks about my going under various aliases, is no doubt intended to cast a slur upon my character; but Sir Halliday knows, no one better, that every Chinaman has four names at least to which he is entitled. 1st, the name one's parents bestow on their child. 2nd, the name given by the schoolmaster. 3rd, the name a young man wishes to be known by when he goes out into society. 4th, the name he takes when he is married. The only constant part of the name is the first syllable—the surname, really the family name; the other part of the name varies according as it is the parent, the schoolmaster, etc., chooses. Whilst upon this subject it may not be without interest to know that my accuser has various aliases by which he is known to the Chinese. In addition to the name Ma-Ta-Yen, which means Macartney, His Excellency, he is also known as Ma-Ka-Ni, and as Ma-Tsing-Shan, showing that no name is constant in China except the family name.

From The Speaker, October 31st, 1896.

The Dungeons of Portland Place.

Sir Halliday Macartney is an official in the service of the Chinese Government. That fact seems to have deprived him of any sense of humour he might otherwise have had, which, we imagine, would in no circumstances have been conspicuous. The Secretary of the Chinese Legation has struck an attitude of injured innocence in *The Times*. He is like Woods Pasha, when that undiscerning personage stands up for the Turkish Government in an English newspaper. What in a true Oriental would seem natural and characteristic, in the sham Oriental is merely ridiculous. Sir Halliday Macartney assures the world that the Chinese medical gentleman who was lately released from the Portland Place Bastille was not inveigled into that institution. To the obvious suggestion that Sun Yat Sen would never have walked into the Chinese Embassy of his own accord, had he known the real identity of his entertainers, Sir Halliday vouchsafes no reply. It is unquestionable that he saw the captive, and took no measures to set him at liberty, till a peremptory requisition came from the Foreign Office. If it was not intended to deport Sun Yat Sen to China, why was he kept a prisoner? Sir Halliday Macartney is in the pitiable position of an Englishman who is forced by his official obligations to palliate in London what would be the ordinary course of justice at Canton. A purely Chinese emissary would have said nothing. Having failed in his manoeuvre, he would have accepted the consequences of defeat with the fatalism of his race and native climate. The spectacle of Sir Halliday Macartney fussing and fuming in the *Times* like an Englishman, when he ought to hold his peace like a Chinaman, can only suggest to the authorities at Pekin that their English representative here is a rather incompetent person.

On the other hand, there is something in this Chinese kidnapping which is irresistibly diverting. Englishmen can never take the Chinaman seriously, in spite of Charles Pearson's prediction that the yellow man will one day eat ns up. The personality of Ah Sin, especially when he wears a pigtail and his native costume, is purely comic to the average sightseer. If the men who decoyed Sun Yat Sen were pointed out to a London crowd, they would be greeted not with indignation, but with mildly derisive banter. It might go hard with any Europeans who had tried the same game; but Ah Sin, the childlike and bland, is a traditional joke. His strategy excites no more resentment than the nodding of the ornamental mandarin on the mantelpiece. The popular idea of Lord Salisbury's intervention in this case is probably that the Chinaman's pigtail has been gently but decisively pulled, and that such a lesson is quite sufficient without any public anger. Had a German or a Frenchman been kidnapped in similar circumstances, the situation would at once have been recognised as extremely serious. The capture and incarceration in Portland Place simply excite a smile. The newspapers have treated the incident as they treat the announcement that Li Hung Chang, promoted to be Imperial Chancellor of China, had at the same time been punished for an unauthorised visit to the Empress Dowager. How can you be angry with a people whose solemnities frequently strike the Occidental mind as screaming farce? It is impossible to pass No. 40 Portland Place with a romantic shudder. That middle-class dwelling, of substantial and comfortable aspect, is now a Bastille *pour rire*, and excites the mirth of tradesmen's boys, who must feel strongly tempted, by way of celebrating the Fifth of November, to ring the bell and introduce a Celestial guy to the puzzled servitors of the Embassy, with a fluent tirade in pigeon-English.

As for Sun Yat Sen, it cannot escape his notice that there is little curiosity to know the precise reason why he is obnoxious to the Chinese Government.   He is said to have taken part in a conspiracy against the Viceroy of Canton, a statement which conveys no vivid impression to the popular mind.   Political refugees—Italians, Poles, Hungarians—have commonly inspired a romantic interest in this country. They have figured in our fiction, always a sure criterion of public sympathies. When the storyteller takes the foreign conspirator in hand, you may be sure that the machinations, escapes, and so forth touch a responsive chord in the popular imagination. But no storyteller is likely to turn the adventures of Sun Yat Sen to such account, though they may be really thrilling, and though this worthy Celestial medico may have been quite a formidable person in his native land. Even the realistic descriptions by travellers of Chinese administration, the gentle coercion of witnesses in the courts by smashing their ankles, the slicing of criminals to death, have not given a sinister background to the figure of the Heathen Chinee. The ignominious defeat of the Chinese arms in the late war has strengthened the conception of the yellow man as a rather grotesquely ineffectual object.   If Sun Yat Sen were to deliver a lecture on his adventures, and paint the tyranny of the Viceroy of Canton in the deepest colours, or if Sir Halliday Macartney were to show that his late prisoner was a monster of ferocity, compared to whom all the Western dynamiters were angels in disguise, we doubt whether either story would command the gravity of the public. The Chinese have their virtues; they are a frugal, thrifty, and abstemious people; they practise a greater respect for family ties than Western nations. The custom of worshipping their ancestors, though one of the chief stumbling-blocks to the Christian missionaries, probably exercises a greater moral influence than the reverence for genealogy here. But no audience in England or America would accept these virtues as rebukes to the short-comings of the Anglo-Saxon civilisation. So deep is the gulf between Occident and Orient that the pride of neither will learn from the other, and both are indifferent to the warnings of prophets who foretell the triumph of the Caucasian in the Flowery Land or the submergement of Europe by the yellow flood of immigration. All Western notions are regarded in China with a contempt which even the travels of Li are not likely to dispel; and No. 40 Portland Place can never recover that prestige of harmless nonentity it enjoyed before the pranks of the Chinese Embassy made it a centre of the ludicrous.

The following is a copy of the letter I sent to the newspapers thanking the Government and the Press for what they had done for me:

To the Editor of the—

Sir,—Will you kindly express through your columns my keen appreciation of the action of the British Government in effecting my release from the Chinese Legation? I have also to thank the Press generally for their timely help and sympathy. If anything were needed to convince me of the generous public spirit which pervades Great Britain, and the love of justice which distinguishes its people, the recent acts of the last few days have conclusively done so.

    Knowing and feeling more keenly than ever what a constitutional Government and an enlightened people mean, I am prompted still more actively to pursue the cause of advancement, education, and civilisation in my own well-beloved but oppressed country.

Yours faithfully,
Sun Yat Sen.

46 Devonshire Street,
  Portland Place, W.,
     Oct. 24

The End.

中國國民黨
中央委員會黨史委員會編訂

國父全集 第五冊（全六冊）

版權
所有

定價：精裝本 每部新臺幣 八百元
　　　平裝本 　　　　　六百元

出版者：中國國民黨
　　　　中央委員會 黨史委員會

中華民國六十二年六月出版

經銷者：中央文物供應社

地址：臺北市中山南路十一號

劃撥帳戶：二一八一號

承印者：中華印刷廠

地址：臺北市安東街二一六號

主要参考文献

《孙中山全集》第1卷，中华书局1981年版。

《孙中山全集》第6卷，中华书局1985年版。

《孙中山集外集》，上海人民出版社1992年重印本。

陈锡祺主编《孙中山年谱长编》，中华书局1991年版。

罗刚：《中华民国国父实录》，台湾正中书局1988年版。

《中华民国史事纪要》，台湾"中华民国史料研究中心"1961年版。

罗家伦：《中山先生伦敦被难史料考订》，商务印书馆1930年版。

冯自由：《革命逸史》，新星出版社2009年版。

曾纪泽：《出使英法俄国日记》，载钟叔河编《走向世界丛书》，岳麓书社2008年版。

郭嵩焘：《伦敦与巴黎日记》，载《走向世界丛书》，岳麓书社2008年版。

薛福成：《出使英法意比四国日记》，载《走向世界丛书》，岳麓书社2008年版。

出版说明

　　孙中山先生一生著述十分丰厚，他的著作主要是政治理论、哲学思想，以及大量有关政治军事活动方面的文字，而《伦敦蒙难记——我被伦敦中国公使馆拘押和释放的经历》却是他唯一的一篇完整的纪实散文作品，也是他唯一的英文著作，是一本记述他流亡英伦时被逮捕、险遭不测经历的书。

　　孙中山领导第一次反清运动即乙未（1895）广州起义遭到清朝政府血腥镇压之后，即逃亡海外。1896年10月当他流亡到英国伦敦时竟遭到清政府驻英公使馆的阴谋绑架，险被偷运押送回国处决。后来经他在香港学医时的英国老师康德黎先生和孟生博士的全力营救，终于在英国政府的帮助下脱险获得释放。孙中山获释后即写下了这本使他蜚声国际政坛的《伦敦蒙难记》；而这一次蒙难经历，更坚定了他推翻腐败的封建王朝，在中国建立民主政治的远大信念。

　　孙中山的这篇回忆是用英文撰述的，而且是在他的老师康德黎先生的帮助下完成的，这一点孙中山在书的序言里已有说明。原书于1897年1月在英国伦敦和布里斯托尔出版，由于当时面对的是英国以及欧洲的读者，所以在叙述角度以及风格上都不同于孙中山的其他文字，以后他自己也没有译成中文。现在收入《孙中山全集》（中华书局版）的中文译本是民国元年（1912年）商务印书馆出版的一个做了大量删节的文本，并且是用文言意译的，许多地方未尽如人意，个别译文亦未能表达出孙中山原意。这一篇名著从1897年问世后至今，一百多年来都没有一个比较完善的中文版本，这无疑是近代史料研究的一个亟待弥补的欠缺。

本书译文是根据台湾1973年版《国父全集》第五册"英语著述卷"所刊原著翻译的。有关翻译方面的情况，可参看本书"译者前言"里的说明。考虑书中所述已是一百多年前所发生的事情，为便利今天的读者阅读，本书不仅对初译进行了全面的修订，而且对原著中提到的人物、事件、组织等相关内容作了详细的注解，这是《孙中山全集》译本或其他刊本所不具备的。本书还选编了与孙中山伦敦蒙难事件相关的大量详实的文献资料，增加了丰富的第一手资料，以帮助读者了解当时的时代背景。本书还配有一百余幅原始图片，而且其中一些是很罕见的文献图片，如绑架孙中山的主谋、清政府驻英国公使馆、英籍参赞马卡尼的照片，全力营救孙中山的康德黎及其夫人的照片，孙中山被拘押时机智传出的求救密信手迹，孙中山被拘押的牢房，不同历史时期的中英文版本，等等，钩沉史料，图文并茂，以求全面还原孙中山在伦敦被绑架的细节，是既有利于阅读和研究，同时又适合于藏家、图书爱好者收藏的文献版孙中山自述。

庾燕卿、戴桢两位译注者均为资深的文史研究专家、长期从事英语教育和翻译的教授，编者周楠本先生是中国鲁迅研究会的理事、鲁迅博物馆的研究员。不论在翻译方面，还是在编注方面，他们严谨的治学精神令我们非常钦佩，他们兢兢业业、精益求精的译注工作大大提升了本书的质量。

2011年适逢孙中山先生诞辰145周年（1866—2011）及辛亥革命100周年（1911—2011），我们谨以这一名著的新译本纪念我们民族的这位伟人，纪念推翻封建专制王朝一百周年。

中国社会科学出版社

2011年4月